Women 1870–1928

Women 1870–1928

A SELECT GUIDE TO PRINTED AND
ARCHIVAL SOURCES IN THE UNITED KINGDOM

Margaret Barrow

Mansell Publishing
Garland Publishing, Inc., New York

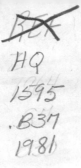

ISBN 0 7201 0923 X
ISBN 0-8240-9450-6

Mansell Publishing, a member of Bemrose U.K. Limited,
3 Bloomsbury Place, London WC1A 2QA

Distributed in North and South America by
Garland Publishing, Inc., 136 Madison Avenue,
New York, N.Y. 10016, U.S.A.

First published 1981

© Margaret Barrow, 1981

British Library Cataloguing in Publication Data
Barrow, Margaret
    Women 1870–1928.
    1. Women – Great Britain – Social conditions
    – Information services
    2. Women – Great Britain – Social conditions
    – Bibliography
    I. Title
    301.41'2'07   HQ1593

    ISBN 0–7201–0923–X

Typeset by Computacomp (UK) Ltd, Fort William,
Scotland. Printed in Great Britain by The Anchor Press
Ltd, and bound by Wm Brendon & Son Ltd, both of
Tiptree, Essex.

To Brad

CONTENTS

ACKNOWLEDGEMENTS

This work could not have been completed without the help of the many archivists and librarians who allowed me access to their collections and thanks must go to all those who gave their time and assistance. In particular, mention must be made of the following: the staff of the Social Sciences Library, Manchester Public Library, who retrieved literally hundreds of volumes from their stacks; the past and present staff of the Fawcett Library, London, including the archivists Rosemary Collier and Geoffrey Dwyer who managed to find something extra every time I visited the Library; Peter Liddle of the 1914–18 Archive at Sunderland who made me so welcome and gave me the freedom of his collection; Miss T. M. Thatcher of the South Asian Archive, Cambridge, who also allowed me to consult her collections; Eve Johansson and James G. Ollé for their help with the official publications material; and finally Helen Davies for her suggestions and encouragement in the early days of this project.

INTRODUCTION

BACKGROUND

This pioneer survey was undertaken because of the lack of a general guide to sources of information relating to women and their place in the rapidly changing society of the United Kingdom during the late nineteenth and early twentieth centuries.

The growth of the women's movement has been international, and perhaps its most obvious manifestation was the 1975 International Women's Year which brought about an added interest in women's role in societies throughout the world. At a national level, the concern about women's role in modern British society can be seen in the campaign for equal rights for women, where the implementation of equal pay legislation has meant that a new assessment of women's place in the economy is taking place. The interest shown in women's place in history, and, more particularly, in the part played by women in the great social changes of the past and the resulting changes in their status within society, also demonstrates this concern.

At present considerable research is being undertaken on the role of women in British society during the past century: subjects range from the general to the specific. The results of this research are reflected in recent literature. The range of materials available to researchers is wide and includes extensive collections of archival material as well as large quantities of contemporary printed documents. Various attempts to document printed sources have been made. These include O. R. McGregor's excellent 'The social position of women in England, 1850–1914: a bibliography' (*British Journal of Sociology*, 6 March 1955, pp. 48–60) which, despite its obvious exclusion of recent publications, is still a major source of information. A limited attempt to update this was made by Glenda Horne in 'The liberation of British and American women's history: a bibliographical essay' (*Society for the Study of Labour History Bulletin*, No. 26, Spring 1973, pp. 28–39), but like McGregor's work it includes no reference to archival material. Glenda Horne's essay does, however, have the advantage of listing research in progress at the time of publication. Despite these two works and other bibliographies contained in various histories, there has been no overall guide to the material available to researchers. Consequently the tracing of material has been a haphazard affair with researchers relying largely on personal knowledge and contacts.

AIM

By including both printed and archival sources of information relating to women, this guide is intended to aid the researcher and to facilitate the task of locating both types of material. The aim is to lead the researcher to the relevant collections of archival material and to indicate the scope of the material available. A select list of the printed material available indicates its scope and range. The amount of material available on each topic varies greatly: for some facets of women's role and place in society there is substantial published source material, ranging from parliamentary papers and contemporary accounts to the ephemeral publications of various organizations and societies, while for other facets little printed source material exists. Throughout the aim has been not to list every periodical article and pamphlet but rather to indicate the amount and type of material available on each topic and to list a representative selection. In particular, the aim has been to include major works on particular subjects.

DATES

Coverage has been limited to the period from 1870, when the Married Women's Property Acts was passed, to 1928, when full enfranchisement of women on equal terms with men took place. Within this period all the major advances of the feminist movement were fought for and in the main achieved, for although by 1928 women's place in British society was not on an equal footing with men's, the major inequalities in property ownership, education, suffrage and, to a certain extent, employment had been overcome. The year 1870 is a convenient starting date because it saw the eventual passing of the Married Women's Property Acts, which enabled married women to own property, both inherited and purchased. When she married, a woman's entire assets as well as any income she earned, had previously become the property of her husband; and the passing of the Acts was seen as a major advance by the women's movement of the time. This decade also saw the beginning of the suffrage movement and the campaign against the Contagious Diseases Acts; while the movement to secure university education gathered momentum with the foundation of women's colleges at Oxford and Cambridge.

With regard to women's studies, the years from 1914 to 1928 have been neglected although the years after the First World War saw employment opportunities become more available for women – if only for single women – as a result of the changes in society brought about by the war. Although the war enabled large numbers of women to find employment in trades and professions, which had previously been entirely male preserves, and to prove they were physically and mentally able to undertake tasks hitherto considered too strenuous, women were expected to return to their former status when the men came back after the war. Unemployment was aggravated for women by the depression of the 1920s and 1930s and the resulting general unemployment. It was many years before women – particularly married women – were given equal opportunities with men, and sixty years after the First World War before equal pay became a legal requirement.

SUBJECTS

In its subject coverage the guide aims to include the relevant sources, both primary and secondary, of information relating to many aspects of women's place in British society during the period 1870–1928. However, the coverage within this general framework has of necessity varied because some subjects have more source material available than others. There is, for example, no major academic work investigating women's employment for these years, nor is there a major work on women's role in the home, although Patricia Branca's *Silent Sisterhood* (Croom Helm, 1975) goes a long way in filling this gap. Primary source material relating to many aspects of women's life can be difficult to locate, but with the recent interest in oral history, more firsthand information is becoming available.

It is the social and economic position of women in British society and the various changes during the period rather than any literary aspects or the literary interpretation of that role that have been covered. Women as portrayed in the literature of the period are excluded, as well as literary women and criticisms of their work, because the amount of material would constitute a volume in itself. Women in the arts have also been excluded, with the notable exception of Ethel Smyth who was an extremely active suffrage worker.

The term 'women' has generally been taken to exclude girls. Some anomalies have arisen, however, principally in education for primary schools have been *excluded* and secondary schools *included*. This is because the movement to obtain higher education for women became deeply involved in the provision of secondary education for girls, in order to raise standards so that the newly formed women's colleges would receive suitably qualified entrants and to provide a basis from which women could apply for a wider range of employment opportunities. It has also been particularly difficult to separate women from girls in the coverage of official publications since much of the employment legislation, and therefore the relevant documentation, relates to both women and children.

In order to determine the appropriate subject headings, a historical study was made of the period 1870–1928. This revealed that, although by far the best known issue was the campaign for women's suffrage, women were involved with many other movements which not only changed their way of life but often attempted to change society as a whole.

These issues ranged from the fight for higher education to the temperance movement and Josephine Butler's campaign for a less appealing cause, the repeal of the Contagious Diseases Acts. By 1870 women were becoming aware that their position in society needed to be revised and their role defined. The 'woman question' became one of the most important topics of the last quarter of the nineteenth century, and women of all persuasions put their opinions in print, so that the number of publications increased greatly. Interest intensified until the Edwardian years when part of the suffrage movement turned to militancy and thus alienated itself from the majority of the feminist movement. At the time the militants believed the vote for women would be a panacea for all their inequalities.

Unfortunately this did not turn out to be the case, and while some campaigns for better status and more opportunities for women had been successful, others still remained to be fought and won after 1928.

ARRANGEMENT

The guide is divided into four Parts, which reflect the decision to include as much material as possible from primary and secondary sources of information and archival and printed material. An introduction precedes each Part which explains the full scope and range of materials in addition to criteria and methods of selection and the arrangement. Each Part is subdivided as appropriate under such headings as: education, emigration, employment, moral and social issues, and suffrage. These subdivisions have often been divided further to provide a more specific approach; for example, employment has in many sections been broken down into individual trades and professions.

1. *Archives.* The personal archives include letters, diaries and other documents, written or collected by individuals active in the various women's organizations of the period. The institutional archives vary from organization to organization but generally include some, if not all, of the following: minutes of committees (frequently the original handwritten minutes), annual reports, letterbooks, correspondence, accounts and agendas of meetings.

2. *Printed Works.* This section includes books, pamphlets and periodicals which have been arranged according to type, i.e. bibliographies, biographies (and diaries), official papers, periodicals and subject histories. The official papers encompass reports of Royal Commissions, committees, relevant Bills and Acts, Returns and Annual Reports. Whilst the majority of the official material included relates specifically to women, in the absence of specific documents, general documents have been reviewed if they include substantial relevant information. General material, such as censuses, is noted and its usefulness discussed.

3. *Non-book Material.* Because valuable primary information can be found in such sources as films, photographs and tape recordings, and newspaper-cuttings, this material has been included.

4. *Libraries and Record Offices.* This section gives the addresses and facilities of the libraries and record offices which have material relating to women. Because of the sheer volume of material, the Fawcett Library and the Blackburn Collection have their own special subsections.

FAWCETT LIBRARY

During compilation many sources of information were consulted and many institutions visited and it became increasingly obvious that the major source of information was the Fawcett Library, now housed in the City of London Polytechnic. The Fawcett Library contains by far the largest number of printed works on women in the British Isles, having in its stock works that are not available elsewhere, in addition to its unique archive collection. However, it is still in need of financial assistance to enable the collection to be fully catalogued and to update its stock.

INDEX

The many different types of material and the wide range of subjects which have been included in order to provide an adequate overall view of the subject have resulted in an arrangement of the text similar to that which might be found if the material were housed in an actual library. A detailed subject/name index enables the user to locate all the various types of material relating to a particular topic, individual or organization. This index, which is arranged word by word, allows a greater degree of specificity than could be provided by a subject arrangement of the text itself. There is also an author/title index.

PART I

ARCHIVES

PART 1   CONTENTS

INTRODUCTION

The archives discussed in this Section relate to the organizations and the women involved in the changing role of women between the years 1870 and 1928. However, it excludes those records held in the British Library, Manuscripts Division, (with the exception of the Marie Stopes collection) because to have included all relevant material there would have swelled the work to unmanageable proportions. The indexes to the British Library manuscript collections are excellent and they should always be consulted as a first step.

With regard to tracing archives, the National Register of Archives (whose address and facilities are given in the Libraries and Record Offices Section) is invaluable, particularly as it has full organization and name indexes. The staff are most helpful and are able to advise on the possible locations of archives and to outline any of the Register's deficiencies.

In the search for archive material many organizations were contacted with varying degrees of success; the main difficulty was that many organizations and societies have long since ceased to exist. Some organizations in which women played a major role have not been included as their archives are not available to the public. The most notable example was the Salvation Army which will not allow access to its records to non-members, and no other records relating to the Army could be traced. This is unfortunate as from its inception women were allowed an equal part in the affairs of the Army.

Access to the archives relating to the movement for the higher education of women in the colleges of Oxford and Cambridge Universities is restricted, and the colleges are conservative about whom they will allow to consult their archives and what they will make available.

The material listed in this Part has been arranged in subject order and then under holding institution. The subject headings are those used throughout and where necessary subdivisions are introduced. If appropriate, the material listed under holding institution or archive has been further divided firstly into material relating to organizations and secondly personal papers. The type of material is also indicated, i.e. minutes, annual reports, correspondence, etc., and dates are given wherever possible. Cross references have been made to material of related interest in the other Parts.

Locations are given and the addresses and facilities of the libraries, record offices or other repositories will be found in Part 4.

EDUCATION

The subject of women's education warrants further research because there is only a small amount of archive material at present located and readily available to researchers. The archives relating to the two leading female educationalists – the papers of Frances Mary Buss at the North London Collegiate School for Girls and of Emily Davies at Girton College, Cambridge – are an exception and well-preserved in their respective establishments. Material relating to the founding of other women's colleges at Oxford and Cambridge, on the other hand, is difficult to trace and access is often restricted. The material located has been arranged under the headings: universities, schools, school mistresses' and other associations.

UNIVERSITIES

Cambridge

Emily Davies Collection, Girton College

The material in the Emily Davies Collection can be divided into two separate groups. Firstly there are the archives relating to the education of women and the founding and early days of Girton College. Secondly there is the collection of archives relating to the suffrage movement and Emily Davies's interest in it. Both groups of papers are valuable sources of information. The education material is particularly interesting as it contains items which show the vital role played by Emily Davies in the founding and the development of Girton College.

The Collection contains a large amount of material, both manuscript and printed, and was used by Barbara Stephen for her book, *Emily Davies and Girton College*.

Degrees for women: correspondence with Professor Sidgwick regarding efforts to persuade Cambridge University to confer degrees on women for May, June and July 1887; with Henry Jackson concerning further efforts, 1887; on the same subject, including letters from head mistresses who signed her memorial for presentation to the University.

Letters from various colleges and Scottish universities regarding the number of women enrolled and the history of women in these colleges.

Printed copies of memorials, from head mistresses, mistresses, old students, local examining boards, sent to Cambridge University, in the campaign for degrees; accounts for the campaign funds, including printers' bills etc; press-cuttings relating to the campaign, 1887.

Typescript of an [article?] by Louisa Stevenson on women students in Scottish universities.

Drafts of the circular and memorials in Emily Davies's handwriting, and correspondence about them with Professor Sidgwick; printed circulars and memorials, 1886.

Founding of Girton College: correspondence between Emily Davies and Madame Bodichon, 1862–9; regarding foundation and early days of the college; and regarding courses; minutes of the first meeting, 1862, of the committee for the purpose of founding of a college for the higher education of women; a collection of newspaper cuttings on the foundation, and on university education for women; memorandum of 1903 on relations of staff and committee and the reply to the memorandum.

Cash books; early Girton College circulars; collection of miscellaneous newspaper cuttings, 1873, 1877, 1879.

Emily Davies; obituary notices and letters of sympathy received by the College.

London Association of School-mistresses: Minutes 1860–88.

London School Boards: correspondence 1870–3 and documents.

Schools Inquiry Commission: correspondence 1864–70, and printed documents.

University examinations: committee for Admission of Women to University Examinations, minutes 1862–9; correspondence with various local examining boards regarding the admittance of girls to university examinations, 1858–65; original petition of 1864 submitted to the Vice-Chancellor and the Senate of Cambridge University for the admittance of girls to University local examinations; documents connected with this campaign.

See also Papers, Emily Davies below.

Letters: from Emily Davies to Miss Bradley, 1869–70; from Emily Davies to Mrs Oliver, 1872, explaining the differences between Girton and Queen's College; correspondence with Miss Crewdson (Bursar) regarding alterations and accounts for Girton, 1903; letter from Emily Davies to Mary Clover regarding Trinity College, Dublin, degrees, 1904; from Emily Davies to Mrs Bertram, 1905–15, including two items regarding the appointment of Mrs Bertram as organizing secretary for the Central Society for Women's Suffrage; letter from Emily Davies to Rosalind Nash, 1907; from Emily Davies at Hitchin to Mrs Banbury; correspondence between Emily Davies and Henry Jackson regarding the appointment of Miss Constance Jones as School Mistress.

Collection of newspaper-cuttings, 1863–6.

Emily Davies's handwritten copy of a family chronicle 'to the history of John and Mary Davies, their ancestors and descendants. It will include if time permits the account of the part taken in public movements by the two of their children who survived them'. Written and dated October 1903. Filed in envelopes as follows; up to 1847, undated – (1848–60), 1861–5, 1865–6, 1866 and 1868. There is a handwritten index to each envelope which includes copies of letters, newspaper-cuttings, etc.

London

Westfield College

The most important material held by the College are the diaries, 1866–1935, of its founder, Constance Maynard. They are in various sequences and are a complete record of her life and work.

The College has a complete run of the college journal, *Hermes*, from 1892. This is particularly useful as they contain details of the positions obtained by past students. *The Directory of Old Students*, (1950) listing students in chronological order, also traces the activities of former students. The *Annual Report* and its predecessor, the *Calendar*, contain details relating to past students as well as Council reports, lists of lecturers and lectures. These give information about the subjects taught in the early days of the college. The College owns a complete run of both the *Calendar* and the *Annual Reports*.

Oxford

Bodleian Library

The Library contains some material relating to women at Oxford. The main guide is *The bibliography of printed works relating to the University of Oxford* by Edward H. Cordeaux and D. H. Merry (Oxford, Clarendon Press, 1968). The following is also held by the Bodleian.

Pamphlets, leaflets, petitions, etc, on the debate for the admission of women to degrees (G. A. Oxon C34 and 6125).

The Bodleian has the archives from Colleges and Halls and copies of College Reports, although some sets are incomplete.

Copies of charters and statutes relating to the Colleges.

Miscellaneous papers concerning women students, including newspaper-cuttings, relating not only to academic but also to social matters. Collection includes a copy of the statute allowing degrees to be conferred on women.

Lady Margaret Hall

The college archives are not organized and can only be consulted where there is a genuine need and the material cannot be obtained from other sources.

Reports of the Old Students' Association from 1892. These list occupations and whereabouts of past students as well as having articles on topics of interest to women which give an indication of how the Association viewed the major breakthroughs in women's position. Some of the articles are by past students on their work or experiences, and provide an interesting sidelight on their lives and their pioneering work in women's education at home and abroad.

College Registers from 1879 give a resumé of a member's academic qualifications, occupation and achievements. The arrangement is chronological but an alphabetical index refers to the year. The register lists past and present Principals, Fellows and members of staff.

Somerville College

The printed Register covers the years 1879–1930, although a new edition is due which will include new entries and update the previous edition and give dates of death. The Register, arranged in chronological order of year of coming up, consists of abbreviated reprints of the principal's original entry and gives details of positions obtained by ex-members of the College, and of their published work. It also lists members of staff and research staff. The original records are not available for consultation. The Register is useful for tracing the activities of particular students and for detecting trends in such matters as the employment of former students.

Annual Reports from 1879.

Lists of examination results of students and their appointments; also library reports.

Reports of the Somerville Students' Association, as it was originally named, and from 1925 the Association of Senior Members. This is of more value then the Annual Reports as it is more concerned with old students and gives full biographical information.

Photographs of students (incomplete) are held by the library; photographs of early college buildings; water colours of the early days of the college.

SCHOOLS

Frances Mary Buss Foundation

Camden School for Girls

The archives are not catalogued and it is unlikely that money will be available to arrange the collection in the foreseeable future. Unfortunately some of the material is very fragile. It is housed in three large scrap books; items cover all aspects of school life – letters, newspaper-cuttings, application forms, time tables, etc.

Minutes of teachers' meetings 1872–1902.

Miscellaneous items, including prizes awarded by the school in 1897–8; photographs of pupils and early buildings.

North London Collegiate School for Girls

Founded in 1850 by Frances Mary Buss, as a day school with the emphasis on academic achievement, it became a public school in 1871 but Miss Buss remained as Head Mistress. The School achieved such a high reputation that it was used as a model for girls' high schools throughout the country.

Material relating to the schools and their foundation: prospectuses from 1850; time tables from 1860; minutes books from 1870; letters received by Miss Buss.

Photographs of early pupils on prize days, supporters of the school and of the original premises at 14 Camden Street; certificates, prize day programmes and book plates.

Personal material: this includes Christmas cards sent by Miss Buss, letters from her brothers, letters to her family and invitations received. It is in a scrap book compiled by her brother Septimus.

Other Schools (Public Record Office)

School Inspectors' reports on girls' schools 1870–1928, listed alphabetically and with the PRO reference number:

Blackheath High School for Girls 1903–21, Ed 35/1720.
Camden School for Girls, Ed 35/1749.
Cheltenham Ladies' College 1899–1919, Ed 35/862.
Clapham High School for Girls 1903–21, Ed 35/1778.
Haberdashers' Aske's Hatcham Girls' School, Ed 35/1644.
James Allen's Girls' School, Dulwich, Ed 35/1607–09.
Manchester High School for Girls, Ed 35/1352–4.
North London Collegiate School 1876–1903, Ed 27/3194; 1889–93, Ed 27/3199: 1901–21, Ed 35/1755–6.
Perse School for Girls, Cambridge 1905–21, Ed 35/156.
Roan School for Girls, Greenwich 1901–21, Ed 35/1663.
Sydenham High School for Girls 1902–19, Ed 35/1733.

SCHOOL MISTRESSES' AND OTHER ASSOCIATIONS

Association of Assistant Mistresses

Founded in 1884 as the Association of Assistant Mistresses in Public Secondary Schools, in 1922 it widened its scope to include all secondary schools and changed its name accordingly. It was set up to improve professional status and to protect the professional interests of teachers. In 1919 the Association joined those of the Headmasters, Head Mistresses and Assistant Masters to form the 'Joint Four'.

During the Second World War the Associations' offices suffered bomb damage and except for the annual reports 1884–1940, all records were destroyed.

Association of Head Mistresses

Founded in 1874 by Frances Mary Buss as the Association of Head Mistresses of Endowed and Proprietary Secondary Schools, it took the professionalism of women very seriously, both at home and abroad. In 1907 it formed a colonial sub-committee and in 1911 the Colonial Intelligence League, together with the Committee of Colonial Intelligence for Educated Women. In 1919 it joined the Associations of Head Masters, Assistant Masters and Assistant Mistresses to form the 'Joint Four' which represents the views of the associations in dealing with government departments. This Association is still extremely active.

Minutes: annual conferences 1874–1916, 1922–38; Conferences 1886–90 –
  Miss Buss's book; Conferences; special 1890–94 – Miss Buss's book.
Executive committees 1879–1933.
Sub-committees: Boarding schools 1919–21; Education, May, Oct 1933;
  Examinations 1907–33; Examinations and curricula 1908–14.
Finance 1902–34; General purpose 1903–8; India and overseas 1913–32;
  Openings 1909–16; Overseas 1907–16; Pensions 1910–20; Pensions and
  salaries 1917–33; Science and art: compulsory afternoon school 1903–7;
  Qualifications for members 1905–7.
Annual reports 1895–1925 (up to 1916 they are bound with the miscellaneous
  pamphlet publications).
Attendance records: Annual conferences 1881–95; general meetings 1896–1907;
  conferences 1908–14; 1930–57.
Copies of early printed pamphlets issued by the Association.
Photograph albums: Members attending the 1890 conference; all past presidents of
  the Association.

Leeds Education Association (Leeds Central Library)

Annual reports 1871–80; minutes 1865–72; annual and committee meetings
1872–80.

Leeds University Women's Appeal (Leeds Central Library)

Committee minutes 1925–7; printed notices 1925.

Yorkshire Ladies' Council of Education (Leeds Central Library)
Founded on an informal basis in 1866 as a committee of the West Riding Board of
Education to organize the Cambridge Local Examination for girls. In 1870 the
West Riding Board of Education became the Yorkshire Board of Education and
enlarged its ladies' committee into the Ladies' Honorary Council of the Yorkshire
Board of Education, with the object of providing general elementary education for
working girls and women as well as encouraging higher education for girls.

In 1867 an independent group of ladies organized a course of lectures on
astronomy. This was the first step in the foundation of the Leeds Ladies'
Educational Association, a more formal body than the ladies' committee, which
took over the running of the Local Cambridge University examinations.

As often happens in such circumstances, the same women were concerned with
the running of both organizations, and although the two bodies cooperated in some
fields, including the founding of the Leeds Girls' High School, the common interest
in the higher education of women caused some friction, particularly as strong
personalities appear to have been involved.

Eventually, however, the Ladies' Honorary Council established its priority; it
separated from the Yorkshire Board of Education and in 1875 became the
Yorkshire Ladies' Council of Education. In 1879 the Registry of Governesses
started by the Leeds Ladies' Educational Association was handed over to the
Yorkshire Ladies' Council and in 1880–81 the two organizations appear to have

merged. The following are the complete records of the Council; those specifically relating to employment have also been included in the employment section.

Yorkshire Board of Education, Ladies' Honorary Council: Minutes of committees: annual and executive 1871–5; executive and health, including details of lectures 1872–5; annual reports 1871–5; subscribers' lists 1871–5; reports on the library at annual meetings 1874–5.

Yorkshire Ladies' Council of Education: Minutes of Committees: annual and executive 1875–1928; British overseas house sub-committee 1923; business and secretarial training 1899–1906; Cambridge Local Examinations 1881–1908; decorative and useful arts 1888–1908; education 1908–24; education and sanitary – later higher education, students' library and kindergarten 1885–1908; elementary education sub-committee 1905–8; employment of gentlewomen 1879–98; executive and health 1872–82; finance 1905–27; health and science school 1889–92; hostel 1905; house 1926–8; interim 1904–5; Leeds branch 1902–4; members' room sub-committee 1932–3; office 1908–13; public health and welfare executive 1910–13; public service 1909–14; technical instruction under County Council grants, Leeds sub-committee, 1892–1905; training school sub-committee 1919–27; war economy campaign sub-committee 1918; war service 1915.

Reports: annual 1876–1902, 1905–16, 1919–20; executive committee 1913, 1917, 1918, 1920, 1923, 1930–2; business and secretarial 1925–6; Cambridge Local Examinations 1877; education and sanitary committee 1885–6; health department 1882–8; health and science school committee 1889–92, 1898–1908; notes and reports on work of Yorkshire Ladies' Council (health education and library) 1884–99; prospectuses and reports on courses of health lectures in Leeds with question papers, 1872–89; register of governesses, 1878; library at annual meetings 1875–9; on reception of sanitary lectures 1872–3; public health and welfare associations (committee of the Yorkshire Ladies' Council) on infant mortality in Leeds, 1911; technical instruction Committee of Yorkshire Ladies' Council on classes in Leeds aided by City Council 1896–1904; technical instruction and training schools committees, 1902; Sheffield Branch, 1902; Leeds branch, 1903; administrative committee for technical instruction under county councils, 1903–6; technical work in West Riding 1904–5.

Balance sheets and reports of the executive 1913, 1917, 1918, 1920, 1923; ledger 1875–93.

Prospectuses, notices and other printed pamphlets covering the various aspects of the Council's work, 1889–1909.

Constitution; Rules, 1872; memorandum and Articles of Associations, 1904.

Correspondence: letter book – incoming 1922–3; correspondence over many years of Mrs Ina Kitson Clark on various topics; of Mrs Frances Lupton, Miss Lucy Wilson, Mrs Eddison on various topics; regarding the National League of Physical Education, 1906.

Diaries: Yorkshire Ladies' Council; Annual and committee meetings and lectures of Yorkshire Ladies' Council, 1887–99; extracts from a diary of Mrs Frances Lupton 1849–91.

Various printed and typescript histories of the Council; manuscript account of the life and work of Mrs Anna Paulina Eddison.

Inventories of furniture, etc, 1909; 18 Blenheim Terrace, Sheffield, 1928.

List of Council committees 1876–84.

Album of newspaper-cuttings relating to the Council and in particular to Mrs Kitson Clark 1906–61; women in the First World War, 1915–18.

Notebook made during an international council at The Hague, 1922.

Photographs of women connected with the Council, annotated.

See also Employment, below.

Affiliated and associated organizations

Association for Home Study in Chapel Allerton and District: Reports on lectures and programmes 1889–92.

Congress of the Sanitary Institute at Leeds: Minutes and report on the conference 1897.

Leeds Invalid Kitchen (although originally started in 1857 this was taken over by the committee of the Yorkshire School of Cookery in 1880): rules and register of medical men, 1857; ledger 1896–8.

Minutes of sub-committees: Infant Welfare Federation 1920; lectures 1910–11; literature 1910–11; provision of lodging-houses for women 1911–12.

Yorkshire Bureau for the Employment of Women: minutes of general, executive and committee meetings 1908–20; library sub-committee 1921; register of suiting fees 1908–20.

Yorkshire Exhibition of Women's Industries: committee minutes 1885.

Yorkshire School of Cookery: Minutes of executive committee 1884–1890; Leeds Branch, general, executive and subcommittee 1874–93; dairy committee papers; donations and subscriptions 1874–87; ledger 1873–89; programmes of public demonstrations, 1893–1908; prospectus 1886.

EMIGRATION

The Fawcett Library is the main source of primary material; details can be found in Part 4 below. There is no comparable collection although some material can be found elsewhere. This is listed below in alphabetical order by organization with the holding library or record office in brackets. The addresses and the facilities of these Libraries and Record Offices are given in Part 4.

ASSOCIATIONS AND SOCIETIES

British Women's Emigration Association
Ardagh Papers (Public Record Office, 30/40 Box 118). The Papers were collected by Susan Harris, Countess of Malmesbury, for a biography of her first husband (*The Life of Major-General Sir John Ardagh*, John Murray, 1909). She also took a leading part in women's emigration, and was particularly involved with the South African Colonization Society. Sir John Ardagh prepared proposals regarding emigration of women to South Africa when the BWEA was considering its South African policy, which was to result in the formation of the South African Colonization Society in 1901–2. Box 118 contains correspondence and papers concerning the British Women's Emigration Association and the emigration of women to South Africa.

Charity Organization Society (Greater London Council Record Office)
Minutes of Sub-committees: Emigration 1898–1914, 1936–43; Miss Stude's Home 1875–6.

Church Colonization Society and Church Emigration Society (Lambeth Palace Library)
The Archbishop Benson papers contain correspondence from 1887.

Girls' Friendly Society (Records to be deposited in The Public Record Office)
In 1885 the Society opened its emigration department but did not cater for large numbers of women.
Agenda books: emigration department; Aid and reference committee 1903–14.
See also Moral and social issues, below.

Englishwomen in India (all papers are held by the South Asian Archive, Cambridge, unless indicated otherwise)

During the period 1870–1928 many English women lived in India and led peculiarly English lives in a strange, and, particularly during the nineteenth century, remote land. They were in the main either the wives and daughters of Indian Civil Service officials, or missionaries sent out by one of the denominational missionary societies.

The India Office Library and Records have the most important collection of official sources relating to South Asia found outside the Indian sub-continent. These consist primarily of the archives of the East India Company and of the India Office, and include many official papers on topics relating to women. Information on the sources available can be found in a typescript 'Sources for Women's Studies in the India Office Library and Records', available from the India Office; this was produced as a contribution to a bibliography of archival sources relating to women now being produced under the editorship of Professors Patterson and Forbes of the Department of South Asian Languages and Civilizations at the University of Chicago.

In addition to the personal papers listed below, the South Asian Archive holds papers relating to women in India until Independence in 1947; these have not been included in this guide because of the cut-off date of 1928. Although 1928 is a date of some significance to women in England in that they were then granted full enfranchisement, it had no significance for Englishwomen in India, as their life in the sub-continent remained unchanged until the outbreak of the Second World War. The Centre for South Asian Studies, which was launched in 1966 to collect archive material relating to the area, has a project currently being undertaken to collect and index the letters and memoirs written by Englishwomen living in India 1900–1947. This project is under the supervision of Miss Thatcher to whom application should be made to consult the archival records in the Centre. In addition to archival material, the Centre has a library which is available for reference, and perhaps more importantly a collection of film material and tape interviews. This is fully described in Part 3, Oral history.

Mrs Jemmina Aimée Allan's letters to her sisters in Edinburgh describing social and domestic life in an English home in India, 1879–84. Mrs Allan was the wife of Alexander Allan, proprietor of Glenmore and Pillar Coffee Estates, Coomer, South India.

Lady Jean Anderson's letters, written while touring with her husband round Alipur and Sitpur in the 1920s.

Miss Eva Bell's letters describing country and camp life in Kashmir in 1920.

Papers and diaries of Mrs Annette Beveridge, founder of the Hindu Mahilu Bidyalaya (Hindu Ladies' School) in Calcutta in 1873. (India Office Records, Mss. Eur. c. 176)

Lady Alison Blood's articles, commonplace books 1918–33, programmes and a journal illustrated with photographs, drawings and newspaper-cuttings.

Mrs Irene Bose's memoir of her life in India 1926–74.

Mrs M. O. Dench's 'Memsahib', a description of the journey to India and of her life there as the wife of a sub-divisional officer, 1918–41.

Mrs C. W. Foster's exercise-book containing her housekeeping accounts 1912–20; it also includes recipes, addresses and general household miscellanea.

Mrs Gage's letters, written in 1920 while accompanying her husband on an inspection tour of the Laccadine Islands. The letters describe travelling between the islands, island life, people, domestic life and customs, and are a good example of the experiences of a young Indian Civil Service officer's wife.

Lady Elinor Lyall Grant's memoir, written in 1950 but unfinished, of the years 1900–6. It concerns her engagement and early years of marriage, including journeys to and from England.

Lilian Shillington Haigh's letters written on the voyage to India and about her first experiences in settling in as a missionary, 10 Dec 1886–26 Sept 1887; letters written while on a tour of Northern India 1891 (in Box XIII of the Maxwell papers); manuscript notebooks about time spent in the Nilgiri Hills, South India, and in Kananerse; manuscript of a talk about women's missionary work in India; series of printed missionary letters.

A collection of over 900 letters, written by Miss Agatha S. Hellier, a missionary teacher from the Methodist Missionary Society, to her mother, family and friends from 1923, many letters running to several pages. They provide a very full account of the life of a missionary in India in the 1920s.

Mrs Margaret Murison's memoir of her whole life, 1896–1969. Part 2 is concerned with her life in India, from 1910 (when she went there to be married) to 1925. It includes an account of the journey to India and life in a travelling dispensary.

Mrs N. E. Parry's typescript memoir, 'People and places in Assam', which relates to the life of a District Officer's wife in the 1920s.

Mrs P. T. Pengree's diary; as the wife of a tea planter in Assam 1924–8 it describes a number of expeditions made by boat.

Lady Alice Reading's papers 1921–6 (two boxes). She was Vicereine of India 1924–6 and took an active part in social work in India. (India Office Records, Mss Eur. E. 316).

Lady Beatrix Scott's account of her life as the wife of an Indian Civil Servant, 1910–39.

Christian Showers-Stirling's notes on her life in India 1902–15.

Lady Alice Stokes's commonplace book, 1922–35.

Lady Helen Stokes's letters on domestic and social life, 1872–3.

Constance Wilson's unpublished autobiography, including a description of her work as a nurse in India, 1921–47. (India Office Records, Mss Eur. C.251)

See also Diaries, Englishwomen in India.

EMPLOYMENT

Fabian Women's Group (Nuffield College, Oxford)

The Women's Group was founded in 1908 by Mr C. M. Wilson although the Fabian Society had earlier concerned itself with issues relating to women. This interest is reflected in the publications of the Fabian Society, which after the formation of the Women's Group continued to publish documents of importance to women. The Women's Group did however have its own offices and under its auspices publications appeared including *Women Workers in Seven Professions: a survey of their economic conditions*, edited by Edith J. Morley (Routledge, 1914). Its own material was generally issued for private circulation only. The Group took an active part, independently and in cooperation with other bodies, in the various movements affecting women. It had a particular interest in the suffrage movement, the majority of its members being Suffrage Society workers. The Group's main concern, however, was with conditions of employment and the effect of legislation on women in employment.

Minutes: executive committee 1908–30; board of studies, 1908–13; citizenship sub-committee 1908–12; domestic relief committee 1914–15; Fabian Women's Group meetings 1908–26; parliamentary; Sub-committee on the position of women in trade unions 1915; suffrage section 1911–17.
Various records of resolutions, etc, 1913–14.
Joint committee of the Fabian Women's Group and the Fabian Research Department 1915–17.
Account books 1908–18; attendance lists 1909–21.
Publications of the Fabian Women's Group.
Printed announcements of various women's organizations.
'Women's Progress', an unsigned manuscript.

National Union of Women Workers, Leeds branch (Leeds Central Library)

Minutes 1892–9; Handbook of central conference 1893.

Yorkshire Ladies' Council of Education (Leeds Central Library)

The city library has extensive holdings of the Council's records. The material listed below is related only to the employment of women.

Minutes of meetings: business and secretarial training committee 1899–1906; employment of gentlewomen committee 1879–84, 1884–90, 1890–8; National Union of Women Workers, Leeds Branch 1892–9; Yorkshire Bureau for the

Employment of Women, general executive committee meetings 1908–20.
Business and secretarial committee, Statistics of work 1908–18; summary of
   earnings 1908–13.
See also Education, above, and Midwifery, below.

Margaret Ethel MacDonald (British Library of Political
and Economic Science)

Manuscript letters and papers concerning shop fines, employment of women and
other social questions 1895–1912.

See also Part 2, Biographies.

Dr Helen Wilson (Sheffield City Library, Department of
Local History and Archives)

Donated by Dr Helen Wilson, who had collected these papers during an enquiry
conducted by the Women's Industrial Council into the effects of the industrial
employment of married women in the Sheffield area.

Enquiry form and the 'Hints to investigators'; notes made for this enquiry, giving
   details of worker, family, wages, apparent economic results, characteristics of
   trade; eight case studies of married women workers, by Sister Margaret of Croft
   House Settlement, 1908–9. They concern work, wages, children, social and
   family life.

PROFESSIONS AND TRADES

Armed services

The women's services originated from the nursing services attached to the army
during the Boer War. Queen Alexandra's Imperial Military Nursing Service was
founded in 1902 and in 1909 the First Aid Nursing Yeomanry was founded as a
force of expert horsewomen who would ride on to the battlefield to assist the
wounded. However, during the First World War the horsewomen gave way to the
less romantic but more practical tasks of driving ambulances and nursing in field
hospitals. The Women's Army Auxiliary Corps was founded after the outbreak of
the First World War. It became effective in 1915 and in May 1918 its name was
changed to Queen Mary's Army Auxiliary Corps. The Women's Royal Naval
Service was founded in 1917 by Dame Katharine Furse and disbanded in 1918. It
was not re-formed until the Second World War. The Women's Royal Air Force
was formed in 1918 from flying units in the WRNS and Queen Mary's Auxiliary
Corps, but the service was not fully established until the Second World War.

Miscellaneous papers (1914–18 Archive, Sunderland): includes xerox copies of
   certificates, enrolment and discharge papers relating to WRNS, WAAC and
   WRAF; photographs of WRNS and WAAC.

(The following material is held in The Public Record Office, reference WO 162/ unless numbered otherwise.)

Conferences: On the organization of women employed in the army 1917; Employment of the General Service Section of the VAD in France 1917; Coordinating conference of Women's Corps meetings 1919.

Reports: Women's Services Committee, by Sir George Newson, 1916; Women War Workers Resettlement Committee 1918; Women's Reserve Committee 1920–1 (123/813).

Correspondence on payment of women doctors 1917; employment of women 1917; hostels and accommodation 1918; enrolment of women employed by the army: draft army council instruction 1917; official recognition of Women's Legion as a voluntary reserve transport unit 1917 (114/GEN/6759).

First Aid Nursing Yeomanry (Chelsea Barracks, London; photocopies in the 1914–18 Archive at Sunderland)

Papers concerning the early days of the FANY from 1909; particulars of early members; general information on the history of the FANY.

Lamarck (a dressing station in France) 1915–16, reports, correspondence, personnel and closure considerations. Notes for a report on the work done for the Belgians, 1914, 1915, 1916; convalescent homes 1915–17 for the Belgians, letters, etc; Calais British Convoy, reports 1917, 1918; correspondence regarding sick members; 1919, regarding personnel vehicles, uniform, service recognition, promotions, new arrangements with the Red Cross.

St Omer Unit VIII: Mainly French documents regarding Franco-British administrative cooperation at Port à Buison. FANY report of work for the French wounded; convoys for French, SS Y2, Amiens, Elernay, Chalons SS Y5.

Correspondence and forms dealing with medals and letters of thanks and praise for all units.

Patronage and fund-raising.

Equipment and accounts; includes booklets for ambulances, samples of fabric for uniforms, orders for food and medical supplies.

Organization at headquarters, committees; letters to the Secretary, Mrs Cowlen, and Miss Anderson.

Queen Alexandra's Imperial Military Nursing Service

Report of sub-committee on pay and pensions 1903 (WO32/9340); 1904 (WO32/9341).

Queen Mary's Army Auxiliary Corps

Minutes: Conference between representatives of QMAAC, WRNS and Ministry of Labour 1917–18; issue of great-coats, minutes and memorandum, 1918.

Correspondence concerning discharge on medical grounds.

Papers: demobilization, strength and progress; number of women enrolled 1918; overseas settlement of women; posting of six members of the No. 15 Canadian

Hospital, Taplow, Bucks, 1918; QMAAC working with the American Expeditionary Force 1919; suggestions for recruiting; transfer of members to the WRAF and WRNS 1918; visit of the Duchess of Atholl to France 1918.

Royal Flying Corps

Minutes: recruitment 1917.

Women's Auxiliary Army Corps

Until the formation of the Women's Auxiliary Army Corps in 1917 the women's units were small and mainly run on an amateur basis. The exception to this was the nursing service which since Florence Nightingale's work in the Crimea had become an accepted part of the army. The WAAC recruited and trained girls, mainly domestic servants, although clerks and telephonists were recruited as well. Immediately following their training these girls were sent to France where they relieved men for front-line duty.

Conference held at the War Office 1917.
Correspondence from the National Service Department to the Director on recruiting.
Papers: rates of pay, draft Army Council instructions 1917; administration in France 1917; mobile and immobile branches, Army Council instructions 1917; recruitment, training and conditions of service of women to relieve men of certain army duties 1916–17; proposals regarding uniform and badges to be worn by women holding positions equivalent to commissioned rank 1917; decisions reached concerning organization on a civil or military basis 1917; administrative staff, appointments, pay and conditions of service 1917; forms and memorandum, 'Injuries in war', 1918; lists of motor drivers 1918; letter from Ministry of Labour regarding publication of reports to be made by visiting Commissioners to France 1918; press statements on condition of WAAC in France 1918; recommendations for honours 1918–19.

Women's Royal Army Corps (Women's Royal Army Corps Museum)

Photographs: A fine collection which show the activities undertaken by the women's army during the First World War. These include social activities as well as the more usual service ones.
Recruiting posters and leaflets giving rates of pay and conditions of service.
See also Diaries, First World War.

Health Visitors' Association

Established in 1896 as the Women's Sanitary Inspectors' Association and as a trade union although it was not registered as such until 1918. It changed its name to the Women's Sanitary Inspectors and Health Visitors' Association in 1915, again in 1929 to the Women's Public Health Association, and in 1962 to its present one.

Minutes: Annual meetings from 1928; executive committee 1902–15, from 1926; annual reports from 1906.

Match-manufacturing industries (House of Lords Library A/1 1890–2)

Papers on the conditions of employment of match-box makers in England and Sweden.
Correspondence; newspaper-cuttings; rules of the Match Box Makers' Union; notes on visit to Sweden.

(Trades Union Congress Library).
Correspondence and papers of Lady Dilke referring to the conditions of employment for girls working in match factories, with particular reference to phosphorous poisoning.
See also Papers: Mrs Millicent Garrett Fawcett, below.

Midwifery

Holborn and Finsbury Midwives' Association (Royal College of Midwives)

Minutes 1909–13; correspondence; balance 1913.

Midwives' Association, Gillingham branch (Royal College of Midwives)

Minutes 1921; correspondence and photographs of Rosa Smith, a founder member of the Royal College of Midwives.

Royal College of Midwives

In 1881 the Midwives' Institute was founded to 'raise the efficiency and improve the status of midwives and to petition Parliament for their recognition'. As a direct result of continued petitioning the first Midwives' Act was passed in 1902 and resulted in the establishment of a statutory body, the Central Midwives Board, to govern training and state registration. The Act made it illegal for any unqualified person to work as a midwife. However, because of poor working conditions midwifery attracted few middle-class women, for although some trained in midwifery they frequently changed to district nursing. Membership of the Midwives' Institute gradually increased; in 1941 it became the College of Midwives and in 1947 it was granted a royal charter. At present it has a membership of nearly 17,000 and its prime objective is still 'to promote and advance the art and science of midwifery and to raise the efficiency of midwives'.

Accounts 1893–1941; correspondence 1881–1941.
Royal Maternity Charity letters from recipients and husbands, 1920–34.

Training of Midwives and West Riding Nursing
Association (Leeds Central Library)

Minutes: midwives' committee 1908; executive committee 1909–10; provisional
   sub-committee 1908–9. Pamphlets and news-cuttings concerning its
   foundations 1908. Superintendents' reports 1920–1.

Teaching

For archival material relating to women in the teaching profession refer to the
entries for the Association of Head Mistresses and the Association of Assistant
Mistresses in the Education section above. However, a National Union of Women
Teachers was established in the late nineteenth century with the object of obtaining
equal pay and status for women teachers. When this was achieved the organization
closed, and unfortunately no records have been traced apart from those of the Kent
Organizing Committee held in Kent County Record Office which refer to the
post-1928 period.

Trade Unions

Railway Women's Guild (Labour Party Library)

Correspondence of Mrs Mary A. Macpherson, Secretary, regarding the possibility
of a Women's Labour Federation in association with the Labour Representative
Committee 1904.

Standing Joint Committee of Industrial Women's
Organizations (Labour Party Library)

Minutes 1916, 1919–25; correspondence 1919–25

Women's Labour League (Labour Party Library)

Minutes: Executive committee 1900–11; central London: branch meetings;
   executive committee, 1906–18; Publication and general purposes committee
   1911.
Queries regarding union organization of female labour 1906–8.
Volume containing names of subscribers to, and purchasers of, WLL leaflets,
   1911–17; another containing brief notes about branches 1910.
Cash books 1908–9, balance sheets 1907–8; treasurer's receipts and expenditure
   book 1917–18.

Women's Trade Union League (Trades Union Congress
Library)

The League was founded by Emma Paterson in 1874 to promote trade unionism
amongst women; it developed as a federation of affiliated trade unions. Any trade
union which allowed women members was able to affiliate. The aim of the League
was to encourage women to join men's societies, although often men's unions
closed their ranks to women, whom they regarded as cheap labour. By 1906 there

were 167,000 women members of trade unions, the majority in the textile trades; but those women most in need of trade unions, low-paid home workers, were still, in the majority of cases, unorganized. It was these workers that the League sought to organize. In addition to its organizational activities the League had a provident side, including a Women's Half-penny Bank, and it also had its own library and swimming club. The league was absorbed by the TUC in 1921.

Minutes: Committees: executive 1903–21; Annual Congress 1895–1921. Correspondence 1918–21.

These records are obtainable on microfilm from EP Microfilm Ltd, East Ardley, Wakefield, Yorkshire.

FIRST WORLD WAR

WOMEN'S WORK COLLECTION, DEPARTMENT
OF PRINTED BOOKS, IMPERIAL WAR MUSEUM

Material relating to women is located in several Departments at the Museum:
Documents, Film Archives, Photographs, Printed Books and Sound Archives. The
Department of Printed Books has over a hundred boxes of manuscript letters,
pamphlets, newspaper-cuttings, etc, which were collected at the end of the First
World War from women who were involved in war work of some kind. There is a
bound photocopied index to the Collection, arranged by country and by subject.
The Department also has a good collection of books relating to the role of women in
the First World War.

The material listed here is purely archival; other material at the Museum is
referred to in Parts 2, 3 and 4.

The Department of Documents has a collection of reminiscences and scrap
books and these are listed separately below.

The Department of Exhibits and Firearms has a comprehensive collection of
uniforms.

Armed services

Queen Mary's Army Auxiliary Corps

Scheme for a Women's Army Corps; organization of women; employment of
women with the armies; status of WAAC; conference of employment of women
in France.

Mrs Gwynne-Vaughan's diary of her visit to France, Feb 1917.

Correspondence between Sir Reginald Brade, secretary to the War Office, and
Dame Kathleen Furse 1917, founder of WRNS.

Account of the first year's work. Forms, leaflets and regulations; circulars from
HQ; circular letters; Corps orders.

Various Commands: London; Aldershot, School of Cookery; Eastern; Northern;
Southern; Scottish; Irish.

General reports by the Assistant Chief Controller; notes on conferences held at
headquarters; report of the Commission of Enquiry appointed by the Ministry of
Labour to enquire into the WAAC in France; miscellaneous papers including
articles, programmes, etc.

Women's Royal Air Force

Miscellaneous forms, leaflets, pamphlets, posters, etc; notes from Dame Helen

Gwynne-Vaughan; correspondence; National Political League circular; press-cuttings; Report of the WRAF inquiry on the Hon. Violet Douglas-Pennant; correspondence relating to the termination of her appointment.

Women's Royal Naval Service

Documents and instructions including précis of WRNS series of dockets, orders, regulations; specimen papers of a WRNS division as filed in WRNS registry; special report on women's work in the WRNS; letters of appreciation to WRNS; reports from ports; reports on recreation, etc; WRNS journal; photographs of directors, assistant directors, etc; statistics; schemes for demobilization and permanent service; maps and charts.

WAAC and WRNS official papers, miscellaneous files.

Decorations: press-cuttinngs and photographs of decorations and their recipients; names of women of the British Empire to whom the Military Medal was awarded.

Countries

These files contain information relating to the work of women in various countries, mainly on relief work, they show the massive mobilization of women and the amount of effort put into fund-raising activities.

Armenia: Relief funds.

Belgium: local government boards' reports; war refugees committee; Lady Lugard's hospitality committee; metropolitan asylum board; Women's Emergency Corps; local relief committees (items relating to some 256 local committees established for the relief of Belgian refugees); employment in Great Britain (of Belgians); relief funds (organized for Belgians in Great Britain by the British); relief funds organized by Belgians in Great Britain; Red Cross hospitals: home, including VAD hospitals; abroad, including Pervyse Allies Dressing-Station; organizations for the relief of Belgian civilians, records of eleven funds; prisoners and internees; W. E. Dowding, includes Belgian relief; press-cuttings; Lycée de Londres.

Colonies: press-cuttings: Australasia; Australia; New Zealand; Canada; Canadian women; South Africa, various funds and societies; Gold Coast Imperial War Fund.

Czecho-Slovakia: Lady Paget's Mission.

France: French Red Cross hospitals run by the French Red Cross; canteens; ambulances; women organizing emergency canteens; sanatorium; relief funds; French funds.

See also Nursing services and hospitals, below.

India: India's part in the war; women's work; women – press-cuttings.

Italy: British Red Cross in Italy; Italian Red Cross Society; British-Italian League; press-cuttings.

Montenegro: Red Cross and Relief Fund.

Poland: miscellaneous.

Roumania: Red Cross Society, press-cuttings.

Russia: Anglo-Russian Hospital; Russian Relief Fund; Millicent Garrett Fawcett
    Maternity Unit for Russia, minutes and correspondence.

Serbia: Relief Fund; press-cuttings.

Syria and Palestine: Relief Fund.

United States of America: Societies and Relief Fund.

Employment

Government reports from various Departments including Health, Unemployment,
    etc, relating to women workers during the war.

Queen's Work for Women Fund, leaflets, newspaper-cuttings, etc.

Schemes by Dame Katharine Furse for national service for women.

Notes on work already performed by Employment Exchanges on recruiting women
    for various occupations, together with suggestions and proposals for enrolment of
    women for national service.

Substitution: reports; correspondence; charts; Home Office correspondence with
    Miss Anderson, senior surgeon of the Endell Street Military Hospital run by the
    Women's Hospital Corps.

Agricultural work: Press-cuttings, arranged by area; speeches; National Political
    League; Women's National Land Service Corps, HQ file 1915–18,
    demobilization; Women's Land Army, Wood production department;
    pamphlets, Women's Institutes; local records: 460 town files.

Civil Service, subdivided into Departments and the type of work undertaken by
    women.

Clerical work in banks and insurance.

Food: Ministry of Food reports and literature; Patriotic Housekeeping Exhibition
    1916; National Food Economy League.

Health, 23 various reports.

Housing reports.

Industrial work: Gas Light and Coke Co; London Electric Railway Co; London
    General Omnibus Co; South Metropolitan Gas Co; W. G. Tarrant, Sons & Co,
    – women carpenters in France; General Post Office; Royal Mail van drivers.

Munitions and shipbuilding: General information concerning munitions exhibitions,
    catalogues, etc.

Files on Ministry of Munitions depots: Bolton; Crewe; Lemington-on-Tyne;
    Newbury; Woolwich Arsenal.

Anti-gas Department, including Miss M. Carey Morgan's report.

Cardonald National projectile factory; Georgetown Scottish filling factory; Gretna ordnance factory; Hewlett & Blondeau, aeroplane manufacturers.

Kingsnorth Airship Station: accounts of work done by women in the chemical laboratory and engineers' drawing office.

Accounts of the work of women mathematicians in the New Design Branch, Technical Department's aircraft production.

White City naval airships.

Miss D. G. Poole's account of her career from a munition worker to a Dilution Officer in the Ministry of Munitions.

Welfare in munition factories, Ministry of Munitions' Women's Service Committee, Minutes of Evidence 23, 24 and 28 Nov, 1, 5 and 8 Dec 1916, result of evidence report.

Annual reports of the National Projectile and Shell factories; reports and lists of supervisors.

Reports from Armstrong Whitworth & Co; Barr & Stroud; National Amatol Factory; North British Rubber Co. Ltd; Woolwich Arsenal.

Shipbuilding: Harland & Wolff; John Brown & Co; Palmers, Jarrow.

Observations on the effects of TNT on women workers.

Police: women volunteers; Patrols' Committee, miscellaneous papers, reports, leaflets, badges, Reports 1914–36; police service; patrols, press-cuttings.

Railway Executive account of women's work during the war: Great Central; Lancs. and Yorkshire.

Scientific work undertaken by women: National Physical Laboratory, anti-gas research and correspondence with Mrs G. Nicholson relating to her patent for improvements relating to mine-sweeping apparatus.

Trade Unions, articles, leaflets and press-cuttings.

Nursing services and hospitals

Joint Women's Voluntary Aid Detachment Department; Great Britain: Reports 1908–17; minutes of the Committee 1915–17; press-cuttings 1912; Dame Katharine Furse's papers, including ideals, organizations, complaints, reforms, etc.

Experiences of a VAD at Dublin Castle during the rebellion.

Abroad: VAD work in France; miscellaneous reports by Dame Katharine Furse and Miss Rachel Spoody on Convalescent homes for QMAAC and nurses; VAD detention stations; VAD hostels; VAD recreation huts at convalescent camps; VAD rest stations.

List of VAD officers serving in France 1918.

VAD work in Italy, Holland, Switzerland, Egypt, Malta.

Material relating to the various hospitals for the wounded; and to the hospital units staffed by medical women: Endell Street Military Hospital, Women's Imperial

Service League Hospital, Scottish Women's Hospital, lists of members and photographs.

Army and nursing services: Bridgeman Report and Nurses' Registration Bill; Committee for the medical history of the war; Edith Cavell Home of Rest for Nurses; miscellaneous work of army nurses; National Fund for Nurses; National Union of Trained Nurses; QAIMNS and Reserve; Territorial Force Nursing Service.

Ambulances and motor transport: Hospital Motor Squadron; London Ambulance Column; LCC Ambulance Service; RAC War Service: Volunteer Motor Mobilization Corps.

Territorial Force: St Andrew's Ambulance Corps; Scottish Women's First Aid Corps.

Miscellaneous material, including press-cuttings.

Material relating to these organizations in the provinces.

Suffrage and politics

British Dominions' Women's Suffrage Union; Catholic Women's Suffrage Society; Conservative and Unionist Women's Franchise Society; International Women's Suffrage Alliance; League of the Church Militant (formerly Church League for Women's Suffrage); Liberal Women's Suffrage Society; National Union of Women's Suffrage Societies, London branches, country branches; Professional Women's Patriotic Service Fund; Women Writers' Suffrage League; Women's Freedom League; Women's International League; Women's Municipal Party; Workers' Party; Workers' Suffrage Federation.

Election addresses: Mrs Corbett Ashby, Mrs Dace Fox, Mrs Alison Garland, Mrs How-Martyn, Miss Mary Macarthur, Mrs McEwan, Miss Violet Markham, Miss Christabel Pankhurst, Mrs Pethick-Lawrence, Mrs Oliver Strachey.

Pamphlets: suffrage debates; newspaper-cuttings on women and local government.

Volunteer Corps

Home Service Corps, Liverpool; Royal Automobile Club; Voluntary Service League; Women signallers: Lady Instructors' Signals Company; School of Women Signallers; Women Signallers' Territorial Corps; Women Volunteer Motor Drivers; Women's Auxiliary Force; Women's Emergency Corps, Bournemouth and Edinburgh branches; Women's Volunteer Reserve.

War work by students

Various documents, including reports and registers relating to the war work done by students from the following universities and colleges:

Bristol; Cambridge: Girton, Newnham; Leeds; Liverpool; London: Bedford, Royal Holloway, King's College, Household and Social Science Department,

School of Economics, Westfield; Manchester: Victoria University; Oxford:
Lady Margaret Hall, St Hugh's, Somerville; Sheffield; Swinley.
Federation of University Women.
Press-cuttings: schoolchildren, universities; pamphlets.

Welfare

Benevolent organizations

Miscellaneous papers and press-cuttings relating to the many organizations and
comfort funds organized by women for the benefit of the troops, their dependants
and women workers. These vary greatly in scope from HRH Princess Mary's
Gift Fund to the Silver Thimble Fund and Lady Gladys Storey's Bovril Fund.
There are some sixty files relating to these funds, although many contain only a
small amount of information. The material in these files is often the only source
of information for many of the smaller and therefore lesser-known organizations.
Entertainments: material relating to various entertainments and organizing
committees.

Children

Press-cuttings; literature distributed by societies at the National Baby Week
Council; Day nurseries; Children's Jewel Fund.

Clubs and canteens

At home: Soldiers on leave, motor transport volunteers, London station buffets,
etc; Abroad: Corner of Blighty, British Army and Navy League Clubs, etc.
Clubs and hostels for wives of soldiers and sailors and for women workers.
Press-cuttings; files on individual clubs, including the Girls' Friendly Society and
the Travellers' Aid Society.

Patriotic associations

'Fight for right' movement; League of Honour; Navy League; Girl Guides, etc.

Prisoners

General file; Lady Dobbs' Prisoner of War Funds; RAF Prisoners' Funds; local
funds (approximately 80 individual files); press-cuttings.

Relief

British refugees from Turkey; National Food Fund; Society of Friends: War
Victims Relief Committee; Maternité Anglaise at Chalons-sur-Marne;
Emergency Committee for the assistance of Germans; Austrians and Hungarians
in distress.

Religious and temperance organizations

Additional Curates' Society War Fund; Baptist Women's League; Catholic Club;
Catholic Federation of the Archbishop of Westminster; Catholic Women's

League; Chaplains' Fund; Church Army; Church of England Temperance Society; (National) British Women's Temperance Association; Salvation Army; Scottish churches.

DEPARTMENT OF DOCUMENTS, IMPERIAL WAR MUSEUM

General

Lieutenant F. A. Brettrell's correspondence with his future wife 1915–16. She was a driver with the Women's Legion, and gives home front news and views on female emancipation.

A. Bryan's letter from Salonika, 1918.

C. Burleigh's memoir, letter and photographs, 1914–16.

C. A. Hill's miscellaneous papers. She was a secretary in MI5, 1915–18.

Constance Miles, *see* Diaries, First World War, below.

P. E. Plaistow's passport and brief manuscript. She was a secretary at the Allied Mission.

Mrs E. E. Quinlan's memoir and miscellaneous papers. She was a clerk with the WAAC in France, 1917–19.

D. I. K. Stevenson's papers. She was a volunteer welfare worker in France, 1916–18.

A. S. Tait, *see* Diaries, First World War, below.

G. West, ditto.

G. L. Wilby's letters to Ethel, his fiancée, which include violent opposition to her doing 'man's work'.

Agricultural work

M. Bale's brief account of the Women's Land Army, 1916–19.

R. Freedman's memoir of the Women's Land Army.

G. Mazey's papers, including handbooks.

Helen Bowen Wedgwood's letters which relate to the Land Army and to conscientious objectors.

Armed services

Mrs M. Brunskill Reid's papers and correspondence, 1915, pamphlets, membership lists, etc, of Women Signallers Territorial Corps.

B. Gordon's letters. She was a WRNS wireless telegraphist.

The Hon. Dorothy Pickford's letters, 1918–19. She was Assistant Administrator, WAAC and QMAAC.

C. F. Shave's papers and photographs, Women's Volunteer Reserve, 1917.

M. Simmonds's QMAAC notebook.

W. Waller's autograph book, WAAC.

Munition work

Mrs M. H. Adams's account (written in 1970) of life as a driver for Vickers arms
  factory.
A. Darter's typescript – a munition worker.
P. L. Stephens's memoir of a munition factory, engineering and motor-cycling.
U. A. Williams's typescript of a munition worker's career at Gwynnes Ltd,
  Chiswick, 1915–19.

Nursing services and hospitals

Mrs M. Battrum's post cards and photographs, 1915; an account of her career as a
  nurse, and of Edith Cavell's career; letters written by Edith Cavell, and
  correspondence with soldiers who had been helped.
M. W. Cannan's work with the British Red Cross VAD No. 12, 1909–19.
M. Cottam's letters and memoir, Scottish Women's Hospital, Serbia 1918.
I. Edgar's letters, photographs and miscellaneous items, QAIMNS.
A. Garland, *see* Diaries, First World War, below.
Miss A. Glenny's letters, a VAD in Montenegro, 1915 and 1920.
Nurse Elsie P. Grey, *see* Diaries, First World War, below.
R. Haire-Foster's account of her life and work as VAD Commandant, Salonika
  1918.
E. Hastings, see Diaries, First World War, below.
Mrs D. Hay's letters from Red Cross Hospital Unit, Serbia 1915, and Italy 1917.
Dr L. Henry's full account of her work at the Scottish Women's Hospital,
  Royaumont, 1917–18.
Beryl Hutchinson's account of her work as FANY driver, 1914–19.
Mrs D. Irving-Bell's papers and photographs, VAD West Country hospital,
  1916–20.
Mrs G. A. Jones, *see* Diaries, First World War, below.
R. I. Leared's account of service as a WAAC ambulance driver, 1914–17.
D. H. Littlejohn's letters, 1914–15, cook with Scottish Women's Hospital in
  France.
G. McDougal's typescript of 'Five years with the Allies, the story of the FANY
  Corps'.
Mrs G. MacKay Brown's scrap books and photographs, VAD Rouen, 1915–19.
M. L. McNeill, *see* Diaries, First World War, below.
K. S. MacPhail's letters and postcards – Serbian Relief Fund in Marne, Corsica
  and Haute Savoie, 1916.
C. Meade's miscellaneous papers, 1917, 1918 and 1919 – Ambulance Unit and
  FANY.
R. M. de Montmorency, *see* Diaries, First World War, below.
E. J. Morgan's letters, photographs, etc.
Mrs A. Mullineaux, *see* Diaries, First World War, below.
M. B. Peterkin, ditto.

E. J. Rice's letters, QAIMNS.
Dr Jean Rose, *see* Diaries, First World War, below.
F. Scott's letters, photographs and a memoir, Red Cross nurse 1915.
D. C. Spickett's small collection of official papers and letters – VAD in a hospital ship.
M. G. Trembath, *see* Diaries, First World War, below.

1914–18 ARCHIVE, SUNDERLAND

In addition to the papers listed below this archive contains a substantial collection of tape-recordings made in recent years by women involved in the First World War. These are listed in Part 3, Oral history. The papers below have been divided into those relating to the war front and to the domestic front, in accordance with the arrangement of the Archive itself.

See also Diaries below.

Domestic front

Miss K. Alexander's diary, 1914–18, written from her home. The Archive also has her brother's diaries, as well as tape recordings by herself and her brother.
Miss Olive Armstrong's diary, written in Dublin 1915–18.
Dame Elizabeth Cockayne's recollections, and documents relating to nursing.
Dame Margery Corbett-Ashby's letters and typescript recollections. She was an active suffrage worker.
E. A. Macleod's letters, diary and diary extracts, describing life at her home in Cambridge, at Dartford College, and various forms of war work. The Archive also has the papers of her mother, her brother and her sister.
Mrs E. Macleod's household accounts, 1914–18, letters and papers.
Miss M. L. Macleod's letters, diary for 1916–18, recollections of home life in Cambridge, at Gypsy Hill College, and various types of war work.
Miss D. McMurdo's housekeeping book, 1917.
Lady Mabel Napier's diary recording her husband's death at Gallipoli in 1915; letters 1914–18.
Mrs Robb's diary of a girl working in a photographic shop in Kirkwall, Orkney, 1911–18.
Lady Olive Stedman's recollections of an air raid.
Papers relating to agriculture, including photographs and photocopies of the Public Record Office papers on the Women's Land Army.
Papers relating to clerical work during the war, including recollections of Miss Jenkins who did cipher work for the Admiralty.
Recollections in the form of letters to Mr Liddle from individuals relating to the effect the First World War had on their lives. They include some from women describing war work on the land, VAD nursing, etc.

War front

Mrs Pat W. Beauchamp's photographs and typescript recollections. She was the author of *FANY goes to war*.

Nurse A. C. E. Beaumont's photographs and autograph album. She was a member of Queen Alexandra's Nursing Corps.

Nurse G. K. Brumwell – an article.

Nurse M. Chisholm's typescript memoir.

Mrs Charlotte Cook's photographs and typescript recollections. She was a nurse with the Friends' Ambulance Service.

Nurse G. V. Crowder's certificates and letters.

Mrs Disney-Simons's Women's Legion badge, documents and a photograph.

Nurse M. A. C. Gibson (QMAAC) – xerox letters.

Mrs E. Hogg (*née* Hallam), a VAD – diary extracts, 3 Aug–19 Nov 1918, 23 Nov–19 Dec 1918.

Mrs Peggy Heaton, a VAD – letters from France to Miss Phillips and letters from Miss Pinkie Fenwick.

Miss Hutchinson, a FANY nurse – scrapbook of newspaper-cuttings relating to the FANY; typescript recollections of the Calais and St Omer convoys.

Miss M. M. James, a Sister in the Territorial Force Nursing Service – diary, 29 Oct 1914–15 Jan 1916.

Nurse S. Kitson – a few official documents, including identity papers.

Lady Lenanton's tape-recording, photographs and various papers.

Mrs McCann, a VAD nurse – autograph album, photographs and tape-recording.

Nurse G. Milburn, British Red Cross – letters, papers, diaries, artefacts and a tape-recording.

M. Parker, British Red Cross driver – manuscript recollections.

Miss Puckle, British Red Cross and FANY – letters, photographs and typescript recollections.

Nurse M. Ranking's letters to her brother while training.

Mrs Dorothy Smith's brief diary, 1914–20 as a VAD in Salonika, Constantinople and Cologne.

Nurse Suffield, a VAD – xerox copies of papers, letters and leaflets (originals in Sunderland Museum).

Miss Violet Thurstan, a nurse on the Eastern front – diaries 1914–19, copies of letters, papers and newspaper-cuttings.

Mrs B. M. Trefusis's diary, 1914–16.

Baroness de T'scrclaes's slides. She was the author of *The cellar house of Pervyse*.

Dr M. Verney, on the Eastern front with the Scottish Women's Hospital – xerox letters from Macedonia and Serbia.

A. Wherry's photographs, certificates, newspaper-cuttings and typescript recollections.

Sara Wilsdon (*née* Apporley) – illustrated diary, 1 Jan 1918–4 Sept 1919.

Nurse Wynne-Eyton's photographs.

MORAL AND SOCIAL ISSUES

BIRTH CONTROL

Family Planning Association

In 1921 the Malthusian League established the Walworth Women's Advisory
Clinic and the North Kensington Women's Welfare Centre to provide birth control
information. These clinics differed from one established in 1921 by Marie Stopes in
that at the North Kensington and Walworth Clinics all women were seen by a
medical practitioner. In 1924 the committee of the Walworth Clinic adopted the
name 'Society for the Provision of Birth Control Clinics', and encouraged the
formation of new clinics. By 1929 twelve clinics had been opened in different parts
of the country, despite fierce opposition from local Catholic communities. In 1930
the National Birth Control Council was established; the name was changed in 1931
to National Birth Control Association, and finally in 1939 to the Family Planning
Clinic.

The Clinic has papers relating to the Association from 1930, as well as early
records from other clinics received in response to an appeal by the Association for
early records; these do however relate to the post-1928 period.

Marie Stopes Memorial Centre (now housed in the British
Library Manuscript Division)

The Society and Clinic for Constructive Birth Control was founded in 1921 by Dr
Marie Stopes as part of her campaign for a comprehensive birth control service and
a clinic for mothers. In 1960 the name was changed to the Marie Stopes Memorial
Clinic and in 1968 to the Marie Stopes Memorial Centre.

The Marie Stopes Collection is currently being organized. The Centre itself
retains the Society's first minute book, together with other miscellaneous records.
Many of the early records were destroyed because of lack of space.

See also Part 2, Biographies, Marie Stopes.

CONTAGIOUS DISEASES

The archives of the Association for Moral and Social Hygiene and of other societies
campaigning for repeal of the Acts are housed in the Fawcett Library and are
described in Part 4, Section 1. The material below consists chiefly of the letters and
papers of Josephine Butler and Henry J. Wilson, the two leading figures in the
campaign.

Mrs Josephine Butler, (Liverpool University Library)

Letters: To her son, Arthur Stanley Butler, and his wife Rhoda, 1871 ?–1906; to Fanny Forsaith, secretary of the British Federation for the Abolition of Government Regulation of Prostitution 1892–1906; to her grandchildren 1890–1904?

(St Andrews University Library)
The Library has 102 letters most of which are addressed to Mrs Josephine Butler. Almost all are written by important figures of the second half of the nineteenth century and relate to the social reform movement as it concerned women's rights, particularly the campaign against the state regulation of prostitution in this country and abroad.

Henry J. Wilson

He was Liberal MP for Holmfirth 1885–1912 and actively involved in the campaign for the repeal of the Contagious Diseases Acts and with the question of the State Regulation of Vice, both at home and abroad. He first met Mrs Josephine Butler in 1870 when he invited her to address a meeting in Sheffield; he was to contribute much to her campaign. Henry Wilson was a most methodical man and dated every letter he received from Josephine Butler, often adding the place from which it was written. This habit has made the job of the researcher easier, because Mrs Butler herself did not date her letters and frequently used the salutation 'Dear Friend'. His dating and numbering of letters enables one to link up the material held in the Fawcett Library, Sheffield City Library and the Sheffield University Library.

(Sheffield City Library)
Letters 1886; notices and circulars of repeal mettings 1883–5; circulars, press-cuttings and handbills 1883–1907; circulars, leaflets, etc, 1884–1909; speeches and notes for speeches 1876–8; press cuttings 1876–89; material relating to a visit to the United States 1876.

(Sheffield University Library)
The Library has six boxes of archival material relating to Henry J. Wilson, the majority not relevant to the campaign for the repeal of the Contagious Diseases Acts as it relates to local political matters. The only items of interest are a typed copy of a letter written to his children in 1885 describing the effect of the publication of W. T. Stead's article in the *Pall Mall Gazette*, and a letter from Emma Paterson on behalf of the Vigilance Association for the Defence of Personal Rights on the organizing of evidence to the Royal Commission on the Factory and Workshop Acts regarding the employment of women.

MISSIONARIES

Baptist Missionary Association
The women's branch of the Baptist Missionary Society was founded in 1867 and

called, the Ladies' Association for the Support of Zenana Work and Bible Women in India. In 1897 this was shortened to the Baptist Zenana Mission. Like many other female missionary organizations the Society was controlled by a committee of women and was financially independent. At first it was a basically India-based organization. In its first year it opened stations in Calcutta and Delhi and by 1877 it had ten stations, all in the Indian sub-continent. In 1893 it sent its first women workers to China although revolutionary activities in 1901 and 1911 subsequently caused the withdrawal of female missionaries. In 1908 in conjunction with the London Missionary Society the Society opened the United Missionary Training College for Teachers with Miss Ethel Dyson as Principal. In 1909 it formed the Girls' Auxiliary. The Society went from strength to strength and by 1917, the year of its golden jubilee, had women working in Europe, Ceylon, the Congo as well as India and China.

Minutes: Women's Missionary Association 1867–1936; field base sub-committee 1920–4; home base committee 1924–6; finance sub-committee 1921–6.
Girls's Auxiliary 1918–48: agenda books 1903–58.

Church Missionary Society

Although women first offered their services as overseas missionaries to the Society as early as 1815 when three ladies from Bristol volunteered, it was not until 1887 that women were accepted and sent abroad as missionaries. Until this date women were restricted to fund-raising activities within the society although wives and sisters were occasionally allowed to accompany their menfolk abroad and to give instruction to native women. Two societies (later to merge with the Church Missionary Society) did, however, send women abroad. The Church of England Zenana Missionary Society, founded in 1880, sent women to various countries, including China and Japan. The other organization was the Female Education Society, founded in 1834 as the Society for Promoting Female Education in the East, which sent women mainly to India. In 1900 the Society disbanded and the CMS took over its twenty-three missionaries.

Minutes: Church of England Zenana Missionary Society Committee 1880–1957; candidates committee 1880–1957; finance minutes and papers 1881–1957; home organization committee 1889–1957; Female Education Society 1834–99; women's foreign committee 1895–1901, 1912–14.
Correspondence, 1921–57.
Female Education Society, annual reports, 1858–9; finance ledgers, 1860–99.

London Missionary Society Ladies' Committee (School of
Oriental and African Studies Library)

Although the LMS had lady missionaries on its staff from 1864 it was not until 1875 that a Ladies' Committee was formed with responsibility for work among women. In 1890 when the Board of Directors of the LMS was reconstituted with women then being eligible to be directors, the women's committee handed over responsibility for its work to the Board. The work of the Ladies' Committee was in the main in India where it organized girls' schools, 'industrial homes' and 'training schools' as well as sending lady doctors out to missionary stations. By 1899 the society had seventy-two lady missionaries in the field.

Minutes 1875–1907.

Methodist Missionary Society

The earliest female Methodist Missionary Society was the Ladies' Committee for the Amelioration of the Condition of Women in Heathen Countries, founded in 1858. This later changed its name to the Wesleyan Women's Auxiliary. The Committee was founded as a result of a letter received from a Mrs Batchelor, working with girls in India, requesting help. Other female Methodist missionary societies were founded: in 1892 the Bible Christian Women's Missionary League; in 1897 the Ladies' Missionary Association of the United Methodist Free Church; in 1899 the Methodist New Connexion Ladies' Missionary Association; and in 1909 the Primitive Methodist Women's Federation. These various societies, belonging to the different traditions of Methodism, were united in 1930 to become 'Women's Work'. They now work in close cooperation with the Methodist Missionary Society.

Minutes: Women's Work Committee 1858–1932; Women's Methodist Missionary Society Candidates Committee 1912–32; Joint Women's Methodist Missionary Society and Women's Auxiliary Committee 1916–21.

Society for the Propagation of the Gospel, Women's Work Committee

The Society was founded in 1701 and from the beginning women contributed to the funds but it was not until over two hundred years later, in 1921, that women were admitted to full membership of the Society. However in 1866 the Ladies' Association was formed and it sent its first missionary abroad in 1867. The Association's work was mainly of an educational nature. In 1894 it changed its name to the Women's Missionary Society. In 1897 it added medical work to its activities and by 1900 there were over 186 women missionaries in the field. Although an independent body from the Society for the Propagation of the Gospel, with its own funds, it was closely linked with the Society and eventually in 1904 the two merged and a committee for women's work with the SPG was formed.

Minutes: Ladies' Association committee 1866–1903; women's work committee 1903–13; advisory sub-committee 1906–20; finance sub-committee 1903–21; foreign group 1921–31; Furlough groups from foreign sub-committees 1910–19; files and roll of women missionaries from 1866.
Finance: Women's work candidates department ledger 1906–18; training fund 1919–30; ledger 1921–6; probationers' training fund 1921–30.
In addition there is a great deal of material relating to overseas members of the Association, in Africa, Canada and Asia. These records are subdivided by country and include letters from women at missionary posts.

Women's Missionary Association

The Association was founded in 1878 and sent women to many countries, particularly China, where by 1914 there were 252 Presbyterian women missionaries. As with other women's missionary societies it raised its own funds and administered its own finances.

Minutes: Women's Missionary Association 1878–1964; executive, and advisory committee 1901–52; joint Women's Missionary Association and foreign missions advisory committee 1899–1917.
See also Emigration, Englishwomen in India above.

ORGANIZATIONS

Girls' Friendly Society

Founded by Mrs Townsend in 1874 at a meeting at Lambeth Palace, it was the first Anglican organization to be run by women. It was intended for single girls; the Mothers' Union was founded for the married GFS members. One of the aims of the GFS was to improve the status of domestic service and consequently a large percentage of its members were recruited from the servant class. It ran 48 employment registry offices and in 1905 opened a central employment office. By 1880 the GFS had 489 branches and over 47,000 members. In 1883 the Society opened an emigration department but did not cater for large numbers; it also opened branches abroad, particularly on the Continent. The Society was completely non-political; its journals ignored the major political events and the Society played no part whatsoever in the suffrage campaign. After the First World War the GFS declined as it failed to adapt itself to changed conditions.

There is a great deal of correspondence on a wide range of subjects but most dates from 1928.

Agenda books: central council 1885–1938; executive committee 1907–24; various committees 1910–19; Central Lodges Fund sub-committee 1911–33; Committees of council 1913–33.
Minute books: Central Council 1875–9 including drafts of the constitution, 1880–1950; executive committee and sub-committee 1879–1954; general sub-committee 1880–1912; finance committee 1875–1948.
GFS in Europe, Diocesan Council 1890–8, 1904–13, 1926–9, 1938–44.
Committees: literature, later publications, 1890–1939; deputation 1895–1920; special committee 1903–9; standing committee 1911–20; colonial 1896–1904.
Department of Registry Work 1903–20: Central employment office committee 1905–36; central needlework depot 1905–48,
Lodges and Lodging Department 1906–23; aid and reference committee 1913–17; sick funds central sub-committee: signed minutes 1914–46, draft minutes 1913–51.

Diocesan Committee 1920–67.

War Emergency Committee: minutes 1916–21; address book; register of subscribers to the Wartime Fund, and receipts; centres of work, place-names with names of officers; presentation of purses to Queen Mary.

Brabazon Home: printed reports 1885–1905; minute books 1886–1954; log book 1910–28; accounts 1938–47.

Accounts: ledgers 1900–49; journals, cash books 1896–1958.

Hostels: Material relating to those run by the GFS 1925–50; correspondence 1916–50.

Dioceses: record books [?] 1904–21.

See also Emigration above.

National Council of Women of Great Britain

This is the coordinating body for a number of women's organizations. It originated in the 1870s with the foundation of Ladies' Associations for the Care of Friendless Girls. These associations held conferences from 1888 onwards on a wide range of topics relating to women. It was also at about this time that women workers' unions were being formed. From 1892 the activities of both these types of organizations were coordinated by a Central Conference Committee. In 1894 the Central Conference Council of the National Union of Women Workers was established; the following year this became the National Union of Women Workers of Great Britain and Ireland. This organization changed its name once again in 1918 to the National Council of Women of Great Britain and Ireland, and finally, in 1928, to the National Council of Women of Great Britain.

Minutes 1892–1900. This is the only archival material to have survived. The activities of the organization can, however, be traced through the printed reports (the Council has a complete set). These include reports of the Central Conference of Women Workers from 1888, including transcripts of the papers delivered.

National Federation of Women's Institutes from 1917

The first Women's Institute in Great Britain was formed in Anglesey in 1915 with the aim of improving the quality of the country woman's life. The National Federation was founded in 1917 with 137 member Institutes.

Minutes: executive committee from 1917; files on over 9,000 member Institutes.

Women's Cooperative Guild

Founded in 1883 on the initiative of Mrs Alice Acland, it held its first meeting at the Cooperative Congress in Edinburgh in June of that year. During the following years branches were established throughout the country until by 1893 there were a hundred. These were linked together by the Central Committee and the Honorary Secretary. In 1889 the movement was divided into sections and districts with sectional councils. In addition to its interest in consumer affairs, the movement campaigned for reforms in women's suffrage, divorce law, for a minimum standard wage of cooperative employees, and for the inclusion of maternity grants for women in the National Insurance Bill of 1911. In 1963 it changed its name from Women's Cooperative Guild to Cooperative Women's Guild.

(British Library of Economics and Political Science)
The material relating to the Women's Cooperative Guild was given to the Library by a friend of Margaret Llewelyn Davies. Margaret Davies was General Secretary 1889–1921 and was responsible for the widening of the Guild's interest in consumer affairs to cover broader questions of the feminist movement. The material consists of eleven volumes, for the years 1890–1944, as follows:

Vol. 1 1890–1944, including printed, typed and manuscript material.
Vols 2–5 1902–4, Coronation Street branch of the Sunderland Cooperative Society.
Vol. 6 The 'Sheffield' enquiry of 1902 and the promotion of the Peoples' Stores in Bristol 1905–6.
Vol. 7 Photographs, etc, of visiting Belgian cooperators in 1906.
Vols 8–9 relate to the retirement of Miss Davies and Miss Hamisin from the Guild in 1921.
Vol. 10 Drafts of speeches made by Miss Davies.
Vol. 11 Miscellaneous papers.

(Hull University Library)
Minutes: central committee from 1883; joint meetings of the central committee and section secretaries 1938–65; Guild convalescent fund 1908–42; annual reports from 1883.

Women's Local Government Society (Greater London County Record Office, A/WLG)

Originally founded in 1888 as a committee to promote the election of women to County Councils and to support in particular Lady Sandhurst and Miss Jane Cobden. In 1893 it became the Women's Local Government Society with the aim of securing for women the right to be eligible to serve on County Councils in all capacities. Mrs Fawcett was treasurer of the Society for two years. The Society supplied speakers for various other women's organizations and campaigned in a variety of ways.

Minutes: committee 1888–9; executive committee and some sub-committees 1889–1915; council 1915–25; annual general meetings 1915–24; Education Bill and County Councillors Bill 1896–7; reorganization of local government 1909; parliamentary sub-committee 1911–17; sub-committee for the performance of 'Atalanta in Calydon' 1911; parliamentary and legal committee 1917–20; election consultative committee 1918–20.
Annual reports 1888–1925; letters 1892–8; printed notices, memoranda and hand-bills, 1888–1925; volume containing notes of 'work to be done' 1900–3; certificate of incorporation of the Society; certificate authorizing the Society to commence business.
See also Section 4, Fawcett Library

TEMPERANCE

The following diagram shows the changes in name of women's temperance associations:

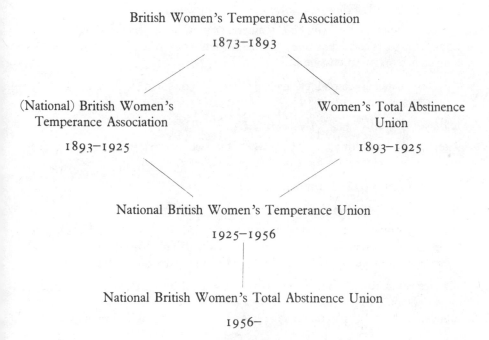

British Women's Temperance Association

1873–1893

(National) British Women's
Temperance Association

1893–1925

Women's Total Abstinence
Union

1893–1925

National British Women's Temperance Union

1925–1956

National British Women's Total Abstinence Union

1956–

(The National British Women's Total Abstinence Union has the archives of each of these associations and unions.)

British Women's Temperance Association

Founded in 1873, the Association's object was 'to form a union or federation of women's temperance societies existing in various districts within the United Kingdom'. It was open to individuals as well as to organizations, but at the time it was unique as its membership was wholly female. In 1893 the British Women's Temperance Association split over a matter of policy into two separate organizations.

Minutes: 1873–9, includes a copy of the constitution, 1879–80, 1890–93.

Church of England Temperance Society (Lambeth Palace Library)

Founded in 1863 and while not an exclusively male organization, the Society mainly confined women to organizing fund-raising events.

Minutes: Central Women's Board 1892–1901, 1901–14, 1914–35; Ellison
Lodge Home for Female Inebriates, executive committee 1897–1907; Temple
Lodge Home for Female Inebriates, Torquay 1907–25. Women's Union
Congresses minutes are included in the executive committee minutes 1885–7,
1888–91.

(National) British Women's Temperance Association

When the split in the women's temperance movement occurred in 1893, the
original founders carried on under this name until 1925 when the separate women's
temperance organizations merged.

Minutes: national committee meeting 1893–1902; national executive 1893–
1925; sub-committee 1893–7, 1897–1928.

National British Women's Temperance Union

The Union was formed in 1925 when the two existing women's temperance
organizations reunited to form one temperance society.

Minutes 1925–51; Sub-committee 1928–45.

Women's Total Abstinence Union

When the women's temperance movement divided, in 1893 with her supporters
Lady Henry Somerset formed the Women's Total Abstinence Union. This
organization remained active until 1925 when the two societies reunited.

Minutes: executive committee 1894–1907; general committee 1900–26 (the first
two volumes are missing).
Huddersfield Branch: minutes 1908–25 (Huddersfield Public Library)

Although at the height of the temperance movement there must have been many
women's temperance branches and organizations, by and large, records have not
survived and this point is made by Brian Harrison in 'Drink and sobriety in
England', *International Review of Social History*, XII, 1967, Part 2, pp 204–76.
One of the reasons he cites was the frequent change in headquarters made by the
temperance organizations and the consequent clearing out of unwanted papers.

SUFFRAGE

See also Part 4, Section 1, Fawcett Library, Suffrage.

The majority of suffrage archive material outside the Fawcett Library is held in two places; the Suffragette Fellowship Collection at the London Museum, and the Archive Department of Manchester Central Library. The material held in these collections is listed here in alphabetical order: organizations first, followed by individuals' papers. On the whole material relates to the central offices of the suffrage organizations rather than to local branches.

Despite the large number of local associations at the height of the suffrage campaign very few branch records have survived. The Women's Social and Political Union arranged its branches into twenty districts, while the National Union of Women's Suffrage Societies had over three hundred branches. There is scope for an attempt to be made to trace the branch records of the various suffrage organizations, for these records could include undiscovered aspects of the movement; for instance, the effect of suffragist or suffragette activities in a small community and the way in which the activities of individual women were received by their families in a closely-knit society. Local records could also show whether or not branches always followed the 'party-line' advocated by headquarters, particularly with regard to violence.

In addition to the records listed below, material of relevance to the suffrage movement can be found in the Papers of eminent contemporary politicians. The limited use of these Papers made by historians in writing the history of the suffrage movement has been noted by Andrew Rosen in the introduction to his book, *Rise up women!* Among the Papers of relevance to the suffrage movement are those of Arthur Balfour, Prime Minister during the early days of the militancy campaign, and the Papers of Sir Henry Campbell-Bannerman, who succeeded Balfour as Prime Minister. These Papers are in the British Library. Lloyd George's Papers include some correspondence on the subject of women's suffrage. They were previously owned by the Beaverbrook Library, but are now in the Public Record Office, as are the Papers of Edward Grey, who, as Secretary of State for Foreign Affairs, was involved with the incident with Christabel Pankhurst and Annie Kenney which marked the beginning of the militancy campaign. The Papers of George Lansbury, who fought the Bromley and Bow by-election of 1912 on the suffrage question, are in the British Library of Political and Economic Science. The Papers of Reginald McKenna of the 'Cat and Mouse Act', The Prisoners' Temporary Discharge for Ill-Health Act 1913, are in Churchill College, Cambridge, and contain correspondence relating to his time as Secretary of State for Home Affairs, 1911–13. The Papers of W. M. Dickinson in the Greater London

Record Office contain some material relating to his role in the Men's League for Women's Suffrage.

ORGANIZATIONS

East London Federation of the Suffragettes (Internationaal Instituut voor Sociale Geschiedenis, England North American Department)
Minute books

International Women's Suffrage Alliance
See Papers, Mrs Millicent Garrett Fawcett, below.

Manchester (National) Society for Women's Suffrage (Manchester Central Library Archive Department, M20)
Annual reports, printed, 1868–80, 1881–93, 1907–14, 1914–18; letter book 1874–7, including circulars from 1870; pamphlets, circulars, programmes, etc, 1906–17.

Manchester Women's Suffrage Society (Manchester Central Library, Archive Department M20)
Correspondence, incoming: Vol. I 1867–85 includes letters from Emily Davies in 1867 regarding the organization of a petition and an article later published in the *Contemporary Review*. It also includes letters from Clementina Taylor, 1867, regarding the title of the Manchester Society; letters from Henry Fawcett and C. P. Villiers supporting a Bill for women's suffrage in 1867; a letter from Josephine Butler giving addresses of people to contact; and a letter offering Lydia Becker the post of paid Secretary to the National Society for Women's Suffrage. Vol. II contains letters from MPs and others regarding plans for a meeting, most sending their apologies. There is correspondence from Frances Power Cobbe, letters dated 1899 from Lady Bective and others refusing to act as vice-presidents.
Correspondence, outgoing: Lydia Becker's letter book 21 Mar–29Nov 1868. This is a full record of all 496 letters sent by the Society during these months, and although the index is incomplete the letters are a very valuable source of information regarding the early days.

National Society for Women's Suffrage Central Committee (Manchester Central Library Archive Department, M20)
Reports: executive committee 1888–9–1890–91.

National Union of Women's Suffrage Societies (Labour Party Library, LP/WOM/12)
Correspondence of Arthur Henderson with NUWSS 1912.

(Manchester Central Library Archive Department M20.)

Minutes: executive committee 1913–18 (incomplete); election fighting fund committee July–Aug 1916.

Information bureau department, tabulated information; press department, News Sheets 1915 and 1917 (2 documents only).

Proceedings of the Annual (London) and Half-yearly Provincial Council, Nov 1914–Feb 1917.

Papers, programmes, etc, relating to demonstrations and exhibitions, including programmes for the 'Great Suffrage Pilgrimage' of 1913; also a souvenir number of *Common Cause*. These give details of the routes taken into London. Some programmes relate to the Women's Kingdom exhibition held from April 1913.

Circular letters, memos and miscellaneous papers. A number of circular letters relate to the canvassing of MPs to vote for Bills in the House of Commons. There are also circulars outlining schemes of work suggested by the NUWSS and other societies and individuals on the outbreak of war in August 1914.

'Women's work in the time of war', draft syllabus by the NUWSS; circular on its attitude to the war and various other documents related to a dispute within the organization as to the role of the NUWSS during the war, including copies of the Parliamentary election addresses given at the meeting held on 15 Feb 1915.

Manchester Branch: minutes 1912–14.

(Bertrand Russell's Papers in Mill Memorial Library, McMaster University, Ontario)

In 1907 Bertrand Russell became a member of the Executive Council of the NUWSS and although he left the Society two years later he had agreed in 1907 to contest the Wimbledon by-election for the NUWSS as a Women's Suffragist candidate.

Letters, telegrams etc, 1907–16; pamphlets, circulars, press-cuttings 1909; press-cuttings, posters and other documentary material relating to the 1907 Wimbledon by-election.

North of England Society for Women's Suffrage

See Manchester Society for Women's Suffrage

Suffragette Fellowship Collection (London Museum)

This material, which was presented to the London Museum in 1950, deals with the militant aspect of the suffrage campaign and consists not only of archive material but also photographs, postcards, newspaper-cuttings and other miscellaneous items. The archive material is listed under the relevant organizational headings, or under an individual's name where appropriate, but some additional material which will not fit readily into either category is listed below.

The museum has approximately 100 biographical notes on imprisoned women and while they only represent a fraction of the total of 1,000 women who were imprisoned during the campaign for the vote, they are a good collection. They are not arranged in alphabetical order, so the whole list has to be checked. The notes vary in length: some merely give an outline of activities in the militant campaign, others are longer and more detailed. Most appear to have been compiled by the individuals themselves. They cover a wide range of suffragettes, from wellknown figures like Mrs Pethick-Lawrence to many unknown members of the movement. As information relating to some of the less known figures is scarce, these biographical notes are invaluable.

Letters: relating and testifying to forcible feeding, violence by prison guards, trials and experiences during imprisonment.
A collection of typescripts of several of the trials in which suffragettes were involved.

Women's Freedom League (London Museum. Suffragette
Fellowship Collection)

Founded by Mrs How-Martyn, Mrs Charlotte Despard, Mrs Teresa Billington-Greig and Irene Fenwick Miller in 1907 as a result of the split in the ranks of the Women's Social and Political Union, it was not associated with any political party. Although its policies were similar to those of the Women's Social and Political Union it did not follow the extreme militancy of the WSPU in 1913–14.

Correspondence relating to the split in the ranks of the Women's Social and Political Union over militancy and the formation of the Women's Freedom League, including letters from Mrs Pankhurst.
Papers: Constitution; agenda and resolution from the special conference held for the purpose of founding the League.

Women's Social and Political Union

Founded in Manchester by Mrs Pankhurst in 1903, the WSPU became the most militant of the suffrage organizations with its members undertaking a campaign of extreme militancy during 1913–14. Her daughters Sylvia and Christabel were also prominent members of the Union. On the outbreak of the First World War the WSPU suspended its militancy in favour of patriotism.

(London Museum. Suffragette Fellowship Collection)
Correspondence: relating to the split in the WSPU that led to the formation of the Women's Freedom League; to demonstrations and meetings organized by the WSPU; and to the disruption of meetings by the WSPU.
Papers relating to the constitution and policy of the WSPU; instructions for demonstrations, 1910–14.

(Manchester Central Library Archive Department, M20)
Letters of Mrs Pankhurst, 1906–8; leaflets 1906–10; annual report 1907.
Canning Town Branch: Minute book 1906–7.

Women's Tax Resistance League
See Papers, Millicent Garrett Fawcett, below.

PAPERS

Emily Davies (Emily Davies Collection, Girton College, Cambridge)

Cuttings from the *Manchester Guardian*, 1905, collected by Emily Davies.

Suffragettes' march, by Margaret Kennedy (aged 11 years) (manuscript copy in an adult hand).

Letters to Emily Davies on women's suffrage, from various people including Lord Robert Cecil; also a letter from Beatrice Graves, Secretary of the London Society for Women's Suffrage, enclosing a resolution by the society's organizing committee.

Manuscript notes of articles on the emancipation of women, and other subjects; draft letter to *The Times*, 1913; copies of articles, petitions and pamphlets on women's suffrage, 1889–1918.

Letters from George Eliot to Emily Davies 1867–71; extracts from Emily Davies' letters describing visits to George Eliot.

See also Cambridge University, Emily Davies Collection above.

Flora Drummond (London Museum. Suffragette Fellowship Collection)

Correspondence.

Millicent Garrett Fawcett (Manchester Central Library, M20)

Correspondence: general 1870–1912; conciliation committee 1910–12, letters between Mrs Fawcett and Henry Noel Brailsford, hon. secretary for the Committee; International Women's Suffrage Alliance 1908–18, including letters from officials to Mrs Fawcett, draft replies, etc. The majority of the letters are concerned with the journal *Jus Suffragii* and its publication of 'pacifist' articles in 1916; phosphorous poisoning: investigations personally undertaken by Mrs Fawcett into conditions at the Bryant & May factories; University degrees for women 1880–1920, including correspondence with Emily Davies; Welfare of women, 1886–93; Women's Tax Resistance League 1910.

Papers: analysis of parliamentary discussions on suffrage issues 1867–83; women in the medical profession 1873–96.

Publications: Conciliation Committee Bill; education 1882–92 annual report, articles of association relating to women's colleges; employment of children in theatres; government reports and statistics 1884–1919; sanitary conditions of the British Army in India; social, moral and legal issues relating to women 1873–1920; suffrage; welfare of women; white slave trade; Women's Tax Resistance League pamphlet; speeches 1890–93.

Ada Flatman (London Museum. Suffragette Fellowship Collection)

Correspondence.

Mary Gawthorpe (London Museum. Suffragette Fellowship Collection)

Typescript of autobiography.

Constance Lytton (London Museum. Suffragette Fellowship Collection)

Correspondence 1909–12; MSS of her book, *Prisons and prisoners: some personal experiences*; statement of her treatment in prison while using the name 'Jane Walton'.

Kitty Marion (London Museum. Suffragette Fellowship Collection)

An actress and suffrage worker, Miss Marion later worked for the birth control movement in the United States and sold their publications in New York.

Diary; letters 1909–14; typescript autobiography.

Catherine Marshall (Labour Party Library)

Correspondence, 1912; and with Arthur Henderson regarding Election Fighting Fund for Women's Suffrage, 1912.

Hannah Mitchell (Manchester Central Library, Archive Department)

Manuscript copy of *The hard way up: the autobiography of Hannah Mitchell, suffragette and rebel* (ed, G. Mitchell, etc, Faber, 1968).

Evelyn Sharp Nevinson (Bodleian Library)

Known as both a suffrage worker and a journalist, she was very active in the suffrage movement from 1905 to 1918. She was imprisoned and there went on hunger strike. As a journalist she contributed to many leading papers. She was also an active member of the Labour Party and the National Council of Civil Liberties.

Letters 1892–1955; diaries 1920–45; notebooks and scrap books 1907–27; drafts of published and unpublished manuscripts; miscellaneous manuscripts; press-cuttings 1909–46; photographs.

Sylvia Pankhurst (Internationaal Instituut voor Sociale Geschiendenis)

Pre-1900 material, including papers of Dr R. M. Pankhurst, her father; eight volumes of newspaper-cuttings, letters from Lydia Becker, and various personal documents.

(London Museum. Suffragette Fellowship Collection)
Letters: On forcible feeding; to her mother while in prison.

Emmeline Pethick-Lawrence (London Museum. Suffragette Fellowship Collection)

Correspondence.
See also Sylvia Pankhurst above.

Myra Sadd Brown (London Museum. Suffragette Fellowship Collection)

Papers relating to imprisonment and forcible feeding.
See also Part 4, Section 1, Fawcett Library, Special Collections.

S. J. Stevenson (London Museum. Suffragette Fellowship Collection)

Manuscript autobiography.

Mrs Terrero (London Museum. Suffragette Fellowship Collection)

Diary 1912; letters.

Marion Wallace-Dunlop (London Museum. Suffragette Fellowship Collection)

She was the first woman to go on hunger strike.
Correspondence relating to her imprisonment.

Olive Walton (London Museum. Suffragette Fellowship Collection)

Diary 1912.

E. R. Willoughby Marshall (London Museum. Suffragette Fellowship Collection)

Manuscript account of suffragette escapes and adventures.
See also First World War, Suffrage and Politics, above.

DIARIES

Diaries are a valuable source of the sort of information that cannot be found in general histories. This is particularly true with regard to women, as their role in society has until recently been neglected by historians. As is the case with biographies and autobiographies, diaries tend to emanate from the middle and upper classes. Diaries are frequently destroyed for a variety of reasons but usually because surviving relatives underestimate their value. Happily this attitude seems to be on the decline and more and more diaries are being donated to local record offices. Published diaries can be traced through standard bibliographical works although there are problems of recognition and of separating diary material from autobiographies.

This section lists manuscript diaries, divided into subject sub-divisions, giving details of author, title (if any), dates and location of the work; if necessary a reference number is given. The facilities and full addresses of the libraries and record offices are given in Part 4, Section 2.

The two most useful guides to diaries are William Matthews, *British diaries* (Cambridge University Press, 1950) and John Stuart Batts, *British manuscript diaries of the nineteenth century* (Fontwell, Sussex, Centaur Press, 1976). Matthews covers British diaries written between 1442 and 1942. He claims to have searched the major libraries of the United States and the British Isles and to have circulated local libraries. He has excluded types of material that are not day-to-day accounts, or are reminiscences, autobiographies and memoirs; he has also excluded parliamentary, explorers' and travellers' diaries. He has, however, included some diaries that form part of published works such as biographies or histories, when they are substantial enough to stand on their own. The work is arranged chronologically by year of first entry, with diaries beginning in the same year arranged in alphabetical order. The entries for each diary give author's name, type – i.e., religious, country, etc – followed by dates and a brief description of the contents, publication details (if appropriate) or location. There is an author index, and a chronological index of diaries covering a span of more than ten years.

Batts' work extends and updates Matthews' work for the nineteenth century, and follows the same format, but only includes unpublished diaries. This has meant that valuable material has been excluded because many late nineteenth-century diaries were published, titles like *Anna Kingsford: her life, letters, diary and work*, by Edward Maitland (G. Redway, 1896).

Other guides are A. A. W. H. Ponsonby's *British diarists* (Benn, 1930), *English diaries* (Methuen, 1923) and *More English diaries* (Methuen, 1927).

General

Mary K. Bell. Personal diary 1869–72 (Edward Hall Coll.).

Stella Benson. Private diary 1902–33 (Cambridge University Library, Additional MSS 6762–6802).

Mary Billingshurst. Personal diary (Fawcett Library).

Mrs W. T. Blathwayt. Private diary 1879–80. (Gloucestershire Record Office, Dyrham Park MSS D1799 F260).

Martha Braithwaite. Private diary in 30 volumes 1842–95 (Society of Friends, MS volumes S302–331).

Mrs Harriette P. W. Bund. Private diary 1872–3 (Kent Archive Office, MSS 705 : 36).

Margery Capper. Personal diary and sketchbooks, early 1900s (Edward Hall Coll.).

Catherine Courtney. Private diary 1875–1919 (British Library of Political and Economic Science R (SR) 1003).

Sybil M. Curtis. Private diary 1907–10 (Edward Hall Coll.).

Mrs F. Dixey. Personal diary 1886–1916 (privately owned).

Mrs Louisa Galton. Personal diary 1875–96 (London, University College Library, MSS Galton 1 item 2).

Lady Angela F. H. Herries. Social and family affairs 1870, 1872–3, 1877, 1883 (West Yorkshire Record Office, MSS DDEV/61/36/40).

Mrs M. Hewitt. Private diary 1884–1924 (William Salt Library, Stafford).

Miss E. A. Jones. Personal diary 1889–1900 (Minet Library, Lambeth, MS 8/25 (S1655)).

G. E. Kennaway. Private diary 1894 (Devon Record Office, MS 8961 M Add/F14).

E. Knatchbull-Hugessen. Private diary 1873–93 (Kent Archive Office, Ms KNATCHBULL – 4951 F30/1–9).

Hon. Frederica M. Lascelles. Private diary 1878–80 (Edward Hall Coll.).

Mrs McCracken. Private diary 1882–1934 (Berkshire Record Office, manuscript on loan from Mrs B. M. N. Powell and Miss G. C. S. McCracken).

M. Main. Private diary 1896–1952 (privately owned).

Countess Morley. Social diary, 1877–8 (British Museum, Additional MSS 48263–4).

Mrs L. M. Simpson. Private diary 1878–80 (Edward Hall Coll.).

C. M. Slade. Diary of a young girl, 1885 (West Sussex Record Office, MS 1260).

Lillian D. Sykes. Private diary 1919 (owned by diarist).

Lady Templeton. General diary 1897–1906 (Warwickshire Record Office, MSS CR 426).

M. A. Ward. Personal diary 1885–7, 1892–8 (University College London Library, MSS Add 202).

Constance E. Weld. General diary 1874, 1876 (Dorset Record Office, MSS D10/F109).

Alice Williams. Private diaries, 1920s (Fawcett Library).

Education

Constance Maynard. Various sequences 1866–1935 (Westfield College).

Emigration

Lady Knox. Diary, including letters from emigrants (Fawcett Library).
Frances Thornton. Diary of voyage on an emigrant ship to New Zealand 1882
   (Devon Record Office, MS 877 M/FI).
See also Organizations, Lady Louisa M. Knightley, below.

Employment

A. Schluter. Diary of a lady's maid at 10 Downing Street 1877–90 (British
   Museum, Additional MSS 46271).

Englishwomen in India

Mrs M. L. Ferrer. Indian diary, 1913 (South Asian Archive).
Fanny Knyvett. Diary extracts (South Asian Archive).
W. G. Waterfield. Diary of her mother's visit to India, Apr–Dec 1906 (South
   Asian Archive).
See also Emigration, Englishwomen in India, above.

First World War

Miss K. Alexander. *See* 1914–18 Archive, Sunderland, Domestic front, above.
Miss Olive Armstrong. ditto.
Elsie Bowerman. Service with the Scottish Women's Hospital Service in Russia,
   1916–17 (Fawcett Library).
Mrs S. J. Brown. Diaries 1915, 1918 (1914–18 Archive, Sunderland).
Edith Cavell. Diary entries of her work in Brussels clinic helping wounded over the
   frontier to Holland (Imperial War Museum).
Y. C. Coen. Diary 1916–17 (1914–18 Archive, Sunderland).
H. V. D'Abernon. Diary of Red Cross work, 1914–18? (British Red Cross
   Society).
Lady R. Dobbs. War diary 1914–16? (British Library).
Mrs A. Garland. VAD at military hospital 1916 (Imperial War Museum).
E. G. Gibson, *née* Bates. Memoir of work on a Lincolnshire farm 1916–18
   (1914–18 Archive, Sunderland).
Nurse Elsie P. Grey. New Zealand Expeditionary Force 1916–17 (Imperial War
   Museum).
L. J. D. Griffith. 1914–19 (Imperial War Museum).
Miss Pat Hanbury, (Lady Cunninghame Graham). Schoolgirl diary 1914–19
   (1914–18 Archive, Sunderland).

E. Hastings. Territorial Nursing Force in Glasgow and Salonika 1914–18 (Imperial War Museum).

Mrs Ella Hogg, *née* Hallon. *See* 1914–18 Archive, Sunderland, War front, above.

Miss M. M. James. Ditto.

Mrs G. A. Jones. Semi-official diary while Deputy Controller WAAC responsible for Expeditionary Force canteen in France 1918–19 (Imperial War Museum).

Miss E. A. Macleod. *See* 1914–18 Archive, Sunderland, Domestic front, above.

Miss M. L. Macleod. Ditto.

M. L. McNeill. Five diaries relating to the Scottish Women's Hospital in Salonika, 1916–19 (Imperial War Museum).

Constance Miles. War diary 1914–18 (Imperial War Museum).

G. Milburn. *See* 1914–18 Archive, Sunderland, War front, above.

R. M. De Montmorency. Diary 1915 (Imperial War Museum).

Mrs A. Mullineaux. American Red Cross 1918–19 (Imperial War Museum).

Lady Mabel Napier. *See* 1914–18 Archive, Sunderland, Domestic front, above.

M. B. Peterkin. Diary 1914–18 Red Cross in France (Imperial War Museum).

Mrs Robb. *See* 1914–18 Archive, Sunderland, Domestic front, above.

Dr Jean Rose. Diary 1917–18 Scottish Women's Hospital in Macedonia (Imperial War Museum).

Mrs Dorothy Smith. *See* 1914–18 Archive, Sunderland, War front, above.

A. S. Tait. Work with Red Cross 1914–18 (Imperial War Museum).

Miss Violet Thurstan. *See* 1914–18 Archive, Sunderland, War front, above.

M. G. Trembath. Short diary of voyage to India 1917–18 (Imperial War Museum).

Mrs D. M. Trefusis. *See* 1914–18 Archive, Sunderland, War front, above.

Mrs Helen Gwynne-Vaughan. Diary of her visit to France in 1918 (Imperial War Museum).

G. West. Work with refugees, VAD, women's police in munition factory 1914–17 (Imperial War Museum).

Sara T. Wilsdon. *See* 1914–18 Archive, Sunderland, War front, above.

Missionaries

Miss Baring-Gould. Diary kept while with her father, a missionary for the Church Missionary Society 1894–1939 (CMS MSS Acc 21 FP).

A. Fisher. Missionary activities in West and Central Africa 1891–3 (Rhodes House Library, Oxford, Microfilm copy 409 (original in Rhodesian National Archives)).

See also Emigration, Englishwomen in India, above.

Organizations

Lady Louisa M. Knightley. Private diary relating to her activities with the Girls' Friendly Society (Northamptonshire County Record Office).

D. M. Ward. Work with the Passmore Edwards Settlement (London, University College Library, Add. MSS 202).

Politics

C. Courtney. Political and other events 1875–1919 (British Library of Political and Economic Science, Courtney Collection R (SR) 1003/21–38).

Suffrage

Lydia Becker. Diary of appointments etc, 1873 (Fawcett Library).

Elsie Duval. Prison diaries, 1911–12, 1913 (Fawcett Library).

Vida Goldstein. Diary whilst visiting England, 1908 (Fawcett Library).

Edith How-Martyn. Diary, undated (1900s?) (Fawcett Library).

Kitty Marian. Suffrage 1909–14 (London Museum. Suffragette Fellowship Coll. 50 82/1120).

Mrs J. Terrero. Suffragette diary for 1912 (London Museum. Suffragette Fellowship Coll. 50 82/1116).

Olive Walton. Suffragette diary for 1912 (London Museum. Suffragette Fellowship Coll. 50 82/1131).

Olive Wharry. Notebooks kept by her during imprisonment at Holloway and Winson Green Prisons 1911–14 (British Museum, Additional MSS 49, 976).

Travel

Julia M. Bandinel. A journey through Switzerland 1878–98 (Birmingham University Library, MSS 7/iii/11).

Mrs M. A. Belliss. Travels in Palestine (privately owned).

Mary Billinghurst. A pedestrian ramble through Oxford, Chester and North Wales, 1854 (Fawcett Library).

Catherine L. Braithwaite. A continental journey, March–April 1892; a journey to Norway, June–August 1897 (Society of Friends, MS Vols. S 298 and S 299).

Martha Braithwaite. A journey to the Continent, 1875 (Society of Friends, MS Vol. S 332).

M. S. G. Brooks. A journey to France, 1880–81 (Bedfordshire Record Office, MS LL 17/291).

Helen Caddick. Travel diaries 1889–1914 (Birmingham Public Library 336851).

Dr H. M. Davis. San Francisco to India: by sea across the Pacific via Japan, China, etc. Two and half months in India, including seven weeks in the jungle 1927–8 (South Asian Archive).

Mrs C. Gladstone. A journey to France, 1883 (British Museum, Add Manuscripts 46269).

Emily Greenstreet. A journey to France and Switzerland, undated (Greater London Council Record Office, MS P.82/ALB/139).

Rachel Hamilton-Gordon. A journey to New Zealand, 1882 (British Museum, Additional MSS 49271).

M. C. Minto. Travel diary 1894–1904 (Rhodes House Library, Oxford MS CAN t.1,2).

Evelyn Sharp Nevinson. Holiday in Ireland 1921; Russian travel 1922; German travel 1923; holiday 1924; holiday 1926 (all Bodleian Library).

Diane Ramsden. Travels in Australia, *c.* 1890 (Edward Hall Coll.).

Miss Riggs. Travel diary, date unknown (Thomas Cook Ltd).

Jane C. Sanderson. Travels on Cook's tours 1871–2 (London, University College Library MSS ADD 179/83 a–c).

I. G. Verney. Travel diary, 1889 (Edward Hall Collection).

W. G. Waterfield. Tour in Shalopur District of India, 1903 (South Asian Archive).

S. E. Whitehouse. Travels to Kenya, 1898 (Rhodes House Library, Oxford, MS Afr. S1055).

PART 2

PRINTED WORKS

PART 2 CONTENTS

INTRODUCTION

The wide range of materials has resulted in this section being divided primarily by type of publication; where necessary each division has been further subdivided under the subject headings used throughout the guide. An attempt has been made to evaluate the material, as many of the earlier works are reminiscences rather than histories, and their titles can be misleading. The majority of the more recently published works tend to be based on extensive research and are thus more useful to researchers. Many of the earlier publications are included, however, as they are the only source material available. The recent interest in the women's movement as part of an era of great social change rather than as isolated campaigns involving individuals, has resulted in many subject histories being published that provide an in-depth study, by contrast with the superficial works published in the 1920s and 1930s.

A select bibliography of general subject histories has been included in order to provide an overall view of the period. This is not comprehensive: it aims to indicate the standard historical works or books of particular interest.

Biographies of the leaders of campaigns and movements are another area where the recent interest in women's history has produced new publications and often new assessments of the achievements of individuals. Earlier biographers had had a tendency to reminisce and to sentimentalize great achievements; notable exceptions to this, however, were the two major biographies of Florence Nightingale – by Sir Edward T. Cook and Mrs Woodham-Smith – and Violet Markham's *May Tennant*. More recent works, like Georgina Battiscombe's life of Elizabeth Wordsworth (*Reluctant pioneer*), place the life-story in its social context. Although every endeavour has been made to ensure that this subject history section is as up to date as possible, a deadline had to be applied; this is 30 September 1978. Very little published after that date has been included.

One particular aspect of Part 2 is the amount of parliamentary material that has been included. A detailed survey of parliamentary papers relating to women revealed a large amount of little-used material, especially concerning women in employment. But legislation which simply resulted in minor changes to hours of work for women in specific trades has been omitted.

The periodicals listed are those which were published for, and by, women, with the exception of women's magazines of a general and trivial nature. These have been adequately covered by Cynthia White in *Women's magazines 1693–1968* and to have included them would have meant repetition of Dr White's work. However, a brief list of current journals which regularly contain relevant material has been included.

The subject arrangement complements that of the other Parts and the comprehensive index will help to trace material on a particular topic.

BIBLIOGRAPHIES

While no comprehensive bibliography relating to women for the period 1870–1928 has been published, there are some specific bibliographies, often contained in published monographs. Where there are several bibliographies on a particular subject they have been arranged in alphabetical order by author, with a brief summary to indicate scope, coverage and usefulness.

GENERAL

BiblioFem is produced by the library of the City of London Polytechnic, and is the combined catalogue of the Fawcett Library and the continuing bibliography on women compiled from recently catalogued works in the Fawcett Library and the holdings of the library at the Equal Opportunities Commission. The acquisitions of both libraries are added to the catalogue, which is issued on 42X COM microfiche at monthly intervals, with each set cumulating and replacing the previous set. There are two sequences: an alphabetical index of authors, titles, etc, and a classified index arranged according to Dewey system, 18th edition. The subject coverage is wide and includes the arts, civil rights, clothing and fashion, medicine, religion and sex roles. The intention is that *BiblioFem* should be comprehensive on all subjects relating to women.

Boston Public Library, *Catalogue of the Galatea Collection of books relating to the history of women*, USA, Boston, Mass, 1898.

This has a strong American bias and its usefulness is restricted because of its early publication. The Galatea Collection was donated to Boston Public Library in 1896 by Thomas Wentworth Higginson and although the Collection has since been added to no further catalogues have been published. This 1898 catalogue contains approximately 1,000 entries and is arranged according to its own slightly complicated classification scheme.

Blease, Walter Lyon, *The emancipation of English women*, Constable, 1910, pp 271–8.

Includes works which 'marked a definite stage in the progress of Englishwomen, or represent the ideal of a particular school of thought' and covers the period from the Restoration in 1660 to its date of publication. It is useful for literary sources.

Blackburn, Helen and Mackenzie, Antoinette M., compilers, 'A British Bibliography on Women's Questions'.

The editors of the *Englishwoman's Review*, compiled this bibliography in response to the many requests they had received for lists of books. The basis of the bibliography is that the included items had been collected by the authors and had been published in the British Isles. It is arranged in chronological order and includes periodical articles and reports of speeches in addition to published works. The bibliography appeared in the following issues of the *Englishwoman's Review*: 1899: 16 Jan, 15 April, 15 July, 16 Oct, 14 Dec; 1900: 16 July, 15 Oct.

Bullou, P. K., 'Bibliographies for research on women'. *Signs: Journal of women in culture and society*, University of Chicago Press, 3, 2, Winter 1977, pp 436–50.

A review article covering history, literature, anthropology, economics and employment, education, politics and law, sociology, psychology and health. It contains predominantly American published material relating in the main to women in present-day American society.

Gerritsen, Carel Victor and Arlette H., *La femme et le féminisme*, France, Giard & Brière, 1900.

This is a very useful bibliography, particularly for early periodicals. It also has a comprehensive coverage of women's organizations, although the date of publication should be borne in mind both for changes of name and the growth of new organizations after 1900.

Horne, G., 'The liberation of British and American women's history; a bibliographical essay', Society for the Study of Labour History, *Bulletin* 26, Spring 1973, pp 28–39.

The listing is limited to books published since the mid-1950s and is useful in that it does to some extent up-date McGregor's work (see below). It compares the treatment of women's emancipation in England and the USA.

Kanner, S. B., 'The women of England in a century of social change, 1814–1914; a select bibliography', M. Vicinus, ed, *Suffer and be still: women in the Victorian age*, Indiana University Press, 1972, pp 173–206.

A critical bibliography which aims at 'providing a useful catalog for studying the social position of women in England during the nineteenth century'. It is arranged under broad subject headings with the entries arranged chronologically and covers books and periodical articles. It is a select bibliography and includes several references to literary works.

Kanner, S. B., 'The women of England in a century of social change, 1814–1914', Part II pp 173–206 in M. Vicinus, ed, *A widening sphere: changing roles of Victorian women*, Indiana University Press, 1977.

This is the second part of a bibliography begun in *Suffer and be still*, also edited by Martha Vicinus (see above). It includes subjects less well covered by historians and deals chiefly with the private rather than the public lives of women, marriage, the family, and medical factors relating to women, for example menstruation. Like the first part, it is divided into broad subject groups with the references arranged in chronological order. It comments critically on a small selection of the references. It contains references to books and to periodical articles, and several libraries have been searched. The medical section, which includes obstetrics, gynecology and medical psychology, is particularly useful.

McGregor, O. R., 'The social position of women in England, 1850–1914: a bibliography', *British Journal of Sociology*, 6, March, 1955, pp 48–60.

Although it was published over twenty years ago, this is still the major bibliography on women for the late nineteenth and early twentieth century. The bibliography has a critical approach and lists the more important sources which 'fall within the interests of sociologists and sociologically inclined historians'. The coverage is wide in both type and subject of material included.

Webb, Beatrice, 'Awakening women: select bibliography of feminism', *New Statesman*, 1913, (2), Special supplement.

A short but useful bibliography of approximately 150 entries containing contemporary accounts of the suffrage movements and the condition of women.

Bornat, J. 'Women's history and oral history: an outline bibliography', *Oral History*, 5, 2, pp 124–35.

This reviews social investigations which made use of oral history techniques and included in their investigations the lives and experiences of women. In the early days of social investigation concern focused on women on the fringes of society, and the bibliography covers this aspect in detail. It deals chiefly with English works but does include some American examples. Although a selective bibliography it provides a most useful guide to available source material and covers a wide range of subjects.

EDUCATION

Bradbrook, M. C., *That infidel place: short history of Girton College, 1869–1969*. Chatto & Windus, 1969, pp 162–3.
Burstyn, J. N., 'Women's education in England during the nineteenth century: a review of the literature, 1970–6', *History of Education*, 1977, 6, 1, pp 11–19.

Burstyn's review bibliography is a useful critical essay. Bradbrook's book contains a short list of works relating to the history of Girton College.

EMPLOYMENT

Hewitt, Margaret, *Wives and mothers in Victorian industry*, Rockcliff, 1958, pp 226–36.

An extremely good source of information relating to Victorian working mothers and their children, covering official reports and publications, journals, society publications and contemporary literature.

Papworth, Lucy and Zimmern, Dorothy, *Women in industry: a bibliography*, Women's Industrial Council, 1915.

This is an excellent bibliography and especially helpful for tracing material on particular trades up to the First World War; taken as a whole it is a comprehensive bibliography of the employment of women in industry to 1914. It includes only those works which attempt to give a women's point of view, and foreign works which deal with conditions affecting women in England, wherever possible. It is divided into two sections; (i) Women in employment – accidents, dangerous trades, strikes, insurance, etc. (ii) Women's trades, from artificial flower-making to wire mattress-weaving.

'Women in industry – a select list of works dealing with women in industry', *New Statesman*, February 21 1914, Special Supplement.

A useful source for oganizations concerned with women in industry and for trade unions which admitted women. It lists general works, works on specific occupations and official publications. It is, however, overshadowed by Papworth and Zimmern's bibliography, see above.

MORAL AND SOCIAL ISSUES

Rover, Constance, *Love, morals and the feminists*, Routledge, 1970, pp 168–76.

The bibliography in this book covers topics such as contagious diseases, family planning from the suffrage point of view, and it is divided into sections: public documents arranged chronologically; books; newspapers and periodicals arranged alphabetically. It is a starting-point for anyone researching into moral and social issues in relation to women.

Birth control

Banks, J. A. and O., *Feminism and family planning in Victorian England*, Liverpool University Press 1964, pp 135–40.

Covers the 'period of the genesis and development of the Malthusian controversy in Britain' and the bibliography contains 'those writings on the status of woman which are relevant to the controversy'. It only includes separately printed works and excludes all material dealing solely with other aspects of feminism. Although the larger part of this listing covers the pre-1870 period, it is still very useful for background information. It is arranged chronologically.

Banks, J. A., and Glass, D. V., 'A list of books, pamphlets and articles on the population question published in Britain in the period 1793 on to 1880', in D. V. Glass, ed, *Introduction to Malthus*, Watts, 1953, pp 79–112.

Birth control and population problems: a selective list of books ..., compiled by the Society for Constructive Birth Control and Racial Progress, London, National Book Council, 1927.

The Case against birth prevention; a selected list of books ..., compiled by the League of National Life, London, National Book Council, 1927.

Chachuat, M., *Le mouvement de 'Birth control' dans les pays anglo-saxons*, Université de Lyons, 1934.

Himes, N. E., *A guide to birth control literature; a selected bibliography on the technique of contraception and on the social aspects of birth control*, Noel Douglas, 1931.

Peel, J., 'Birth control and the British working-class movement: a bibliographical review', Society for the Study of Labour History, *Bulletin* 7, Autumn 1963, pp 16–22.

Wolfe, A. B., 'The population problem since the world war: a survey of literature and research', *Journal of Political Economy*, XXXVII, 5, Oct 1928, pp 529–59; 6, Dec 1928, pp 662–85; XXXVIII, 1, Feb 1929, pp 87–120.

The Banks' bibliography is the only one which specifically covers material relating the birth control movement to the feminist movement or treats the subject from a feminist point of view, although there are several which are useful sources of information. These have been listed with only a general comment that they all contain some references of value and each has a different emphasis on the subject.

Contagious Diseases

Scott, B., 'A bibliography of the literature of the repeal movement', in Scott, B., ed, *A state iniquity: its rise, extension and overthrow*, Kegan Paul, 1890.

Useful contemporary bibliography which lists among other documents the publications of organizations campaigning for the repeal of the Contagious Diseases Acts, as well as Josephine Butler's published work. It is arranged in alphabetical author order with subdivisions for leaflets, memorials and reports.

Walkowitz, J., *We are not beasts of the field: prostitution and the campaign against the Contagious Diseases Acts, 1869–1886*, unpublished PhD thesis, University of Rochester, New York, 1974.

This contains very useful bibliography which includes material on both prostitution and contagious diseases and not only material relating solely to the campaign for the repeal of the Contagious Diseases Acts, as Scott's bibliography does. In addition to alphabetical lists of published sources and periodicals it includes archival materials and government publications.

PROFESSIONS AND TRADES

Armed services

Department of Employment, Library Checklist, *Women in the war 1914–1918*, (typescript, no date).
Ministry of Defence, Book list, series 464, 'Women's Services, 1914–1918', (typescript, no date).

The former is a useful though short list and the latter is short and of limited value.

Domestic service

Butler, Christina V., *Domestic service: an enquiry by the Women's Industrial Council*, Bell, 1916, pp 142–8.

This has a very useful bibliography of books and contributions to journals, including those published in France and Germany.

Midwifery

Donnison, Jean, *Midwives and medical men; a history of inter-professional rivalries and women's rights*, Heinemann Educational, 1977, pp 225–8.

A select bibliography which lists some of the more important and easily available published works on the subject is included. It is based on a much fuller bibliography in her unpublished PhD thesis 'The development of the profession of midwife in England, 1750–1903', (London University, 1974). The thesis bibliography is extensive and comprehensive and includes archives, official papers, newspapers and periodicals as well as books and pamphlets. Each section is arranged in alphabetical order and although the subject of the thesis is midwifery the sources cover the medical profession as a whole.

SUFFRAGE

Rosen, Andrew, *Rise up women! The militant campaign of the Women's Social and Political Union 1903–1914*, Routledge, 1974, pp 294–301.

Contains bibliography basically relating to the suffragette movement and its importance lies in the archive sources quoted which together with the published sources make this a valuable source of information. Some contemporary accounts are listed and they have been divided into books and pamphlets. A list of periodicals and journals does not include individual articles.

Rover, Constance, *Women's suffrage and party politics in Britain, 1866–1914*. Routledge, 1967, pp 225–31.

This is useful, not only because it was the first bibliography to be published on women's suffrage since 'A British Bibliography on Women's Questions' (see above p 70) but because of the scope of the material included. It has a comprehensive list of periodicals and journals and although it does not list parliamentary papers this is unnecessary as the appendix contains a list of suffrage Bills presented to Parliament. Published sources are divided into contemporary accounts; those published before, and those published after, 1914.

BIOGRAPHIES

This section has been arranged in alphabetical order of name, because the wide range of interests of many of the individuals concerned would have made a subject arrangement difficult and have necessitated a confusing cross-referencing system. Men and women who have in some way affected or changed the position of women during the period 1870–1928 are included. A brief outline of their achievements has been given to compensate for the lack of subject arrangement. The references do not aim to be comprehensive but rather to act as a guide to further sources of information. Where there have been many biographies only the more comprehensive have been included; however an attempt has been made to include all autobiographies. Where appropriate the date of *The Times* obituary has been included as it usually gives a concise and accurate account of an individual's achievements and apart from an entry in the *Dictionary of National Biography* for many women it is the only account of their lives.

Anderson, Elizabeth Garrett 1836–1917

Anderson, Louisa Garrett, *Elizabeth Garrett Anderson*, Faber, 1939.
Bell, Enid H. C. M., *Storming the citadel: the rise of the woman doctor*, Constable, 1953.
Bellis, H., *Elizabeth Garrett Anderson*, Newnes, 1953.
Blackwell, Elizabeth, *Pioneer work in opening the medical profession to women: Autobiographical sketches*, Longmans-Green, 1895.
Fawcett, M. G., *What I remember*, Fisher Unwin, 1925.
Manton, Jo, *Elizabeth Garrett Anderson*, Methuen, 1965.
Wymer, Norman G., *Elizabeth Garrett Anderson*, Oxford University Press, 1959.
The Times, 18 December 1917.

Elizabeth Garrett Anderson, the sister of the suffragist leader Millicent Garrett Fawcett, was the first woman to be admitted to membership of the British Medical Association. She was unable to qualify as a doctor in England and so took her MD degree in Paris. On her return to England she worked to open up the medical profession to women. Of the biographies Jo Manton's is the most extensive, while Wymer's is a pamphlet in the Oxford University Press series 'Lives of Great Men and Women'. Enid Bell's history of women in the medical profession contains information relating to Elizabeth Garrett Anderson's role in opening the profession to women, while Millicent Garrett Fawcett's autobiography contains more personal information.

Anderson, Mary Reid (*née* Macarthur) 1880–1921

Drake, Barbara, *Women in trade unions*, Allen & Unwin, 1920.
Hamilton, Mary A., *Mary Macarthur*, Leonard Parsons, 1925.

Mrs Anderson was a pioneer and organizer of women's trade unions and amalgamated them into the National Federation of Women Workers in 1906. In 1903 she had been appointed General Secretary to the Women's Trade Union League and it is this aspect of her life that is covered by Mary Hamilton. Barbara Drake's history of women in trade unions is also a valuable source of information.

Astor, Nancy 1890–1964

Collis, Maurice, *Nancy Astor: an informal biography*, Faber, 1960.
Sykes, Christopher, *Nancy: the life of Lady Astor*, Collins, 1972.
The Times, 4 May 1964.

Nancy Astor is famous as the first woman to take her seat as a Member of Parliament. Her interests included temperance, education, nursery schools and women police. The biographies by Maurice Collis and Christopher Sykes deal mainly with her life and position in society rather than with the first woman Member of Parliament.

Beale, Dorothea 1831–1906

Kamm, Josephine, *How different from us*, Bodley Head, 1958.
Raikes, E., *Dorothea Beale of Cheltenham*, Constable, 1908.
Shillito, E. H., *Dorothea Beale: Principal of the Cheltenham Ladies' College, 1858–1906*, SPCK, 1920.
Steadman, Florence C., *In the days of Miss Beale: a study of her work and influence*, E. J. Burrow, 1931.
Cheltenham Ladies' College Magazine, Memorial Number, 1906.
Journal of Education, December 1906, January 1907.
The Times, 10, 17 and 19 November 1906 (obituary and tributes).

Dorothea Beale is best known as the Principal of the Cheltenham Ladies' College which she greatly improved and expanded during her time as headmistress. Her interest in women's education was not, however, confined to the College; she was also concerned about the standard and the availability of suitably qualified women teachers. She opened St Hilda's College, Oxford, in order to train women to a suitable standard.

Her influence on education has been discussed by Florence Steadman in her work on Miss Beale's achievements. Biographies by Elizabeth Shillito and Elizabeth Raikes describe her achievements and influence at the Cheltenham Ladies' College, whilst Josephine Kamm's work *How different from us* describes briefly the influence of both Miss Beale and Miss Buss. Useful reviews of her life and work are to be found in the Memorial Number of the *Cheltenham Ladies' College Magazine* and in the obituaries and tributes published in the *Journal of Education*.

Becker, Lydia 1829–90

Blackburn, Helen, *Women's suffrage: a record of the Women's Suffrage movement in the British Isles* ..., Williams & Norgate, 1902.
Holmes, Marion, *Lydia Becker: a cameo life sketch*, Women's Freedom League, 1913.
The Times, 21 July 1890.

Lydia Becker's earliest interest was botany and in her early years if women had been able to follow scientific careers she would have been a botanist. She was a supporter of many feminist causes but is known chiefly for her work with the suffrage movement. She founded the Manchester Society for Women's Suffrage, and was editor of the *Women's Suffrage Journal*. There is as yet no full biography although the Women's Freedom League pamphlet gives a brief review of her life and work and Helen Blackburn's history of the early suffrage movement includes biographical sketches of Lydia Becker.

Belloc, Bessie (*née* Rayner Parkes) 1828–1925

Lowndes, M. A. Belloc, *I, too, have lived in Arcadia*, Macmillan, 1941.

Mrs Belloc was co-founder in 1858 of the *Englishwoman's Journal*. She was well known also as an essayist on women's work. The only work containing information relating to her life and work is her daughter's published reminiscences which contain very little of value.

Besant, Annie 1847–1933

Besant, A., *An Autobiography*, Fisher Unwin, 1893.
Besterman, Theodore, *A bibliography of Annie Besant*, Theosophical Society of England, 1924.
Besterman, Theodore, *Mrs Annie Besant: a modern prophet*, Kegan Paul, 1934.
Nethercot, A. H., *The strange lives of Annie Besant*, Hart-Davis, 1960.
Nethercot, A. H., *The first five lives of Annie Besant*, Hart-Davis, 1961.
Nethercot, A. H., *The last four lives of Annie Besant*, Hart-Davis, 1963.
Shaw, G. B., *Dr Annie Besant: fifty years in public work* (a pamphlet), 1924.
West, Geoffrey, *The life of Annie Besant*, Gerald Howe, 1929.
Williams, Gertrude M., *The passionate pilgrim: a life of Annie Besant*, John Hamilton, 1932.
The Times, 21 September 1933.

Although Annie Besant is probably best known as a supporter of neo-malthusianism and as a defendant in the Bradlaugh-Besant trial of 1877, she had many interests relating to women. She participated in the match-girls' strike against phosphorous poisoning and formed a union for them in 1889. In later life she became famous as a Fabian Socialist, a theosophist and an Indian independence leader. Arthur Nethercot's biographies are the best source of information relating to her many interests. Besterman's bibliography includes biographical works and also her publications to 1924. It is divided into sections which are arranged chronologically: (i) works by Annie Besant, (ii) works partly by, or in collaboration with, Annie Besant, (iii) works edited or introduced by Annie Besant, (iv) periodicals edited by Annie Besant, (v) works translated by Annie Besant, (vi) extracts from her works, (vii) works about Annie Besant.

Blackwell, Elizabeth 1821–1910

Baker, Rachel, *The First Woman Doctor: the story of Elizabeth Blackwell, MD*, Harrap, 1946.
Bell, Enid H. C. M., *Storming the citadel: the rise of the woman doctor*, Constable, 1953.
Blackwell, E., *Pioneer work in opening the medical profession to women*, Longmans Green, 1895.
Chambers, Peggy, *A doctor alone: a biography of Elizabeth Blackwell*, Bodley Head, 1956.
Ross, Ishbel, *Child of destiny: the life story of the first woman doctor*, Gollancz, 1950.
Tabor, M. E., *Pioneer women*, Sheldon Press, 1925–33.
Wilson, Dorothy C., *Lone woman: the story of Elizabeth Blackwell*, Hodder & Stoughton, 1970.
The Times, 2 June 1910.

Elizabeth Blackwell was the first woman doctor of medicine. She had, however, been unable to enter a British university and so had qualified in the United States of America. On her return to England she worked to enable women to qualify as doctors in the United Kingdom. The story of her campaign is told in her autobiography and in Enid Bell's work on the early days of the woman doctor.

Bodichon, Barbara Leigh 1827–91

Bradbrook, M. C., *Barbara Bodichon, George Eliot and the limits of feminism*, Oxford, Somerville College, 1976.
Burton, H., *Barbara Bodichon, 1827–1891*, John Murray, 1949.
Stephen, B., *Emily Davies and Girton College*, Constable, 1927.
The Times, 15 June 1891.

Madame Bodichon was the major benefactress of Girton College and information relating to her part in the founding of that college can be found in Barbara Stephen's work on Emily Davies and Girton College. The biography by Hester Burton also covers Madame Bodichon's part in the passing of the Married Women's Property Acts, while Miss Bradbrook's work places her in the wider context of the feminist movement as a whole.

Bondfield, Margaret Grace 1873–1953

Bondfield, M. G., *A life's work*, Hutchinson, 1949.
Hamilton, Mary A., *Margaret Bondfield*, Leonard Parsons, 1924.
The Times, 18 June 1953.

Margaret Bondfield became the first woman Cabinet Minister when in 1929 she was appointed Minister of Labour, a post she occupied until 1931. Prior to this she had been active in the trade union movement. Her autobiography is a useful source of information as she quotes from personal letters and diaries. Mary Hamilton's biography covers her early life, but as none of the papers Margaret Bondfield refers to in her autobiography can now be traced it seems unlikely that a full biography will be written.

Booth, Catherine 1829–90

Booth, C. B., *Catherine Booth: the story of her loves*, Hodder & Stoughton, 1970.
Booth-Tucker, F. de L. *The life of Catherine Booth: the mother of the Salvation Army*, Salvation Army Press, 1893, 2 vols.
Chappell, Jennie, *Four noble women and their work: sketches of the life-work of Frances Willard, Agnes Weston, Sister Dora and Catherine Booth*, S. W. Partridge, 1898.
Chappell, Jennie, *Women of worth: sketches of the lives of 'Carmen Sylva', Isabella Bird Bishop, Frances Power Cobbe and Mrs Bramwell Booth*, S. W. Partridge, 1908.
Powell, Cyril H., *Catherine Booth*, Epworth Press, 1951.
Stead, W. T., *Mrs Booth of the Salvation Army*, J. Nesbit, 1900.
Unsworth, Madge, *Maiden Tribute: a study in voluntary social service*, Salvationist Publishing, 1949.
The Times, 6 October 1890.

Known as the 'Mother of the Salvation Army', the wife of William Booth was the co-founder of the Salvation Army. It was through her influence that the position and role of women in the Salvation Army were equal to those of men. She also interested herself in other feminist topics and was involved in Josephine Butler's campaign against the Contagious Diseases Acts. Her involvement in this cause is described in Madge Unsworth's work; William Stead's biography also contains information on this aspect of her life. The fullest account of Mrs Booth's work, particularly with the Salvation Army, is to be found in Booth-Tucker's biography.

Burdett-Coutts, Angela Georgina 1814–1906

Burdett-Coutts, A., *Baroness Burdett Coutts, a sketch of her public life and work, prepared for the Lady Managers of the World's Columbian Exposition, by command of Her Royal Highness, Princess Mary Adelaide, Duchess of Teck*, Chicago, A. McClurg, 1893.

Healey, Edna, *Lady unknown: the life of Angela Burdett-Coutts*, Sidgwick & Jackson, 1978.
Patterson, Clara B., *Angela Burdett-Coutts and the Victorians*, John Murray, 1953.

Having inherited the Coutts fortune, Angela Burdett-Coutts devoted herself to philanthropic works. Her interests were wide, but her principal ones were schools and churches; she established various institutions, notably the Art Students' Home for Ladies, in conjunction with Charles Dickens. While her autobiography is mainly an account of her public work, Edna Healey's work covers her private and public life and gives an interesting picture of a previously little-known woman.

Buss, Frances Mary 1827–94

Burstall, S. A., *Frances Mary Buss: an educational pioneer*, SPCK, 1938.
Holmes, M., *Frances Mary Buss*, Women's Freedom League, 1913.
Kamm, Josephine, *How different from us*, Bodley Head, 1958.
Ridley, A. E., *Frances Mary Buss and her work for education*, Longmans Green, 1895.
The Times, 2 January 1895.

Miss Buss was a leading educationalist and a supporter of secondary education for girls. She founded the North London Collegiate School for Ladies in 1850 and in 1871 its sister school, the Camden School for Girls. She was also a supporter of the women's colleges at Cambridge and became the first President of the Head Mistresses' Association. Her biography by Annie Ridley is a valuable source for all aspects of her life. Brief outlines of her achievements can be found in the pamphlets by Holmes and Burstall. Josephine Kamm's work describes the role of both Miss Beale and Miss Buss in the early movement for secondary education for girls.

Butler, Josephine Elizabeth 1828–1906

Bell, Enid H. C. M., *Josephine Butler: flame of fire*, Constable, 1962.
Butler, Arthur S. G., *Portrait of Josephine Butler*, Faber, 1954.
Butler, Josephine E., *Personal reminiscences of a great crusade*, Horace Marshall, 1896.
Crawford, Virginia M., *Josephine Butler*, Josephine Butler Centenary Committee, 1928.
Fawcett, M. G. and Turner, E. M., *Josephine Butler: her work and principles*, Association for Moral and Social Hygiene, 1928.
Hay-Cooper, L., *Josephine Butler and her work for social purity*, SPCK, 1922.
Holmes, Marion, *Josephine Butler: a cameo life-sketch*, Women's Freedom League, 8th ed., 1913.
Johnson, George W. and Lucy A., eds, *Josephine E. Butler: an autobiographical memoir*, Bristol, Arrowsmith, 1909.

Petrie, G., *A singular iniquity: the campaigns of Josephine Butler*, Macmillan, 1971.

Turner, E. M., *Josephine Butler*, Association for Moral and Social Hygiene, 1935.

The Josephine Butler Centenary 1828–1928, Josephine Butler: an appreciation, Association for Moral and Social Hygiene, 1927.

The Times, 2 January 1907.

Although Josephine Butler was interested and involved in many feminist movements, including the campaign for the right of married women to separate property, she is best known as the leader of the campaign first to repeal and later to abolish the Contagious Diseases Acts. Mrs Butler's autobiographies are extremely valuable for information relating to her life and achievements. *Personal reminiscences of a great crusade* describes her work for the repeal of the Contagious Diseases Acts and her *Autobiographical memoir* is devoted to more personal aspects of her life. The more extensive biographies are those of Enid Moberley Bell and Glen Petrie which deal predominantly with her role in repealing the Contagious Diseases Acts. The bibliography in Enid Bell's biography lists not only works by and about Josephine Butler but also gives the locations of manuscript material relating to her. Arthur S. G. Butler's work adds little new to others despite his being her grandson and having had access to family papers.

Chisholm, Caroline 1808–77

Anstruther, George E., *Caroline Chisholm: the emigrant's friend*, Catholic Truth Society, 1916.

Kiddle, Margaret, *Caroline Chisholm*, Melbourne University Press, 1950.

Mackenzie, E., *Memoirs of Mrs Caroline Chisholm and sketches of her philanthropic labours in India, Australia and England*, Webb, Millington, 1852.

The Times, 26 March 1877.

Caroline Chisholm was connected with the nineteenth-century emigration movement, and established the Family Colonisation Loan Society, thereby assisting the wives and children of ex-convicts in Australia to emigrate there. Margaret Kiddle's biography, based on material in both the United Kingdom and Australia, is a valuable source of information, and the fullest account, Eneas Mackenzie's *Memoirs of Mrs Caroline Chisholm*, includes a history and review of the organisation founded by Mrs Chisholm. The Catholic Truth Society's publication is merely a brief outline of her life.

Clough, Anne Jemima 1820–92

Clough, B. A., *A memoir of Anne Jemima Clough*, Edward Arnold, 1897.

The Times, 29 February 1892.

A leading educationalist, she was a founder-member of the North of England

Council for Promoting the Education of Women. In 1870, together with five other students, she formed the nucleus of Newnham College, Cambridge. Her biography, written by her niece, who herself became a Principal of Newnham College, is an authoritative work.

Cobbe, Frances Power 1822–1904

Cobbe, F. P., *Life of Frances Power Cobbe*, R. Bentley, 1894.
The Times, 4 April 1904.

A philanthropist and religious writer, Frances Power Cobbe campaigned for the Matrimonial Causes Act of 1878 and for the granting of degrees to women, and in later life against vivisection. There is as yet no biography of Frances Power Cobbe but information relating to her life and work can be found in her autobiography.

Davenport-Hill, Rosamund 1825–1902

Metcalfe, Ethel E., *Memoir of Rosamund Davenport-Hill*, Longmans, 1904.

An educational administrator, Rosamund Davenport-Hill was a member of the London School Board for nearly twenty years, 1879–97, where she was well known for her policy of trying to obtain the best possible education for children. Her other interests included the improvement of prisons and reformatories, but unfortunately her biography, written in 1904, concentrates mainly on her personal life.

Davies, Emily 1830–1921

Stephen, Barbara, *Emily Davies and Girton College*, Constable, 1927.
The Times, 19 July 1921.

Although best known as the founder of Girton College, Cambridge, she was also the founder of the London Schoolmistresses' Association, and active in suffrage work. Barbara Stephen's excellent biography describes Emily Davies's role in founding Girton College, and includes an invaluable bibliography of her writings.

Dilke, Emilia F. S. 1840–1904

Askwith, B. E., *Lady Dilke: a biography*, Chatto & Windus, 1969.
Jenkins, R. H., *Sir Charles Dilke: a Victorian tragedy*, Collins, 1958.
The Times, 25 October 1905.

Lady Dilke was president of the Women's Trade Union League but is probably more famous as an art historian and art editor of the journal *Academy*. Information relating to her life and work to improve conditions of employment for women in factories is to be found in the biography by Betty Askwith; in his biography of her husband, Sir Charles Dilke, Roy Jenkins makes reference to Lady Dilke.

Fawcett, Millicent Garrett 1847–1929

Chappell, Jennie, *Noble work by noble women: sketches of the lives of Baroness Burdett-Coutts, Lady Henry Somerset, Miss Sarah Robinson, Mrs Fawcett and Mrs Gladstone*, S. W. Partridge, 1900.

Fawcett, M. G., *What I remember ...*, Fisher Unwin, 1925.

Fawcett, M. G., *The women's victory – and after: personal reminiscences, 1911–1918*, Sidgwick & Jackson, 1920.

Strachey, Ray, *Millicent Garrett Fawcett*, John Murray, 1931.

The Times, 6 August 1929.

In 1867 Mrs Fawcett became a member of the London National Society for Women's Suffrage, one of the first women's suffrage committees and thirty years later, in 1897, became the president of the National Union of Women's Suffrage Societies and undisputed leader of the suffragist movement. In addition to her suffrage work she was interested in the education of women and in conditions of employment for women, as shown by her interest in the match-girls's strike. In 1901 she led a commission of women to South Africa to inquire into conditions in concentration camps. Her autobiography, *What I remember*, contains information relating to all these aspects of her life; *The women's victory* is devoted to reminiscences of the suffrage campaign. Her biography has been written by Ray Strachey although there is still scope for further work based on the archival material in both the Fawcett Library and Manchester Public Library. A brief account appears in Jennie Chappell's *Noble work by noble women*.

Fenwick, Ethel G. 1857–1947

The Times, 17 March 1947.

A pioneer of nursing reform and leader of the movement for the state registration of nurses, she became the founder and President of the International Council of Nurses. She also helped to found the British Nurses' Association, the Matrons' Council of Great Britain, the National Council of Nurses of Great Britain and in 1926 the British College of Nurses, as well as being the editor of the *British Journal of Nursing*. Despite all these achievements there is as yet no biography of Ethel Fenwick and the only readily available sources of information are the *Dictionary of National Biography* and her obituary in *The Times*.

Furse, Katharine 1875–1952

Katharine Furse became the founder and director of the Women's Royal Naval Service in 1917. She had joined the Red Cross Voluntary Aid Detachment in 1913 and in 1914 was one of the first women to go to France where she organized VAD stations. Later in the war she was appointed Commandant-in-Chief of the VADs. She resigned in 1917 when she became the director of the short-lived Women's Royal Naval Service. No biography of Katherine Furse has yet been published.

Gregory, Alice Sophia 1867–1946

Morland, Egbert, *Alice and the stork, or the rise in the status of the midwife as exemplified in the life of Alice Gregory, 1867–1944*, Hodder & Stoughton, 1951.
The Times, 26 November 1946.

A pioneer for the registration of midwives she also pioneered for their further education and was a co-founder of the British Hospital for Mothers and Babies. Despite the importance of her work for the midwifery profession, there is no adequate biography of her, as Egbert Morland's work does not include much information on her achievements but concentrates on her Christian beliefs.

Grey, Maria Georgina Shirreff 1816–1906

The Times, 26 November 1906.

She was secretary to the Women's Education Union until 1879, the author of two major works on the education of women and the founder of a training college for women teachers in secondary schools which opened in 1878. In addition to her educational activities she was also a supporter of women's suffrage. There is as yet no biography published of her life and this is a gap that could usefully be filled. Her interest in training women as secondary-school teachers was in advance of her time.

Gwynne-Vaughan, Helen 1879–1967

Izzard, Molly P., *A heroine in her time: a life of ...*, Macmillan, 1969.
The Times, 30 August 1967.

The daughter of a Scottish Earl she broke with the conventions of the day to study Geology and Botany at London University. She became lecturer and later Head of the Biology Department of Royal Holloway College and published twenty-five scientific papers between the years 1905 and 1937. She was also interested in the suffrage cause and founded the University of London Suffrage Society. During the First World War she became Chief Controller of the Women's Army Auxiliary Corps after establishing and expanding the organization and was later appointed Commander-in-Chief of the Women' Royal Air Force. She returned to Birkbeck College between the wars, though in 1939 she returned to the armed forces to take control of, and expand, the Auxiliary Territorial Service, the women's branch of the army. All these aspects of her life have been covered by the Izzard biography which gives a clear and well-presented account of her life.

Hadow, Grace Eleanor 1875–1940

Deneke, Helena C., *Grace Hadow*, Oxford University Press, 1946.
The Times, 22 January 1940.

Grace Hadow had two main interests relating to women, first, as an educationalist, and secondly, as one of the principal organizers of the Women's Institutes. She was lecturer in English Literature and Tutor in English at Lady Margaret Hall and Principal of the Society of Oxford Home Students which she helped to found. The biography covers this aspect of her work as well as describing her role in the Women's Institute of which she was an executive member; it is a good source of information relating to her activities and beliefs.

Hill, Octavia 1838–1912

Bell, Enid H. C. M., *Octavia Hill: a biography*, Constable, 1942, Quantum Books, 1965.
Hill, W. T., *Octavia Hill, pioneer of The National Trust and housing reformer*, Hutchinson, 1956.
Maurice, C. E., ed, *Life of Octavia Hill as told in her letters*, Macmillan, 1913.
The Times, 15 August 1912.

A philanthropist with many interests, she was chiefly interested in housing projects for the poor and in later life was actively involved in the foundation of the National Trust. Charles Maurice's biography, as suggested by its title, is based on her letters but gives little indication of how much they reflect her work, whilst Enid Moberley Bell's work tends to have superficial coverage of her works with little in the way of background; William Hill's work deals with her pioneering role for the National Trust and as a housing reformer.

Hilton, Marie 1821–96

Hilton, J. D., *Marie Hilton, her life and work, 1821–1896*, Isbister, 1897.
The Times, 11 April 1896.

A Quaker, she was concerned with working mothers and introduced the crèche system to England in 1871 after having visited Brussels and seen such a system in operation. She was associated with Dr Barnardo's work and also an active member of the temperance movement. Hilton's biography does not do full justice to her dedication to the causes she supported, nor does it set her advanced ideas in the context of the time.

Hubbard, Louisa M. 1836–1906

Pratt, Edwin A., *A woman's work for women: being the aims, efforts and aspirations of 'LMH', Miss Louisa M. Hubbard*, Newnes, 1898.
The Times, 1 December 1906.

A feminist, she was interested in the education and better employment opportunities of women. Louisa Hubbard's main aim was to open new fields of work to women and she was an early supporter of typing as a suitable occupation. She founded the Women's Emigration Society in 1880 and helped to found the National Union of Women Workers, as well as the Matrons' Aid or Trained Midwives' Registration

Society in 1882. She edited the *Women's Gazette* (later *Work and Leisure*), an emigration journal, and also for many years the *Englishwomen's Year Book*. An account of her work has been given by Edwin Pratt although there is still room for a more exhaustive work.

Inglis, Elsie Maud 1864–1917

Balfour, Lady Frances, *Dr Elsie Inglis*, Hodder & Stoughton, 1918.
Gibbs, A., *Elsie Maud Inglis*, Women's Freedom League, 1920.
Lawrence, M., *Shadow of swords, a biography of Elsie Inglis*, Michael Joseph, 1971.
McLaren, E. S., *Elsie Inglis: the woman with the torch*, SPCK, 1920.
Tait, H. P., *Dr Elsie Maud Inglis*, private circulation, (n.d.).

A physician and surgeon, she is best known for her work with the Scottish Women's Hospital, which she helped to found, to provide hospital units during the First World War. She worked with these hospital units in Serbia and Russia and that eventually led to her death. Her less known interests included the founding of a maternity hospital in Edinburgh staffed by women and the formation of the Scottish Women's Suffrage Federation in 1906. Of the biographies Margot Lawrence's work, *Shadow of Swords*, is a valuable source of information as it draws on previously unpublished sources. The pamphlets by Eva McLaren and Aimée Gibbs are only brief outlines of her life, while Francis Balfour's biography and H. P. Tait's privately printed work have now been superseded by Margot Lawrence's work.

Jex-Blake, Sophia Louisa 1840–1912

Bell, Enid H. C. M., *Storming the citadel: the rise of the woman doctor*, Constable, 1953.
Todd, M. G., *The life of Sophia Jex-Blake*, Macmillan, 1918.
The Times, 9 January 1912.

Sophia Jex-Blake believed in, and worked for, women's right to practise medicine. In 1874 with Elizabeth Garrett Anderson she founded the London School of Medicine and in 1886 the Edinburgh School of Medicine for Women. In addition to Margaret Todd's biography some information is to be found in Enid Bell's history of the early days of women doctors, *Storming the citadel*.

Kenney, Annie 1879–1953

Kenney, A., *Memoirs of a militant*, Edward Arnold, 1924.
Pethick-Lawrence, F. W., 'Annie Kenney', *Labour Record and Review*, (n.d.).
The Times, 11 July 1953.

A leading suffragette and one of the few working-class members of the movement, she came to London with Christabel Pankhurst to extend the work of the Women's

Social and Political Union which had been founded in Manchester. She had been imprisoned in Manchester and was to be imprisoned again for her suffragette activities. Her memoirs are interesting as they give a working-class point of view of the suffrage movement. The only biographical work at present is Frederick Pethick-Lawrence's pamphlet, *Annie Kenney*.

Lucas, Margaret Bright 1818–90

Heath, Henry J. B., *Margaret Bright Lucas: the life story of a 'British woman', being a memoir*, George Potter, 1890.
Lucas, M. B., *Memoir of Margaret Bright Lucas*, British Women's Temperance Association (n.d.).
The Times, 5 February 1890.

A temperance pioneer, Margaret Bright Lucas was the sister of John and Jacob Bright and was well known for her work with the temperance movement. She became president of the British Women's Temperance Association in 1878 and later president of the World's Women's Temperance Union. She was also interested in the early campaign for women's suffrage and in the campaign for the repeal of the Contagious Diseases Acts. Her autobiography provides an interesting insight into her motivations and ideals, while Henry Heath's biography gives a review of her life and work.

Lytton, Constance Georgina 1869–1963

Lytton, C. G., *Prisons and prisoners: some personal experiences*, Heinemann, 1914.
Lytton, C. G., *Letters, selected and arranged by Lady Betty Balfour*, Heinemann, 1925.

Lady Lytton was the suffragette who, because she suspected her position had given her preferential treatment in prison, when next arrested gave an assumed name and was then force-fed in prison. She wrote about her experiences which subsequently became famous in the suffragette movement. Her letters, which also deal with other aspects of her life have been edited by Lady Balfour.

MacDonald, Margaret Ethel 1870–1911

Herbert, I.., *Mrs Ramsay MacDonald*, Women Publishers, 1924.
Holmes, I. M., *The girlhood of Mrs Ramsay MacDonald*, Ealing, Middlesex County Times Printing & Publishing Co, 1938.
MacDonald, J. R., *Margaret Ethel MacDonald*, Hodder & Stoughton, 1912.
Women's Labour League, *Margaret Ethel MacDonald*, WLL, 1912.

The wife of Ramsay MacDonald, Margaret MacDonald was interested in politics in her own right, with particular emphasis on the position of women. Several biographies have been written, from Isabella Holmes' pamphlet on her childhood to

Lucy Herbert's and J. Ramsay MacDonald's biographies which deal with her later life. The Women's Labour League published a compilation of her obituaries which contain some information of her work and achievements in addition to the usual appreciations.

McMillan, Rachel 1859–1917
McMillan, Margaret 1860–1931

Ballard, Philip B., *Margaret McMillan: an appreciation*, Rachel McMillan Training College, 1937.
Cresswell, Walter D'Arcy, *Margaret McMillan: a memoir*, Hutchinson, 1948.
Lord, Miriam, *Margaret McMillan in Bradford, with reminiscences*, University of London Press, 1957.
Lowndes, G. A. N., *Margaret McMillan: 'The children's champion'*, Museum Press, 1960.
McMillan, Margaret, *The life of Rachel McMillan*, Dent, 1927.
Mansbridge, A., *Margaret McMillan, prophet and pioneer: her life and work*, Dent, 1932.
A bibliography of the lives and works of Margaret and Rachel McMillan, Rachel McMillan College, n.d.

Rachel McMillan worked with her sister Margaret in the campaign for medical inspection in schools and for the provision of school meals for the undernourished. Some information relating to her life and work can be found in biographies of Margaret as well as in Margaret's biography of her sister.

Margaret McMillan was a forerunner in the provision of nursery education. In 1923 she founded the Nursery School Association and became its first president. In 1930 she founded the Rachel McMillan College at Deptford for the training of nursery school teachers, in memory of her sister. Biographies containing information about her philosophy of education and her achievements have been written by Cresswell, Lowndes and Mansbridge; the College produced an appreciation of her work in 1937 which is a useful starting-point and includes bibliographical details of both sisters; the Fourth Margaret McMillan Lecture (included in Miriam Lord's *Margaret McMillan in Bradford*) contains reminiscences of Margaret's work there.

Maynard, Constance Louisa 1849–1935

Firth, C. B., *Constance Louisa Maynard, Mistress of Westfield College: a family portrait*, Allen & Unwin, 1949.
The Times, 27 March 1935.

Constance Maynard had been one of the earliest pupils at Girton College but being of a strong evangelical persuasion she founded Westfield College in North London in order that there could be a college catering for the daughters of those with similar beliefs. Catherine Firth's biography deals predominantly with her personal life.

Meredith, Susanna 1828–1901

Lloyd, M. A., *Susanna Meredith: a record of a vigorous life*, Hodder & Stoughton, 1903.
Meredith, S., *Saved Rahab! an autobiography*, edited by Mrs Meredith, Nisbet, 1881.

Susanna Meredith worked to aid women in prison and founded the Prison Mission and Princess Mary Homes in order to help women released from prison. Her autobiography contains a record of her work as does M. A. Lloyd's biography.

Nightingale, Florence 1820–1910

Bishop, W. J., and Goldie, S., *A Biobibliography of Florence Nightingale*, Dawsons for International Council of Nurses, 1962.
Cook, Sir Edward T. *The life of Florence Nightingale*, Macmillan, 1913.
Huxley, E., *Florence Nightingale*, Weidenfeld & Nicolson, 1975.
Woodham-Smith, C. B., *Florence Nightingale 1820–1910*, Constable, 1950.
The Times, 15 August 1910.

The daughter of a rich family she broke away from the traditional way of life expected of her, to become the heroine of the Crimea. In addition to her more famous role as founder of the British nursing tradition, she was an ardent supporter of women midwives. There have been many biographies. Cook's is the official biography and the bibliography it contains is extensive; until the publication of Bishop and Goldie's *Biobibliography* it was by far the best and most comprehensive bibliography of her works and writings. It is also useful for works relating to the early days of the nursing profession. It is divided into two main sections: first, the writings of Florence Nightingale, including some privately printed works, arranged in chronological order; and secondly, writings about her, but this includes only 'First-hand authorities or works which seem relevant'. Cecil Woodham-Smith's book, published nearly forty years later, is also an excellent and accurate work. Elspeth Huxley's book is particularly useful for the illustrations it contains. There are many other biographies but they have not been included here as those by Cook and Woodham-Smith make all others superfluous.

Bishop and Goldie's *Biobibliography* has a complete list of Florence Nightingales's published writings, including her contributions to government reports, magazines and newspapers, as well as letters and notes she had privately published for circulation among her friends. It is arranged in subject order; nursing, army, Indian and Colonial welfare, hospitals, statistics, sociology, memoirs and tributes, religion and philosophy, miscellaneous works (including untraced works listed by Sir Edward Cook) and selected writings about Florence Nightingale and her times. This is the definitive bibliography of Florence Nightingale's writings.

Pankhurst, Christabel 1880–1950;
Pankhurst, Emmeline 1850–1928;
Pankhurst, E. Sylvia 1882–1960

Keir, Thelma Cazalet, *I knew Mrs Pankhurst*, Suffragette Fellowship, 1945.
Mitchell, David J., *The fighting Pankhursts: a study in tenacity*, Cape, 1967.
Mitchell, David J., *Queen Christabel: a biography of Christabel Pankhurst*, Macdonald & Jane's, 1977.
Pankhurst, C., *Unshackled: the story of how we won the war*, edited by Lord Pethick-Lawrence of Peaslake, Hutchinson, 1959.
Pankhurst, E., *My own story*, Eveleigh Nash, 1914; Virago, 1979.
Pankhurst, E. S., *The suffragette movement: an intimate account of persons and ideals*, Longmans, 1931; Virago, 1977.
Pankhurst E. S., *The life of Emmeline Pankhurst: the suffragette struggle for women's citizenship*, Werner Laurie, 1935.
Pankhurst, E. S., *The suffragette: the history of the women's militant suffrage movement 1905–1910*, New York, Sturgis & Walton, 1911.
The Times, 15 June 1928.
The Times, 28 and 29 August 1960 (obituary and appreciations).

Christabel was an extreme militant and went to Paris (in order to avoid arrest) to run the Women's Social and Political Union campaign. Her autobiography, edited by Lord Pethick-Lawrence, has an obvious emphasis on the suffragette movement. Information is also to be found in David Mitchell's *The fighting Pankhursts*, about their later lives as well as their activities in the suffrage movement. Sylvia Pankhurst's *The suffragette movement* contains information relating to Christabel Pankhurst's role.

Emmeline founded the Women's Social and Political Union in 1903 and became the accepted leader of the militant women's suffrage movement. She served several prison sentences and went on hunger strike on a number of occasions. In 1914 she rallied her supporters to the war effort. Her autobiography concentrates mainly on her role in the suffrage movement. Sylvia Pankhurst's biography is a useful source of information and Thelma Cazalet Keir's pamphlet, the text of a broadcast, gives a personal account of Mrs Pankhurst.

A militant suffragette and socialist, Sylvia was particularly concerned with arousing the interest of working-class women in the suffrage movement. Her later life was spent in Ethiopia where she became a national heroine; information relating to her full life can be found in Mitchell's work on the Pankhursts. Her own works on the suffragette movement only cover the early part of her life as do general works on the campaign for women's suffrage.

Paterson, Emma Anne 1848–86

Drake, Barbara, *Women in the trade unions*, Allen & Unwin, 1920.
Goldman, Harold, *Emma Paterson, her life and times*, TUC, 1974.

Goldman, Harold, *Emma Paterson; she led women into a man's world*, Lawrence & Wishart, 1974.

The founder and first President of the Women's Trade Union League from 1874–86 and the first woman to be admitted to the Trades Union Congress. She was also the editor of the *Women's Union Journal*.

Pethick-Lawrence, Emmeline 1867–1954
Pethick-Lawrence, Frederick W. 1871–1961

Brittain, Vera, *Pethick-Lawrence: a portrait*, Allen & Unwin, 1963.
Pethick-Lawrence, E., *My part in a changing world*, Gollancz, 1938.
Pethick-Lawrence, F. W., *Fate has been kind*, Hutchinson, 1943.

A militant suffrage worker, Emmeline was treasurer of the Women's Social and Political Union until in 1912 she and her husband Frederick split with the Pankhursts over the violence of their activities. She was imprisoned many times for the cause of women's suffrage, and in 1918 she stood as Parliamentary Labour candidate for the constituency of Rusholme, Manchester.

Also a militant suffrage worker, Frederick was joint editor of *Votes for Women* 1907–14. In 1912 he was jailed for his part in the campaign. He was an active Socialist and the editor of several socialist papers. His autobiography covers both aspects of his life, as does Vera Brittain's study. Emmeline's autobiography has much useful information about her husband's suffrage activities.

Rathbone, Eleanor 1872–1946

Stocks, M. D. *Eleanor Rathbone: a biography*, Gollancz, 1949.
The Times, 3, 4 and 8 January 1946 (obituary and appreciations).

Eleanor Rathbone was the president of the National Union for Women's Suffrage Societies from 1919. She represented Combined English Universities in Parliament and as an MP became concerned with the condition of Indian women. She pioneered many social reforms in the UK, including family allowances. Her biography has been well written by Mary Stocks and is a valuable source of information.

Rye, Maria 1829–1903

The Times, 17 November 1903.

The founder of the Female Middle Class Emigration Society with Emily Faithfull, she had previously helped in the founding of the Victoria Printing Press, and with Isa Craig the Registry Office for Women's Employment. There is no published biography of Maria Rye.

Shirreff, Emily Anne Eliza 1814–97

The Times, 24 March 1897.

An educationalist, she was Hon. Secretary to the Women's Education Union and co-editor of its journal, in addition to being on the Council of Girton College, the Girls' Public Day School Trust and Teachers' Training and Registration Society. She was President of the Froebel Society, as well as a founder and developer of the Maria Grey Training College. No biography of her life has yet been published.

Sidgwick, Eleanor Mildred 1845–1936

Sidgwick, Ethel, *Mrs Henry Sidgwick: a memoir*, Sidgwick & Jackson, 1938. *The Times*, 12 February 1936.

She was Principal of Newnham College, Cambridge, 1892–1910, and was appointed to the Royal Commission on Secondary Education. She had a strong interest in psychical research and contributed the article on spiritualism in the *Encyclopedia Britannica*. These varied interests have been described in her niece's biography of her.

Smyth, Ethel Mary 1858–1944

Smyth, E. M., *As time went on*, Longmans, 1936.
Smyth, E. M., *Female pipings in Eden*, Peter Davies, 1933.
Smyth, E. M., *Impressions that remained: memoirs*, Longmans, 1919.
Smyth, E. M., *Streaks of life*, Longmans, 1921.
Smyth, E. M., *What happened next*, Longmans, 1940.
The Times, 10 May 1944.

Author and feminist, Ethel Smyth was also the first British woman composer to achieve serious recognition, and although she is best known for her opera 'The Wreckers', she also composed an oratorio and concertos. She became a militant suffragette and composed the 'March of the Women', the anthem of the WSPU. Her five autobiographical books are also literary works in their own right and contain much valuable information.

Stead, W. T. 1849–1912

Harper, E. K., *Stead, the man: personal reminiscences*, Rider, 1914.
Robertson Scott, J. W., *The life and death of a newspaper: an account of the temperaments, perturbations and achievements of John Morley, W. T. Stead ... and other editors of the Pall Mall Gazette*, Methuen, 1952.
Robertson Scott, J. W., *The story of the Pall Mall Gazette, of its first editor Frederick Greenwood and of its founder George Murray Smith*, Oxford University Press, 1950.
Stead, Estelle W., *My father: personal and spiritual reminiscences*, Heinemann, 1913.
Whyte, F., *The life of W. T. Stead*, Cape, 1925.

Social reformer and journalist, it was Stead who published the article 'The maiden tribute of modern Babylon' in the *Pall Mall Gazette* on 6 July 1885, which resulted in his imprisonment but also led to the raising of the age of consent to 16. He was editor of the *Gazette* at the time. J. W. Robertson Scott's two books are a useful source of information about the campaign. Biographies have been written by his daughter Estelle, Edith Harper and Frederic Whyte but there is still room for a definitive one.

Stopes, Marie Charlotte Carmichael 1880–1958

Begbie, H., *Marie Stopes: her mission and her personality*, Putnam's, 1927.
Box, Muriel, *The trial of Marie Stopes*, Femina Books, 1967.
Briant, Keith R., *Marie Stopes: a biography*, Hogarth Press, 1962.
Eaton, P. and Warnick, M., *Marie Stopes: a preliminary checklist of her writings*, Croom Helm, 1976.
Hall, Ruth, *Marie Stopes: a biography*, Deutsch, 1977; Virago paperback, 1978.
Maude, Aylmer, *The authorised life of Marie C. Stopes*, Williams & Norgate, 1924.
Maude, Aylmer, *Marie Stopes: her work and play*, P. Davies, 1935.
The Times, 3 October 1958.

Best known for her work in the field of contraception, Marie Stopes was the first woman lecturer at Manchester University. Her two well-known works, *Married Love* (Fifield, 1918) and *Wise Parenthood* (J. Bale, 1934), were best-sellers and she opened a birth control clinic to provide fertility information for married people. A useful pamphlet for information relating to Marie Stopes is Harold Begbie's *Marie Stopes* which in addition to providing a brief history also includes a bibliography of her scientific and popular works. Aylmer Maude's books on Marie Stopes have to a certain extent been superseded by Keith Briant's and Ruth Hall's books.

Eaton and Warnick's bibliography is divided into three sections; science, health and social welfare, and literature and travel. It lists periodical articles in addition to books. This and the bibliography in Ruth Hall's biography provide good general coverage.

Tennant, Margaret Mary Edith 1869–1946

Markham, Violet R., *May Tennant: a portrait*, Falcon Press, 1949.
The Times, 12 July 1946.

A pioneer in social work, Margaret Tennant was secretary to Lady Dilke, became treasurer of the Women's Trade Union League, and an Assistant Commissioner on the Royal Commission on Labour in 1891. She was the first woman factory inspector and was concerned mainly with illegal overtime, bad sanitation and dangerous trades. She was a member of the Central Committee on Women's Employment 1914–39 and chief advisor on women's welfare in the Ministry of Munitions during the 1914–18 war. Her biography deals in detail with these achievements and is a full account of her life and is thus a valuable source of information.

Tuckwell, Gertrude Mary 1861–1951

The Times, 6 August 1951

A worker for the improvement of working conditions for women, Gertrude Tuckwell became president of the Women's Trade Union League, and served on many committees of public and official bodies concerned with industrial matters, including the General Committee on Women's Training and Employment. Unfortunately there has been no biography to record her role in obtaining improvements in conditions of employment for women.

Twining, Louisa 1820–1912

Twining, L., *Recollections of life and work: being the autobiography of Louisa Twining*, Edward Arnold, 1893.
Twining, L., *Recollections of workhouse visiting and management during twenty-five years*, Kegan Paul, 1880.
Twining, L., *Workhouses and pauperism and women's work in the administration of the Poor Law*, Methuen, 1898.

A pioneer in visiting workhouses and it was from these visits that Louisa Twining came to campaign for reforms in workhouses and in particular for the appointment of nurses in the wards; she also campaigned for women to be guardians of workhouses. Her 1893 'recollections' are sources of information for both her life and the conditions in which she worked, while her work *Workhouses and pauperism* gives a good account of her career and contains a bibliography of her writings. However, none of these publications link her work with other social movements of the day.

Webb, Beatrice 1858–1943

Cole, M. I., *Beatrice Webb*, Longmans, 1945.
Muggeridge, Kitty & Adam, Ruth. *Beatrice Webb, a life 1858–1943*, Secker & Warburg, 1967.
Webb, B., *Beatrice Webb's diaries 1912–1924*, edited by M. I. Cole, Longmans, 1952.
Webb, B., *Beatrice Webb's diaries 1924–1932*, edited by M. I. Cole, Longmans, 1956.
Webb, B., *My apprenticeship*, Longmans, 1926.
Webb, B., *Our partnership*, edited by B. Drake and M. I. Cole, Longmans, 1948.
The Times, 1 May 1943.

Beatrice Webb is famous for her work with her husband in public service and historical research. Their most famous books are *History of trade unionism*

(Longmans, 1894), *English local government* (Longmans, 1906–29) and *Industrial Democracy* (Longmans, 1897). Two volumes of autobiography, *My apprenticeship* and *Our partnership*, give a detailed account of her life. Her diaries, edited by Margaret Cole were published in the 1950s. Margaret Cole has also written a biography of Beatrice Webb.

Wightman, Julia Bainbrigge 1815–98

Fletcher, J. M., *Mrs Wightman of Shrewsbury: the story of a pioneer in temperance work*, Longmans, 1906.
How, F. D., *Noble women of our time*, Isbister, 1901.

A great temperance worker and author of many temperance works, Julia Wightman was one of the earliest women temperance workers and founded a total abstinence society in 1857 in Shrewsbury and a working-men's hall. Her book, '*Haste to the rescue*', *or work while it is day* (London, 1862) was enormously influential in the temperance movement and she was respected throughout the entire movement. The story of her work has been told by F. D. How and in James Fletcher's biography.

Wilson, Henry J. 1833–1914

Anderson, M., *H. J. Wilson, Fighter for freedom 1833–1914*, James Clarke, 1953.
Fowler, W. S., *A study in radicalism and dissent: the life and times of Henry Joseph Wilson, 1833–1914*, Epworth Press, 1961.

The Liberal MP for Holmfirth, 1885–1912, Henry Wilson worked closely with Mrs Butler in the campaign for the repeal of the Contagious Diseases Acts. His biographers have covered his life as a whole.

DIARIES

Published diaries can give a detailed picture of the life led by the writers, usually upper and middle-class women, but how much of this picture is true to life is open to conjecture. The publication of diaries, particularly travel diaries, became fashionable during the reign of Queen Victoria. She herself had set the fashion with the publication of *Leaves from a journal of our life in the Highlands* edited by A. Elder. The end of the First World War also saw the publication of large numbers of diaries relating to experiences of men and women serving in the forces abroad. Although these published diaries can be a useful source of information they should frequently be treated more as reminiscences.

Brabazon, Mary Jane, *The Diaries of Mary, Countess of Meath*, edited by her husband, 2 vols, Hutchinson, 1928–9. Private diary for the years 1880–1918.
Bridges, F. D., *Journal of a lady's travels round the world*, John Murray, 1883.

Collier, Mary Jane, Baroness Monkswell, *A Victorian diarist: extracts from the journals of Mary, Lady Monkswell 1873–1895*, 2 vols, edited by E. C. F. Collier, John Murray, 1944, 1946. Social diary for these years.

Brittain, Vera, *Testament of youth: an autobiographical study of the years 1920–1925*, Gollancz, 1933; Virago, 1978.

Hanbury, Charlotte, *The life of Mrs Albert Head*, Marshall Bros, 1905. pp 42–160 includes the religious diary of Mrs Caroline Head for the years 1871–93.

Holden, Edith, *The country diary of an Edwardian lady*, Michael Joseph, 1977.

Knightley, L. M., *The journals of Lady Knightley of Fawsley 1856–1884*, edited by Julia A. Cartwright, John Murray, 1915.

Lucas, Matilda, *Two Englishwomen in Rome 1871–1900*, Methuen, 1938.

Emma, Lady Ribblesdale, *Letters and diaries*, collected by Beatrix Lister, private circulation, 1930. Society diary 1870–1907.

Roberts, K., *Pages from the diary of a militant suffragette*, Letchworth, Garden City Press, 1910.

Schluter, Auguste, *A lady's maid in Downing Street*, edited by Mabel Duncan, Fisher Unwin, 1922.

Swinton, Georgina C. C., *Two generations*, edited by Osbert Sitwell, Macmillan, 1940. pp 147–308 contains Florence A. Sitwell's personal diary.

First World War

De l'Isle, A., *Leaves from a VAD's diary*, Elliot Stock, 1922.

Diary of a nursing sister on the Western Front 1914–1915, Blackwood, 1916.

Farmborough, Florence, *Nurse at the Russian front: a diary 1914–1918*, Constable, 1974; Futura, 1977.

MacNaughtan, S., *My war experiences in two continents*, edited by Mrs Lionel Salmon, John Murray, 1919. War diary for the years 1914–16.

MacNaughtan, S., *A woman's diary of the war*, Nelson, 1915.

Millard, Shirley, *I saw them die: diary and recollections*, edited by Adele Comandini, Harrap, 1936.

Sinclair, May, *A journal of impressions in Belgium*, Hutchinson, 1915.

Thurstan Violet, *Field hospital and flying column: being a journal of an English nursing sister in Belgium and Russia*, Putnam's, 1915.

See also Subject Histories, First World War below.

OFFICIAL PUBLICATIONS

Among the documents of primary importance in the field of women's studies are numerous British government publications issued between 1870 and 1928. It is only possible to list here those of major importance, but by using the various series of government publications, and the indexes to them, named below, researchers will discover many other items of direct or peripheral value.

British government publications are officially divided into two broad groups: Parliamentary Publications and Non-Parliamentary Publications. The latter, which were called Stationery Office Publications up to 1922, do not provide many documents relevant to the present subject, most of which are Parliamentary Papers, included in the sets of House of Commons Sessional Papers described below.

Also below are some brief observations on the major series of British government publications, but of necessity these have had to be brief. Further information, if it is needed, will be found in the standard textbooks on British government publications. In ascending order of complexity these are: James G. Ollé, *An introduction to British government publications* (2nd edition. Association of Assistant Librarians, 1973); John F. Pemberton, *British official publications* (2nd edition. Oxford, Pergamon Press, 1973); and P. Ford and G. Ford, *A guide to Parliamentary Papers: what they are, how to find them, how to use them* (3rd edition. Shannon, Irish University Press, 1972). The Fords' book is specifically designed to help those embarking upon intensive research among British government publications of the past, especially those of the nineteenth century. For those who wish to go beyond government publications, and undertake research among the archives of Parliament, which are accessible to the public in the House of Lords Record Office, the essential aid is Maurice F. Bond, *Guide to the records of Parliament* (HMSO, 1971). For those who wish only to understand the pattern of British government publications, and find the texts of individual titles they have been referred to, the books by Ollé and Pemberton should be sufficient.

PARLIAMENTARY PUBLICATIONS

The principal series of Parliamentary Publications are Hansard, Bills, Acts of Parliament and the series of documents called Papers, the best known of which are the Command Papers.

Hansard, which is probably the most widely known of Parliamentary Publications, is the official record of parliamentary debates. Prior to 1909, the published reports of debates were not always verbatim: some speeches were recorded in full, while others were edited. The period 1870–1928 is covered by the following series:

3rd series   1830–91
4th series   1892–1908
5th series   1909–

The House of Commons and the House of Lords each has its own series of Hansard.

Bills and Acts (sometimes referred to as Statutes) often contain more information than is generally realized. The differing phraseology in the various printings of a Bill reflects the changes made at the Committee stage, or perhaps indicate that pressure on a sponsor has resulted in more acceptable wording of a Bill. A Bill presented to Parliament is published in its original form and then in all its amended forms until it receives the Royal Assent. Bills can be either public, reflecting the official policy of the government, or private, relating to matters of interest to a person or corporation. All public Bills are printed by HMSO. Once a Bill has been passed it can only be amended by a new Act.

Many reports are produced, covering all subjects and varying greatly in scope and content, from the multi-volume reports of Royal Commissions to the short, even occasionally single-sheet, recommendation reports from Select Committees. Royal Commissions are appointed by the Crown to investigate matters of major importance requiring extensive new legislation. Several Royal Commissions have dealt directly or indirectly with matters of vital importance to women. Both Royal Commissions and Departmental Committees deal with issues of importance to a particular department. Members of Departmental Committees are appointed by the Minister concerned; as with Royal Commissions, their membership is not limited to Members of Parliament but may also include subject specialists. In addition, these Committees are not bound to sit only when Parliament is in session.

The documents produced by Royal Commissions and Departmental Committees are of value as in addition to their reports, they often include all the evidence given to Commissioners, not only written submissions, but also oral evidence, which is quoted verbatim. Both oral and written evidence are of great value as the witnesses called are involved in the issue being investigated; for example the Royal Commission on the Contagious Diseases Acts interviewed Josephine Butler, the famous campaigner for the repeal of these Acts, as well as prostitutes and organizers of homes for 'fallen women'. The minutes of the Hobhouse Committee on the Post Office include evidence of conditions of employment for various classes of female employees taken from employees of both sexes. This type of detailed and presumably accurate information can often only be found in the minutes of evidence or reports of such Committees and evidence on all aspects of a subject is to be found within the one report.

Select Committees, which are composed of a limited number of Members of Parliament, are formed to investigate the working of Acts or to examine legislation currently before Parliament; their reports vary greatly in length. Advisory and

Consultative Committees are a relatively new development in parliamentary procedure; they were first used at the beginning of the twentieth century, and were widely employed during the First World War by the Ministry of Reconstruction. The membership of these Committees usually consists of lay specialists rather than Members of Parliament and thus they provide the Minister with expert advice.

Other published material includes correspondence, which is published when a matter is of public interest (as in the Lilian Lenton case), returns, accounts and papers, and annual reports of departments. Departmental annual reports contain much valuable information in a condensed form as they include a review of the previous year's changes and achievements and, where appropriate, statistical data. In addition, they frequently incorporate additional reports on subjects of special interest.

THE HOUSE OF COMMONS SESSIONAL PAPERS

Many of the larger public and university libraries have complete sets of the Parliamentary Publications of the nineteenth and twentieth centuries, either in their original form or, what is more likely, in the Readex Microprint Corporation reprint, a microform set which requires the use of a special reading machine.

In either form Hansard and the Statutes will be filed by themselves, in chronological order of the parliamentary sessions, but the files of the House of Commons Papers, House of Commons Bills, and the Command Papers, three important series of Parliamentary Publications which are known collectively as the House of Commons Sessional Papers, will be in sessional sets, each of which will be arranged according to a simple system of classification devised in 1802. Under this system, throughout the period 1870–1928, all the Bills and Papers were grouped as follows:

Class	Series included	Types of documents
1. Bills	House of Commons Bills	Public Bills
2. Reports from Committees	House of Commons Papers	Reports from House of Commons Committees
3. Reports from Commissioners	House of Commons Papers Command Papers	Reports from other committees, etc.
4. Accounts and Papers	House of Commons Papers Command Papers	White Papers, State Papers, accounts, etc.

Within each class the documents will be arranged under alphabetical subject headings.

A Bill is the draft of a proposed Act of Parliament. It may or may not have become law. A House of Commons Paper is a document which has arisen out of the deliberations of the House, or a document which it has required in connection with its work, which it has ordered to be printed. A Command Paper is a report or statement of policy which has been presented to Parliament by a Minister, in theory by command of the sovereign.

Prior to 1921, all the reports of Royal Commissions and Departmental Committees were issued as Command Papers and will therefore be found in the House of Commons Sessional Papers, but since 1921, for administrative reasons some of the reports of Departmental Committees have been issued as Non-Parliamentary Publications. (This applies particularly to reports on education.) Non-Parliamentary Publications have no place among the Sessional Papers. They are normally filed in libraries under the names of the relevant departments, e.g. Board of Education.

TRACING PARLIAMENTARY PAPERS

Each set of the House of Commons Sessional Papers has its own detailed index. In addition, for the period 1870–99 there are three decennial indexes. For the first half of the twentieth century there is the following cumulative index: House of Commons, *General index to the Bills, Reports and Papers printed by order of the House of Commons and to the Reports and Papers presented by Command, 1900 to 1948–49* (HMSO, 1960). All these are alphabetical subject indexes. Although the indexing system used is imperfect, with a little patience the required documents can usually be found.

In textbooks and periodical articles Parliamentary Papers are sometimes cited by their serial numbers only, and not by their titles. (Some nineteenth-century Papers have no titles anyway.) As House of Commons Papers are numbered within the parliamentary sessions, the dates of which are always given (e.g. H.C. 183 1913) it is not too difficult to locate the text of a required Paper in the Sessional Papers, which have numerical as well as subject indexes. Unfortunately, Command Papers are numbered continuously in long, indefinite series which take no account of the parliamentary sessions. Each series is identified by a prefix taken from the word Command. For the period 1870–1928 the relevant series are as follows:

2nd series	1870–99	C. 1–9550
3rd series	1900–18	Cd. 1–9239
4th series	1919–56	Cmd. 1–9889

As a Command Paper is almost always cited by its serial number alone, to find the date of the parliamentary session in which it was issued and its location in the sets of House of Commons Sessional Papers, it is necessary to consult Edward Di Roma and Joseph A. Rosenthal, *A numerical finding list of British Command Papers published 1833–1961/62* (New York Public Library, 1967).

There is one other problem. It has long been customary to refer to the reports of Royal Commissions and Departmental Committees by the names of their respective chairmen (e.g. the Hadow Report). To find the precise details of a report cited in this way, the work to consult is Stephen Richard (compiler), *British government publications: an index to chairmen and authors, 1900–1940* (Library Association,

Reference, Special and Information Section, 1974). A similar index for the nineteenth century is in course of preparation.

Access to the texts of many important government publications of the nineteenth century has been greatly facilitated by the facsimile reprint of British Parliamentary Papers by the Irish University Press. This 1,000 volume series, which was completed in 1972, is divided into subject sets. Those of particular relevance to women are:

Emigration
Infectious Diseases
Marriage and Divorce

The volumes of particular interest are described under the appropriate headings below. It should be emphasized that while these reprints are useful, they are selective and should not be used without reference to the three relevant decennial indexes to the House of Commons Sessional Papers, i.e. those covering the period 1870–99. These have also been reprinted by the Irish University Press. Full details of the Irish University Press series are in the annotated, classified master index, *Catalogue of British Parliamentary Papers in the Irish University Press 1,000 volume series and Area Studies series 1801–1900* (Dublin, Irish Academic Press, 1977).

CITATION OF REFERENCES

While it is very difficult to trace official publications if the bibliographical details are inaccurate or unknown, it is relatively simple to locate a particular publication where the full title and reference are known. It is therefore very important to have the following information for Bills and Papers which appear in the bound sets of Sessional Papers: title, session, Paper number, volume number and page number. For Command Papers, it is helpful to give a date as well as the Paper number. For Acts, the regnal years and chapter number should be given. Wherever possible, references in this section include the relevant information, and refer to the bound sets of the House of Commons Sessional Papers and not to the House of Lords equivalent.

Further, a library which has a collection of old British government publications is likely to have at least one member of staff who is familiar with them and can help readers to use them.

GENERAL

General parliamentary papers that include data relating to women are briefly reviewed here. Appropriate government department reports have been included with the relevant subject papers. The censuses are most important as they give statistical data relating to women which is unique. The relevant censuses for the period covered are 1871, 1881, 1891, 1901, 1911 and 1921, and there is relevant statistical data in the majority of tables, including figures for the education of women for industrial employment up to and including 1911, and by occupation and industry in 1921 as well as figures for women in institutions, home size, etc. The most useful data is however contained in the supplementary tables, as the main body of the census tables are concerned with population statistics. It must be borne in mind that prior to 1921 the employment data was only classified by industry and not by occupation. It is therefore impossible to distinguish between women employed in actual workshops and those employed in the offices of a specific industry. In the 1921 census the tables were altered to include both industry and occupation figures which was a great improvement.

ARMED SERVICES

Commission of Inquiry appointed to inquire into the Women's Army Auxiliary Corps in France, HMSO, 1918. (Non-Parliamentary.)

Correspondence relating to the termination of the appointment of the Hon. Violet Douglas-Pennant as Commandant of the Women's Royal Air Force (WRAF), 1919, [Cmd. 182], xxix, 20.

Further correspondence relating to the termination of the appointment of Hon. Violet Douglas-Pennant as Commandant of the Women's Royal Air Force, 1919, [Cmd. 254], v, 16.

Court of Inquiry ordered by the Air Council to inquire into the matters raised by Eileen O'Sullivan, Assistant Commandant and Clothing Controller WRAF, 1919, [Cmd. 347], v, 184.

Unfortunately the early days of the women's services seemed to be dogged by scandals and unlucky incidents. The Women's Army Auxiliary Corps was involved in scandal when a Commission of Inquiry reported in 1918 after investigating allegations of immoral behaviour. Also at the end of the First World War the Honourable Violet Douglas-Pennant, whose appointment as Commandant of the Women's Royal Air Force had been terminated, took the Air Ministry to court for wrongful dismissal and demanded an inquiry. As a result the incident became one of public debate. In 1919 the Air Ministry published the relevant correspondence in two parts which does not, unfortunately, appear to give the full reasons for the Honourable Violet Douglas-Pennant's dismissal, only that she was considered unpopular and unsuccessful in her job. However, she lost her case and, because of her conduct during the trial, public sympathy as well. The other parliamentary paper published by the Air Ministry is the report of the Court of Inquiry into matters raised by Miss Eileen O'Sullivan, Assistant Commandant and Clothing Controller, relating to the supply of clothing for the Women's Royal Air Force. This incident also caused bad feeling between officers in the service. Nevertheless the services, which had played a useful role throughout the First World War, still attracted many recruits.

EDUCATION

Elementary Education Act 1870, 33 & 34 Vict., c. 75.
Elementary Education Act 1876, 39 & 40 Vict., c. 79.
Elementary Education Act 1880, 43 & 44 Vict., c. 23.
Elementary Education Act 1891, 54 & 55 Vict., c. 56.
Royal Commission on Secondary Education (Bryce Commission), 1895.
    Volume I, *General report*, 1895, [C. 7862], xliii, 1.
    Volume II, *Evidence*, 1895, [C. 7862-I], xlvi, 1.
    Supplement, 1896, [C. 8077], xlvi, 1.
    Volume III, *Further evidence*, 1895, [C. 7862-II], xlv, 1.
    Volume IV, *Further evidence*, 1895, [C. 7862-III], xlvi, 1.
    Volume V, *Memoranda and answers to questions*, 1895, [C. 7862-IV], xlvii, 1.
    Volume VI, *Assistant Commissioners' reports*, 1895, [C. 7862-V], xlviii, 1.
    Volume VII, *Assistant Commissioners' reports*, 1895, [C. 7862-VI], xlviii, 439.
    Volume VIII, *Index to evidence*, 1895, [C. 7862-VII], xlix, 1.
    Volume IX, *Appendix*, 1895, [C. 7862-VIII], xlix, 213.
Committee of the Privy Council for Education, Annual reports, 1839–99.
Board of Education, Annual reports, 1900–45.
Bill to extend the duties and powers of Educational Authorities with regard to the training of girls, 1910, (70), i, 519.
Bill to give better educational facilities to women, 1911, (153), i, 963.
Special reports on education subjects, Volume I, 1896–7, [C. 8447], iv, 732.
Special reports on educational subjects, Volume II, 1896–7, [C. 8943], vii, 694.
Report on industrial training of girls in the separate and district schools in the metropolitan district, 1900, [Cd. 237], lxxiii, 335.
Employment of women in agriculture in England and Wales, Board of Agriculture, 1920. (Non-Parliamentary.)
Board of Education, *The training of women teachers for secondary schools*, Board of Education, 1912. (Non-Parliamentary.)
Sex Disqualification (Removal) Act, 1919, 9 & 10 Geo. 5, c. 71.
Irish University Press, *British Parliamentary Papers: Education*, 46 volumes (Shannon, Irish University Press, 1970).

The Elementary Education Act of 1870 saw the foundation of School Boards which had the power to make attendance compulsory for children between the ages of five and thirteen for both boys and girls. The 1891 Act also made education free as well as compulsory. Parliamentary documentation relating to the education of girls is to be found in general educational documents, particularly in the minutes of evidence to the Royal Commissions on Education. The Bryce Commission contains evidence

relevant to the secondary education of girls including Miss Collet's memorandum
on the education of working girls in Volume V. The annual reports of the
Committee of the Privy Council for Education and its successor, the Board of
Education, are a source for general information as they give statistical information
on numbers of girls receiving education as well as containing reports on girls'
schools. There was further activity relating to the education of girls in 1910–11
when Bills were presented to Parliament to improve educational facilities.

Other parliamentary material is in the form of reports. *Special reports on
education subjects,* Volume I, contains three papers of relevance: domestic
economy teaching in England by Mrs Pillow, examiner in domestic science subjects
to the London Technical Education Board; the technical education of girls by Miss
A. J. Cooper; and a report by Mr Sidney Wells, Principal of Battersea Polytechnic,
on the secondary day school attached to the Polytechnic which was operating an
experiment in the co-education of boys and girls. This volume also includes a
summary of the arrangements in force at the chief universities in the British Empire
and abroad including details for the admittance of women. *Special reports on
educational subjects,* Volume 2 contains four relevant reports: three relate to
physical education for girls, while the fourth is an extremely valuable report on the
curriculum of a girls' school by Mrs Bryant, Headmistress of the North London
Collegiate School for Girls.

Other reports include: the industrial training of girls which recommended one
year's industrial training; the employment of women in agriculture which
recommended education in agricultural topics; and the training of women teachers
for secondary schools from the Board of Education. The Sex Disqualification
(Removal) Act of 1919 stated that 'Nothing in the statutes or charter of any
university shall be deemed to preclude the authorities of such university from
making provision as they think fit for the admission of women to membership
thereof or to any degree right or privilege therein or in connection therewith', thus
opening up university education for women.

As previously stated, all parliamentary material on education for this period will
contain some relevant material and should be consulted; for the pre-1900 period
the Irish University Press set on education is an invaluable source and brings
together a vast amount of material.

EMIGRATION

*Overseas Settlement Committee report – Openings in Canada for women from the
United Kingdom,* 1919, [Cmd. 403], xxxi, 849.
*Overseas Settlement Committee report – Openings in Australia for women from the
United Kingdom,* 1920, [Cmd. 745], xxii, 299.
*Overseas Settlement Committee report – Openings in New Zealand for women from
the United Kingdom,* 1920, [Cmd. 933], xxii, 232.
Statistical tables relating to emigration from and immigration into the United

Kingdom, 1877–. Contained in the sessional set of the House of Commons Parliamentary Papers.

Reports on the Emigrants' Information Office, 1877–. Contained in the sessional set of the House of Commons Parliamentary Papers.

Irish University Press, *British Parliamentary Papers: Emigration*, Volumes 25–8 (Shannon, Irish University Press, 1971).

The government supported the principle of emigration to the Empire for both men and women to the extent of opening an Emigrants' Information Office in 1886. As a result of the interest, the government produced reports relating to emigration; however, none of these dealt with emigration of women as a separate subject until after the First World War when the problems of 'surplus' women became acute and the Overseas Settlement Committee reports considered the opportunities for women.

The government-published statistical tables on emigration from and immigration into the United Kingdom contain relevant information: Table III, 'Account of the number of passengers of each sex ...' gives details of the numbers of women and the countries to which they emigrated; Table IV gives the marital status of men and women; and Table V gives their occupations. The annual *Reports on the Emigrants' Information Office* do not list women separately, but give percentages of occupations, including female domestic servants. The Irish University Press set on emigration covers the period 1826–99; Volumes 25–8 include the returns and Emigration Information Office Reports for the period 1870–99, which contain information on women.

EMPLOYMENT

The period 1870–1928 saw the passing of extensive legislation on employment, a large proportion of which related to conditions of employment and affected the employment of women either specifically or generally. The relevant documentation is considerable and varies greatly in scope, from general studies to reviews of employment conditions in specific industries, and this is also true of the material on women. Therefore, most of the material is listed under the relevant topics in 'Professions and trades' in order to facilitate usage and to bring together related publications, but there are categories for 'General' and 'Statistics' below to cover less specific material.

The publications listed are source materials for a wide range of topics in women's employment and can be used as a basis for studies relating to women and the changes in conditions of employment that occurred during this period. However, this material has not yet been used fully. Lee Holcombe's *Victorian ladies at work* on the employment of middle-class women is rare amongst works at present published in its use of parliamentary papers. Although this book is strictly limited in scope and covers only five professions, the author has used extensively the relevant reports of Select Committees as well as the tables on occupations in the censuses for the period 1861–1911, and illustrates how valuable such material is to the researcher.

General

Royal Commission on Labour, Reports by the Lady Assistant Commissioners on the employment of women, (Miss Orme, etc), 1893, [C. 6894], xxiii, 545.

Report on changes in the employment of women and girls in industrial centres by Miss Collet, Part I, *Flax and Jute Centres*, 1896, [C. 8794], lxxxviii, 305.

Factories Act 1901, 1 Edw. 7, c. 22.

Accounts of expenditure of wage-earning women and girls, 1911, [Cd. 3963], lxxxix, 531.

Departmental Committee on the employment of women and young persons on the two-shift system, 1920, [Cmd. 1038], xix, 533; [Cmd. 1039], xix, 519.

The report of the Lady Assistant Commissioners to the Royal Commission on Labour is one of the most valuable, frequently cited, reports on women. This report studies conditions of employment for women in different industries in various parts of the country, and considers their pay in relation to men's, any grievances the women may have had, and the effect of industrial employment on their health, morality and home life. A large part of the report was prepared by Miss Clara E. Collet who also compiled Part I of the *Report on changes in the employment of women and girls in industrial centres* which unfortunately was the only part published.

The 1911 *Accounts of expenditure of wage-earning women and girls* was compiled through the combined efforts of various organizations, which induced female wage-earners to send in detailed weekly accounts of their expenditure. Although the report is a detailed analysis of thirty women's expenses for a period of one year, it is not a large enough sample for any valid conclusions and is therefore of limited value.

The First World War saw an unprecedented official interest in the employment of women, because for the first time women's labour had become vital to the economy and defence of the nation. Appropriate reports and papers dealing with women's role in the War have been brought together under the heading 'First World War'. However, a 1920 report which dealt with the employment of women on the two-shift system and which reviewed the workings of the 1901 Factories Act with regard to allowing women to work a two-shift system as had been done in the munitions factories during the War has been included here, as it is of general interest.

Statistics

Labour Gazette, 1893–. Board of Trade, 1893–1905. Ministry of Labour, 1905–.

Report on the statistics of women and girls, 1894, [C. 7564], lxxxi, Part II, 845.
Report on the work of the Labour Department since its formation, with supplement of labour statistics, 1894, [C. 7565], lxxx, 397.
Abstracts of labour statistics of the United Kingdom, 1894–1937, HMSO.
Department of Employment, *British labour statistics, Historical abstract, 1886–1968*, HMSO, 1971.

Official statistical data relating to the employment of women is to be found in a number of sources. Reports of Royal Commissions, Select Commissions, etc, often contain much statistical evidence and the annual reports of the Ministry of Labour contain statistical data on wage rates, hours of work, membership of trade unions, etc. Employment statistics had been published monthly in the *Labour Gazette* from 1893, and summaries of employment statistics appeared in the *Abstracts of labour statistics of the United Kingdom* which was published annually from 1894. Both of these publications contain much statistical information relating to women. A useful work for comparisons of statistical data is the *British labour statistics, Historical abstract, 1886–1968*, which is an abstract of all employment statistical publications. Although the information dates from the early nineteenth century it does not always include detailed figures for women's employment in those early years. It does, however, include average wages for women in 1886, 1906, 1924 and 1928 as well as membership of trade unions for both men and women from 1896, and is extremely valuable for statistical data on women's employment. A useful document for the late nineteenth century is the Board of Trade's *Report on the statistics of women and girls* published in 1894 which is basically a report on the statistics of employment relating to women and girls in various industries. The various publications taken as a whole provide a good statistical review of women's employment for the late nineteenth and early twentieth centuries.

FIRST WORLD WAR

War Office, *Women's war work in maintaining the industries and export trade of the United Kingdom*, HMSO, 1916. (Non-Parliamentary.)
Women's Employment Central Committee, Report, 1914–16, [Cd. 7848], xxxvii, 669.
Committee appointed to consider the conditions of clerical and commercial appointments ..., Report, 1914–16, [Cd. 8110], xii, 1.
Munitions of War (Amendment) Act 1916, 5 & 6 Geo. 5, c. 99.
Munitions of War Act 1917, 7 & 8 Geo. 5, c. 45.
HM Inspector of Factories, *Substitution of women for men during the war*, HMSO, 1919. (Non-Parliamentary.)
Increased employment of women during the war in the United Kingdom, Report, 1918, [Cmd. 9164], xiv, 767.
Women's Employment Committee report, 1918, [Cd. 9239], xiv, 783.

War Cabinet Committee, *Women in industry report*, 1919, [Cmd. 135], xxxi, 241.
   Summaries of evidence, [Cmd. 167], xxxi, 593.
Ministry of Reconstruction, Women's Advisory Committee, Women's
   Employment Sub-committee, *Report on women holding temporary
   appointments in government departments*, 1919, [Cmd. 199], xxix, 153.

The First World War saw a great increase – over one million – in the number of
women employed. Relevant material is mainly in the form of reports although there
were two Acts relating to the employment of women in munitions factories, which
laid down rates of pay and conditions of service. There were a large number of
reports dealing with women's employment in the war which can be divided as
follows:
1. Reports which deal with the problem of unemployed women, such as the
Women's Employment Central Committee, Report in 1916.
2. Reports which deal with the substitution of women for men. The War Cabinet
Committee report published in 1918 covers various industries, including
agriculture, finance and transport, and has useful statistical data. The report of the
Committee appointed to consider the conditions of clerical and commercial
appointments covers the years 1914–16. A general view of the substitution of
women for men is contained in the report of HM Inspector of Factories published
in 1919; it includes a review of each industry but excludes the munitions industry.
3. Reports published at the end of the war which review the jobs required for men
returning to civilian life and the resulting unemployment for women. One area
where women had replaced men was in administrative and clerical posts in the Civil
Service; a Sub-committee of the Women's Advisory Committee investigated the
problem and its report recommended that women temporarily employed in
government departments should be admitted to those posts on equal terms with
men. Two reports published in 1918 covered women's employment as a whole: the
first on the increased employment of women during the war gives detailed statistical
tables which show the increases in women's employment in agriculture, commerce,
the professions and transport; the second, the *Women's Employment Committee
report*, considered the opportunities for the employment of women after the war.
These two reports are particularly important as they lay the foundation stones of the
official attitude to the post-war employment of women.
Finally, the report of the War Office published in 1916 shows the work done by
women during the war and is particularly useful as it contains a large number of
photographs showing women at work.

INSURANCE

National Insurance Act 1911, 1 & 2 Geo. 5, c. 5.
National Insurance Act 1913, 3 & 4 Geo. 5, c. 37.
Widows, Orphans and Old Age Contributory Pensions Act 1925, 15 & 16 Geo. 5,
   c. 70.

The Insurance Act of 1911 was the first major legislative measure on state insurance and was of relevance for women as it provided for a maternity benefit. Although according to the 1911 Act this was payable to the man, it was payable to the woman after the 1913 Act. Although the principle of women's pensions had been accepted in the United States before the First World War, it was not until 1925 that women became pensionable by law in the United Kingdom.

MORAL AND SOCIAL ISSUES

Divorce

Matrimonial Causes Act 1878, 41 & 42 Vict., c. 19.
Matrimonial Causes Act 1884, 47 & 48 Vict., c. 68.
Married Women (Maintenance in Case of Desertion) Act 1886, 49 & 50 Vict., c. 52.
Summary Jurisdiction (Married Women) Act 1895, 58 & 59 Vict., c. 39.
Standing Committee Report on the Marriage, Summary Jurisdiction (Married Women) Bill, 1895, (307), xiii, 13.
Matrimonial Causes Act 1907, 7 Edw. 7, c. 12.
Royal Commission on Divorce and Matrimonial Causes (Gorell Commission).
   Report, 1912–13, [Cd. 6478], xviii, 143.
   Minutes of evidence, 1912–13, [Cd. 6479], xviii, 359.
   Minutes of evidence, 1912–13, [Cd. 6480], xix, 1.
   Index, 1912–13, [Cd. 6481], xx, 1.
   Appendix, 1912–13, [Cd. 6482], xx, 655.
Married Women Maintenance Act 1920, 10 & 11 Geo. 5, c. 65.
Report of the Standing Committee 'C' on the Matrimonial Causes Bill, 1923, (30), vii, 57.
Report of Standing Committee 'D' on the Separation and Maintenance Bill, 1923, (120), viii, 391.
Summary Jurisdiction (Separation and Maintenance) Act 1926, 16 & 17 Geo. 5, c. 61.
Irish University Press, *British Parliamentary Papers: Marriage and divorce*, Volume 3 (Shannon, Irish University Press, 1971).

The parliamentary material relating to divorce is one of the most valuable sources of primary information available to researchers and cannot be ignored as it is only through Parliament that changes could be made in the availability and provision for divorce in this country. The debate on divorce spanned the period 1870–1928, and parliamentary concern is reflected in the fact that there was a Royal Commission under the chairmanship of Lord Gorell. Acts passed in 1878 and 1884 amended the law relating to conjugal rights; the 1886 Act enabled a woman to summon her husband for desertion and to claim alimony; the 1895 Act enabled women to have custody of the children; the 1907 Act gave the courts power to grant maintenance and alimony; the 1920 Act provided for maintenance for children under the age of sixteen; and the 1926 Act enabled women to apply for separation if the husband had been guilty of persistent cruelty to the children. The passing of these Acts resulted in far more women being able to obtain divorce from their husbands in 1928 than was possible in 1870 and also entitled them to greater financial support. The situation was still far from equal for men and women and further Acts were needed before this was achieved. Volume 3 of the Irish University Press set on marriage and divorce contains papers and returns for the years 1830–95 and includes detailed returns of matrimonial suits, marriages, separation orders and divorces for Great Britain.

Married Women's Property Acts

Married Women's Property Act 1870, 33 & 34 Vict., c. 93.
Report from the Select Committee on the Married Women's Property Bill, with proceedings, 1881, (124), ix, 683.
Married Women's Property Act 1893, 56 & 57 Vict., c. 63.
Married Women's Property Act 1907, 7 Edw. 7, c. 18.
Report from Standing Committee 'A' on the Married Women's Property Bill with the proceedings, 1907, (216), vi, 493.
Report from Standing Committee 'A' on the Married Women's Property Bill with the proceedings, 1908, (184), ix, 513.
Law of Property (Amendment) Act 1926, 16 & 17 Geo. 5, c. 11.
Irish University Press, *British Parliamentary Papers: Marriage and divorce*, Volume 2 (Shannon, Irish University Press, 1971).

The campaign for the right of a woman to her own property was mainly active in the 1850s and the 1860s, beginning with the Women's Petition organized by Bessie Raynes Parkes and Barbara Leigh-Smith. The 1870 Married Women's Property Act succeeded in allowing the wages and earnings of a married woman to become her own property rather than her husband's, as had previously been the case. For the first time she could also own her own savings, shares or property. This Act was seen as the first achievement of the women's movement, although it did not fulfil all the claims of the Married Women's Property Society. After 1870 many Bills were presented to Parliament which aimed at extending this Act and several amending Acts were passed. The Act of 1893 enabled women to enter contracts against the security of their property; the Act of 1907 allowed women to dispose of their own property without the permission of their husbands; and the Act of 1926 provided for both married and single women to hold and dispose of their property on the same terms as men. The only relevant reports published after 1870 are those of the Select Committee on the Married Women's Property Bill of 1881 and the proceedings of Standing Committee 'A' published in 1907 and 1908. Volume 2 of the Irish University Press set on marriage and divorce contains the reports from the Select Committee on the Married Women's Property Bills England and Scotland and the minutes of evidence and indexes, 1867–94. It was the Acts resulting from these bills that were heralded as the first victory of the early feminist movement as they enabled women to hold separate property and to have the right to their own earnings. The material in this volume is valuable for the evidence contained in the reports and because it brings together widely dispersed papers.

Prostitution

Metropolitan Police Act 1839, 2 & 3 Vict., c. 47.
Town Police Causes Act 1847, 10 & 11 Vict., c. 89.
Offences Against the Person Act 1875, 38 & 39 Vict., c. 94.
Report from the Select Committee of the House of Lords appointed to inquire into the state of the law relating to the protection of young girls from artifices to induce them to lead corrupt lives and into the means of amending the same, Proceedings, evidence, appendix and index, 1881, (448), ix, 355.
   Report in the following session, *with proceedings, evidence, appendix and index*, 1882, (344), xiii, 823.
An Act to make further provision for the protection of women and girls, etc, 1884, (271) ii, 395.
A Bill to make further provision for the protection of women and girls, 1884–5, (159), i, 281.
Criminal Law Amendment Act 1885, 48 & 49 Vict., c. 69.
Vagrancy Act 1898, 61 & 62 Vict., c. 39.
Defence of the Realm Act 1914, 4 & 5 Geo. 5, c. 29.
Bill to make further provision with respect to the punishment of sexual offences, 1917–18, (7), i, 315.
Bill to prevent the treatment of venereal disease otherwise than by duly qualified medical practitioners, 1917–18, (17), ii, 843, and (38), ii, 847.
Report from Standing Committee 'A' on the Venereal Diseases Bill (Lords) with the proceedings of the committee 1917–18, (77), iii, 887.
A Bill to repeal certain laws relating to prostitutes and to amend the law relating to order in streets and public places, 1924–5, (212), iii, 861.
A Bill to repeal certain laws relating to prostitutes, 1926, (133), iv, 177.
Report of the Street Offences Committee, 1927, [Cmd. 3231], ix, 735.

Information relating to prostitution can also be found under 'Repeal of the Contagious Diseases Acts' and the two sections should be read in conjunction. After the repeal of the Contagious Diseases Acts in 1886 the subject was not discussed in Parliament until 1917 when there was alarm concerning the spread of venereal disease among the troops; as a result Sir George Cane introduced a Bill into the House of Commons embodying the principle of the Contagious Diseases Acts but it was opposed and had to be withdrawn. The Government then introduced Regulation 40D under the Defence of the Realm Act which would have made women suffering from venereal disease liable to imprisonment, but this too met with considerable opposition, and had to be withdrawn within six months. In 1918 two Bills were introduced into the House of Lords to provide for legislation similar to

Regulation 40D but relating to both men and women. The report and proceedings of the Select Committee which considered these Bills contain little of value. Owing to the dissolution of Parliament these Bills did not become law. They were however reintroduced in 1920 but were not proceeded with, and this was the last time that attempts were made to check prostitution through the control of venereal disease by law. In addition, attempts were also made to legislate against solicitation by both men and women, by the introduction of clauses to the Criminal Law Amendment Bills in 1883 and 1885 to amend the Acts of 1839 and 1847. These Bills were, however defeated although the 1898 Vagrancy Act did enable men to be found guilty of soliciting. In 1925 and 1926 Lady Astor reintroduced the topic in Parliament and as a result the Committee on Street Offences was formed; its report of 1927 contains valuable information.

The age of consent was closely linked with the problem of prostitution in that young girls were frequently procured for acts of prostitution; it was thought that raising the age of consent would alleviate the problem. In 1875 the Offences Against the Person Act made sexual intercourse with girls under the age of twelve illegal. Following the revelations by W. T. Stead in the *Pall Mall Gazette* in 1885, the Criminal Law Amendment Act was passed; this Act made it a criminal offence for any person to procure girls and women for the purpose of prostitution and also raised the age of consent to sixteen. Prior to Stead's articles the Criminal Law Amendment Bills had met with little success despite the matter being referred to a Select Committee of the House of Lords which reported in 1881 and 1882.

Repeal of the Contagious Diseases Acts

Prevention of Contagious Diseases Act 1866, 29 & 30 Vict., c. 35.
Contagious Diseases Act 1868, 31 & 32 Vict., c. 80.
Contagious Diseases Act 1869, 32 & 33 Vict., c. 96.
Royal Commission on the Administration and Operation of the Contagious Diseases Acts.
    Volume 1, *Report*, 1871, [C. 408], xix, 1.
    Volume 2, *Minutes of evidence*, 1871, [C. 408-1], xix, 29.
Bill for the prevention of certain contagious diseases, and for the better protection of women, 1872, (42), i, 261.
Select Committee of the House of Commons into the working of the Contagious Diseases Act 1866–69; their administration, operation and effect.
    1878–9, (323), viii, 397.
    1880, (114), viii, 283.
    1880, (308), viii, 361.
    1881, (351), viii, 193.
Annual report of the Assistant Commissioner of the Metropolitan Police for 1879, relating to Contagious Diseases Acts, 1880, (231), lix, 469.
Annual report ... for 1880 ..., 1881, (140), lxxxvi, 691.
Annual report ... for 1881 ..., 1882, (191), liii, 383.

Repeal of the Contagious Diseases Acts 1886, 49 & 50 Vict., c. 10.
Irish University Press, *British Parliamentary Papers: Infectious diseases*, Volumes
  4–7, (Shannon, Irish University Press, 1971).

The campaign to repeal the Contagious Diseases Acts was directed against the
1866–9 Acts which had established a special corps of police under the control of
local authorities for the compiling and updating of a list of prostitutes. This corps
also had the power to arrest any woman whom they had 'good cause to believe' was
a prostitute. Although some protest was mounted against these Acts it was not until
Josephine Butler organized the campaign that the repeal of the Acts was achieved.

   There is a large amount of parliamentary material relating to this campaign. As
well as a Royal Commission on the administration and operation of the Acts in
1871, there was a Select Committee which investigated the operation of the Acts
between 1878 and 1881. Although the Acts were eventually repealed in 1886
eleven unsuccessful Bills were introduced into Parliament between 1873 and the
later date. There had also been a Bill in 1872 to extend the Acts. Other
parliamentary material relating to these Acts are memorials and returns relating to
the military towns and ports where the Acts were in operation. The returns give
details of numbers of immoral houses subject to the Contagious Diseases Acts, the
numbers of women admitted to hospital for diseases covered by the Acts, and
statistics compiled by the Army. These were used to evaluate the effectiveness of
legislation. The memorials were compiled by various organizations and submitted to
the government in support of their point of view. Also worth noting are the annual
reports of the Assistant Commissioner of the Metropolitan Police; these give an
insight into the effectiveness of the Acts and their administration.

   Of the Irish University Press set on infectious diseases which covers cholera,
epidemics, rabies and the findings of the Royal Commission on Vaccination,
Volumes 4–7, which are devoted to the Contagious Diseases Acts, are the most
interesting. Volume 4 contains reports of committees leading to the passing of the
Contagious Diseases Act of 1866 and the Select Committee on the working of the
Act 1868–9; although outside the period 1870–1928, the Select Committee report
still provides valuable information on the Acts as it forms the background to the
start of the campaign for their repeal. Volume 5 reprints the papers of the 1871
Royal Commission investigation which contain the evidence given by both
supporters and opponents of the Acts (including Josephine Butler) as well as
prostitutes on their treatment under the Acts, and by police in garrison towns
covered by the Acts. Volume 6 reprints the reports from the select committees
including minutes of evidence for the years 1878–91 and Volume 7 reprints the
report and minutes of evidence from the 1882 Select Committees.

Sex disqualification

Sex Disqualification (Removal) Act 1919, 9 & 10 Geo. 5, c. 71.
*Report from Standing Committee E (on the Women's Emancipation Bill) with
  proceedings*, 1919, (94), vii, 611.

After the Representation of the People Act of 1918 granted the vote to certain classes of women, another Act was passed which was also to change greatly the position of women in the United Kingdom. The Sex Disqualification (Removal) Act enabled women to be eligible for any profession 'Not disqualified by sex or marriage ... from entering or assuming, or carrying on any civil profession ...' and to perform any public function, or to hold any civil or judicial post. The Act also enabled universities to award degrees to women, but although it allowed the universities to admit women it did not compel them to do so. Thus, although Oxford University granted degrees to women in 1920, Cambridge did not grant them for another twenty-seven years. One major exclusion from the Act was the Civil Service.

PROFESSIONS AND TRADES

Civil Service

Telegraph Act 1869, 32 & 33 Vict., c. 73.

Report by Mr Scudamore on the reorganization of the telegraph system of the United Kingdom, 1871, [C. 304], xxxvii, 703.

Royal Commission on the Civil Service (Playfair Commission).
  1874–5, [C. 1113–1], xxiii, 1.
  Appendix to the first report, 1875, [C. 1113-1], xxiii, 31.
  Second report with appendix, 1875, [C. 1122-6], xxiii, 451.
  Third report with appendix and index to the appendices, 1875, [C. 1317], xxiii, 569.

Royal Commission on the Civil Service (Ridley Commission), 1886–90.
  First report with evidence and appendix, 1887, [C. 5226], xix, 1.
  Second report with evidence and appendix, 1888, [C. 5545], xxvii, 1.
  Third report with evidence, 1889, [C. 5748], xxi, 1.

Royal Commission on the Civil Service (MacDonnell Commission), 1912–15.
  First report, 1912–13, [Cd. 6209], xv, 109.
  Evidence and appendix, 1912–13, [Cd. 6210], xv, 113.
  Second report, 1912–13, [Cd. 6543], xv, 255.
  Evidence and appendix, 1912–13, [Cd. 6535], xv, 259.
  Third report, 1913, [Cd. 6739], xviii, 375.
  Evidence and appendix, 1913, [Cd. 6740], xvii, 279.
  Fourth report, 1914, [Cd. 7338], xvi, 1.
  First appendix, 1914, [Cd. 7339], xvi, 165.
  Second appendix, 1914, [Cd. 7340], xvi, 363.
  Fifth report, 1914–16, [Cd. 7748], xi, 673.
  Evidence and appendix, 1914–16, [Cd. 7749], xi, 725.
  Sixth report, 1914–16, [Cd. 7832], xii, 1.
  Evidence and appendix, 1914–16, [Cd. 8130], xii, 91.

Report from the Select Committee on Post Office Servants with the proceedings of the Committee (Hobhouse Committee), 1907, (266), v, 104, 194.
   Minutes of Evidence, 1907, (380), vi, 1300.
   Appendices, 1907, (380), vii, 100.
Report from the Select Committee on Post Office servants (wages and conditions of employment) with the proceedings of the Committee (Holt Committee), 1912–13, (507), ix, 147.
   Reports, proceedings, evidence, appendices and index, 1913, (268), x-xiii, 1.
Sub-committee of Women's Advisory Committee, Women holding temporary appointments in government departments, 1919, [Cmd. 199], xxix, 153.
Regulations for competition governing the appointment of women to situations in the new reorganization classes in the Civil Service and with regard to the appointment of married women in established situations, 1921, [Cmd. 1116], xxviii, 663.

The Civil Service, which is one of the major employers of female clerical and professional labour in the United Kingdom, had a long history of offering equal opportunities for men and women prior to the Equal Opportunities Act of 1976. Although founded in 1855, it did not employ women until 1869, when the Telegraph Act transferred the telegraph facilities from private companies to the Post Office. This was mainly due to the fact that F. Scudamore, who was in charge of the transfer, favoured the employment of women, which can be seen in his report on the reorganization of the telegraph system.

The Royal Commissions on the Civil Service (Playfair 1874; Ridley, 1886; and MacDonnell, 1912) all took evidence of relevance to women and therefore their Reports are of importance. As already mentioned, the Playfair Commission considered the extension of the employment of women in the Civil Service, while the Ridley Commission took this a stage further and examined the work of women within the various departments. As part of its brief, the MacDonnell Commission was required to consider the special problems of women in the Civil Service and the reports give the official opinion; its evidence included contributions from representatives of the women's trade unions in the Civil Service as well as from other eminent women including Miss Lilian M. Faithfull, Principal of the Cheltenham Ladies' College and Miss Emily Penrose, Principal of Somerville College, Oxford. The Hobhouse Committee of enquiry into the Post Office, 1907 took evidence from the Post Office women's staff association on the conditions of women's employment, and this resulted in a slight improvement in salary scales for women within the Civil Service. The evidence of the Royal Commissions as well as that of the Holt Committee on Post Office servants in 1913 give a very clear picture of the conditions of women's employment in the Civil Services as well as indicating the aims of the women's associations.

The First World War changed greatly the position of women in the Civil Service. As men were called up so women were needed to replace them and fill posts in newly created ministries, such as the Ministry of Munitions. This in turn created a problem at the end of the war as the temporary contracts of these women expired. A Sub-committee of the Women's Advisory Committee reported on this problem in 1919 after considering the action that could be taken regarding the termination of contracts, and recommended that women should be employed by the Civil Service and given equal pay and opportunities.

The other documents relating to the employment of women that also need to be noted are the 1921 Civil Service regulations which concerned the appointment of single and married women.

All the material mentioned above, together with the various Bills between 1910 and 1913 aimed to throw open the various closed sections of the Civil Service to women, are of great value to researchers dealing with the subject of women and the Civil Service.

Domestic service

Report by Miss Collet on the money wages of indoor domestic servants, 1899, [C. 9346], xcii, 1.
Women's Advisory Committee, Report on the domestic servant problem, (Lady Emmott – chairman), 1919, [Cmd. 67], xxix, 7.
Committee on the supply of female domestic servants, Ministry of Labour, 1923. (Non-Parliamentary.)

While domestic servants were plentiful and cheap before the First World War, this situation changed greatly afterwards and they were in increasingly short supply. There are reports on domestic servants for the years both before and after the war:
1.   The report relating to pre-1914 was published in 1899. The extremely valuable information, which was collected by Miss Collet between 1894 and 1899, gives average wages of female domestic servants including rates of pay for different age groups, allowances, holidays and privileges.
2.   The post-1918 reports deal with the shortage of domestic servants rather than their conditions. The first, the Women's Advisory Committee which reported in 1919 under the chairmanship of Lady Emmott, considered the shortage of domestic servants and blamed poor conditions of service and wages. The Committee on the Supply of Female Domestic Servants reported in 1923 under the chairmanship of Mrs G. M. Wood.

Factories

Factory and Workshop (Amendment) Act 1891, 54 & 55 Vict., c. 75.
Employment of Women, Young Persons and Children Act, 1920, 10 & 11, Geo. 5, c. 65.
Royal Commission on Labour, General Reports.
    First report, 1892, [C. 6708], xxxiv, 1.
    Second report, 1892, [C. 6795], xxxvi, Part 1, 1.
    Third report, 1893–4, [C. 6894], xxxii, Part 1, 1.

Fourth report, 1893–4, [C. 7063], xxxiv, Part 1, 1.

Fifth report, 1894, [C 7421], xxxv, 9.

Royal Commission on Labour, Reports by the Lady Assistant Commissioners on the employment of women, (Miss Orme, etc), 1893, [C. 6894], xxiii, 545.

Report by Miss Collet on the statistics of employment of women and girls, 1894, [C. 7564], lxxxi, Part ii, 845.

Report of the Chief Inspector of Factories and Workshops, 1891–. Contained in the sessional set of the House of Commons Parliamentary Papers.

The period 1870–1928 saw the introduction of several Factory and Workshop Acts and many amendments to them. Although of a general nature, these Acts frequently contained clauses relating to the conditions of employment of women. The Acts aimed to improve working conditions generally and therefore benefited women; they also restricted women from working in dangerous and/or unhealthy trades. When tracing legislation relating to women, general Acts must be consulted in addition to the more specific Acts which legislated solely for women, or for women and children.

Not all the legislation affecting women was welcomed by the women's movement. The 1891 Factory and Workshop (Amendment) Act which laid down the hours of employment for women was opposed on the grounds that hardship would result for widows, deserted wives and other women dependent on earning their own living. The Vigilance Association for the Defence of Personal Rights was formed to give evidence to the 1892 Royal Commission on Labour opposing the idea of shorter hours for women. The Acts throughout the period, however, did continue to amend the terms of employment for women, as can be seen in the 1920 Act which included restrictions on women working throughout the night.

The Royal Commission on Labour produced five main reports between 1892 and 1894, but the reports of the Assistant Commissioners were also published separately. The extremely valuable report on women's employment by the Misses Orme, Collet, Abraham and Irwin gives the results of their investigations into the work undertaken by women, the differences in rates of pay for men and women, and the effect on women's health of employment.

Miss Collet later produced the Report on the statistics of employment of women and girls containing statistical tables and giving Board of Trade returns for the rates of wages in the cotton, woollen and worsted industries, which were among the chief employers of female labour.

Other valuable sources of information relating to the employment of women in factories are the annual reports of the Chief Inspector of Factories, which include the reports of the Women Factory Inspectors who covered industries employing large numbers of women. In particular, the appendices list offences under the Factories Act, including those relating to women.

The greatest change in factory employment of women came in the First World War with the opening of munition factories and their subsequent employment of large numbers of women. The relevant material is dealt with separately under the 'First World War' heading.

Flax and jute industry

Report on changes in the employment of women and girls in industrial centres by Miss Collet, Part 1, Flax and jute centres, 1896, [C. 8794], lxxxviii, 305.

In 1898 the first, and only, part of the report on changes in the employment of women and girls by Miss Collet was published; it related to the flax and jute industry. This report is important as it covers the conditions of employment in the industry throughout the nineteenth century, noting changes. In addition its appendices are particularly valuable guides to the rates of pay in the industry.

Hairdressing

Bill to provide for the compulsory closing of hairdressers' and barbers' shops on Sundays, 1926, (118), ii, 481.
Bill to provide for the compulsory closing of hairdressers' and barbers' shops on Sundays, 1927, (39), ii, 113.
Bill to provide for the compulsory closing of hairdressers' and barbers' shops on Sundays, 1928, (43), ii, 425.
  Similar Bill, 1928–9, (14), ii, 1.
  As amended by Committee, 1928–9, (45), ii, 3.
Shops (Early Closing) Act 1920, 10 & 11 Geo. 5, c. 50.

No specific legislation relating to hairdressing was passed, but the Bill introduced in Parliament in 1926 aimed to provide for the compulsory closing of hairdressing shops on Sunday; similar Bills were reintroduced in 1927, 1928 and during the 1928–9 session. There was need for this legislation as hairdressing establishments were not included in the Shops (Early Closing) Act of 1920.

Law

Bill to enable women to become barristers, solicitors or parliamentary agents, 1912–13, (196), iii, 159.
Bill to enable women to become barristers, solicitors or parliamentary agents, 1913, (90), iii, 757.
Bill to remove disqualifications on the ground of sex or marriage for the admission of persons as solicitors and their acting and practising as solicitors under the Solicitors Act, 1914, (100), vi, 339.
Sex Disqualification (Removal) Act 1919, 9 & 10 Geo. 5, c. 71.

In 1873 women made the first attempt to gain admittance to the lectures of the Council of Legal Education but they were rejected. In 1903, having obtained a law degree, Christabel Pankhurst applied for permission to qualify as a barrister and was refused; ten years later four women asked to be admitted to the examinations of the Law Society and they, too, were refused. In the 1912–13 session of Parliament a Bill was presented to enable women to become barristers, solicitors or parliamentary agents but was not passed; the Bill was presented in the following session with the same result. In 1914 a Bill to remove marital or sexual grounds as disqualifying persons from acting and practising as solicitors also achieved nothing. It was not until the Sex Disqualification (Removal) Act of 1919 that women were able to join the legal profession and in 1922 the first woman was called to the bar.

Medicine

Bill to amend the Medical Act 1858, so far as relates to the registration of women who have taken the degree of doctor of medicine in a foreign university, 1875, (103), vi, 13.

Bill to amend the Medical Act 1858, so far as relates to the registration of women who have taken the degree of doctor of medicine in a foreign university, 1876, (36), v, 29.

Medical Acts Amendment (College of Surgeons) Act 1875, 38 & 39 Vict., c. 43.

Bill to remove restrictions on the granting of qualifications for registration under the Medical Act on the ground of sex, 1876, (170), v, 33.

Medical Act 1876, 39 & 40 Vict., c. 41.

Correspondence on the subject of medical registration of women, 1875, (446), lviii, 301.

Women had fought for entry to the medical profession since 1859 when because of her foreign medical degree Elizabeth Blackwell had been accepted on the British Medical Register. This loophole was later closed, as was the loophole discovered by Elizabeth Garrett who, by passing the Society of Apothecaries' examinations, was accepted on the Register. In 1875 a Bill to allow women with foreign medical degrees to be admitted to the Register was presented in Parliament but it was rejected as was a similar Bill presented the following year. However, in 1875 an Act was passed which empowered the College of Surgeons to admit women to the necessary examinations. In 1876 Russell Gurney presented a Bill which became law in the same year and allowed for the granting of medical qualifications to suitably qualified applicants regardless of sex. Because this Act was an enabling act which was not compulsory, the barriers against women in the medical profession were only slowly overcome and by 1895 there were a mere 264 women doctors. In addition to the Bills there is some official correspondence published on the subject of the medical registration of women which is a valuable source of information relating to the fight for acceptance in the medical profession.

Midwifery

Select committee on the protection of infant life, proceedings, minutes of evidence, appendix and index, 1871, (373), vii, 607.

Bill, intituled An Act to amend the Medical Act, 1878, (216), v, 93.

A Bill (as amended by the Select Committee) to provide for the registration of midwives, 1890, (391), vi, 769.
Report of the Select Committee on midwives' registration Bill, 1890, (311), xvii, 1.
Report of the Select Committee on midwives' registration with the proceedings, evidence, appendix and index, 1892, (289 – session 1), xiv, 1.
Report in the following session *with the proceedings and evidence*, 1893–4, (367), xiii, 15.
Midwives Act 1902, 2 Edw. 7, c. 17.
Departmental Committee appointed by the Lord President of Council to consider the working of the Midwives Act 1902.
Report, 1909, [Cd. 4822], xxxiii, 191.
Minutes of evidence and index, 1909, [Cd. 4823], xxxiii, 77.
Draft regulations for the training of midwives, 1919, [Cmd. 353], xxxix, 177.
Regulations for the training of midwives, 1919, [Cmd. 441], xxxix, 185.
Midwives Act 1926, 16 & 17 Geo. 5, c. 32.
Midwives and Maternity Homes Act 1927, 17 & 18 Geo. 5, c. 17.

In opening the profession of midwifery to women as in the case of nursing, state registration and therefore control through a central body were the aims. Many Bills were introduced into Parliament and their wording shows the changes in the attitude of the medical profession to midwifery. The first Bill to introduce the subject of registration of midwives into Parliament was the Medical Act (1858) Amendment Bill in 1878, which contained a clause relating to the registration of midwives.

The main activities in Parliament, however, occurred between 1890 when the first Bill since 1878 was presented and 1902 when the Midwives Act was passed. The scope of this Act was amended and widened by the 1926 and 1927 Acts, of which the latter provided for the introduction and registration of maternity homes.

The fight for registration had been long and difficult with powerful opposition from the medical profession which saw its authority and livelihood being undermined. The 1890 Bill introduced by Mr Fell was supported by William Rathbone and three medical men, and despite being talked out, it was referred to a Select Committee which reported in the same year. The Select Committee on Registration reported in 1892, and published its minutes of evidence in 1894. This was not the first Select Committee concerned with midwifery, as a previous Select Committee on the Protection of Infant Life in 1871 had taken evidence from witnesses who proposed the registration of midwives. Following the passing of the Midwives Act of 1902 a Departmental Committee was appointed to consider the working of the Act; it reported in 1909. Other papers of interest are the regulations for the training of midwives published both in draft and final form in 1919.

Nursing

Select Committee of the House of Lords on Metropolitan Hospitals.
First report, 1890, (392), xvi, 1.
Second report, 1890–91, (457), xiii, 1.

Third report, 1892, (321 – Session 1), xiii, 1.
Select Committee on the registration of nurses.
  Report, 1904, (281), vi, 701.
  Report, 1905, (263), vii, 733.
Bill to provide for the state registration of nurses, 1919, (20), ii, 463.
  As amended by Committee, 1919, (65), ii, 479.
  Similar Bill (No. 2), 1919, (202), ii, 495.
Nurses Registration Act 1919, 9 & 10 Geo. 5, c. 64.
Select Committee on the General Nursing Council, Report, 1924–5, (167), vii, 779.
Select Committee (Registration), Report, 1926, (103), vii, 301.

As with midwives, the struggle for the state registration of nurses was long and difficult. The arguments for and against registration were first aired in parliamentary debate in the evidence heard by the Select Committee on Metropolitan Hospitals and published in three reports.

The leaders of the campaign for state registration, who included Mrs Ethel Fenwick (the founder of the British Nurses' Association), realized after the failure of early attempts to introduce a Bill in Parliament that an independent association to campaign for state registration was needed. The Society for the State Registration of Nurses was founded in 1902 and in 1904 had its first sponsored Bill introduced. This resulted in the establishment of a Select Committee which recommended state registration in its reports of 1904 and 1905. However, despite the introduction of sponsored Bills each year from 1905 to 1914, none was passed, chiefly due to lack of time and pressure of business. The First World War resulted in the government becoming aware of the need for registration and in 1919 a government-sponsored Bill was to result in the Nurses Registration Act. Other parliamentary material concerned with the registration of nurses includes the reports of the Select Committee on the General Nursing Council in 1925 and the Select Committee on Registration in 1926. Both were basically reports on the workings of the Registration Act, and as such contain a considerable quantity of valuable evidence.

Policewomen

Report of the Committee on the employment of women on police duties (Baird Committee).
  Report, 1920, [Cmd. 877], xxii, 1087.
  Minutes of evidence, index, 1921, [Cmd. 1133], xvi, 73.
Report of the Departmental Committee on the employment of policewomen (Bridgeman Committee), 1924, [Cmd. 2224], xii, 193.

The First World War saw the introduction of the first women volunteers who were organized to prevent attempts at white slavery being made amongst refugees from Belgium. The Women's Police Service was a voluntary organization founded by Nina Boyle and Damer Dawson. It attracted many women from the suffrage movement and worked throughout the war. In 1918 the Metropolitan Police

Women Patrols were inaugurated but did not have the range or scope of duties undertaken by the Women's Police Service. The addition of women to the Metropolitan Police Force caused controversy in the press and in 1920 a Home Office Inquiry (Baird Committee) into the whole question of policewomen was held. It reported the same year and recommended the 'urgent need' for policewomen to be employed in connection with the custody of women and children and in the prevention of offences connected with prostitution. This report was not fully implemented and in 1922 the Home Office and the Joint Central Committee of the Police Federation agreed to the removal of all women police officers. In 1924 the Bridgeman Committee reported that the efficiency of the police had been increased by the employment of women and that every police authority should in future employ women.

Retail trade

Bill to provide for regulating the hours of labour of children, young persons and women in shops for the sale of goods and otherwise to extend and amend the Workshop Acts, 1873, (123), v, 141.
Factory and Workshops Acts Commission, report of the Commissioners appointed to inquire into the working of the Factory and Workshops Acts.
Report, appendix and index, 1876, [C. 1443], xxix, 1.
Minutes of evidence, 1876, [C. 1443-1], xxx, 1.
Report of the select committee on the Shop Hours Regulations Bill, 1886, (155 – Session 1), xii, 1.
A Bill to amend the law relating to the employment of women and young persons, 1892, (26), ix, 485.
Shop Hours Act 1892, 55 & 56 Vict., c. 62.
Shop Hours Act 1893, 56 & 57 Vict., c. 67.
Report from the Select Committee on Shops (Early Closing) Bill; with the proceedings, evidence, appendix and index, 1895, (273), xii, 635.
Shop Hours Act 1895, 58 & 59 Vict., c. 5.
Report from the Select Committee of the House of Lords on the early closing of shops; with proceedings, evidence, and index, 1901, (369), vi, 1.
Report from the Select Committee on trade, etc., on the Shop Hours Bill with proceedings, 1904, (217), vii, 271.
Report from the Select Committee of the House of Lords on the Sunday Closing (Shops) Bill, (H.L.) with the proceedings, evidence and appendix, 1905, (344), viii, 9.
Report from the Joint Select Committee on Sunday trading together with the proceedings of the Committee, evidence, appendix and index, 1906, (275), xiii, 29.
Shops Act 1911, 1 & 2 Geo. 5, c. 54.
Shops (Early Closing) Act 1920, 10 & 11 Geo. 5, c. 50.

Report and proceedings of Standing Committee A (on the Hours Bill), 1928, (68), vi, 831.
Departmental Committee on the Truck Acts, Report of the Truck Committee.
  Volume I, *Report and appendices*, 1908, [Cd. 4442], lix, 1.
  Volume II, *Evidence (Days 1–37)*, 1908, [Cd. 4443], lix, 147.
  Volume III, *Evidence (Days 38–66)*, 1908, [Cd. 4444], lix, 533.
  Volume IV, *Précis and appendices*, 1909, [Cd. 4568], xlix, 177.

Although the majority of Bills, Acts and Reports concerning the retail trade do not relate specifically to women, they need to be consulted by anyone working in the field as they are relevant to, and contain information on, the changes in employment conditions for women. As shops were not covered by the Factory and Workshop Acts, there had to be separate legislation in order to improve the working conditions of shop assistants, which can be seen through the Bills, Acts and in particular the Reports. The main grievances were long hours and the discomfort of standing for considerable periods of time. Select Committees were appointed to investigate early closing and shop hours in 1886, 1901, 1904 and 1905, and a Joint Select Committee on Sunday trading was appointed in 1906; all produced Reports. Although the question of early closing was debated for many years, it was not until 1920 that an Act was passed and it was still a matter of parliamentary concern in 1928 when the *Report and proceedings of Standing Committee A (on the Hours Bill)* was published.

Information relating to the retail trade can also be found in the evidence submitted to the Factory and Workshops Acts Commission of 1876, which contained evidence relating to the conditions of work and wages paid to women. The Departmental Committee on the Truck Acts considered, among other aspects of the truck system, the practice of 'living-in' for shop assistants and where this practice was part of the wage structure of the trade. The evidence given to the Departmental Committee is similar to that in many other reports and gives a valuable insight into the way of life of a large number of shop assistants of whom the vast majority were women. The reports frequently include evidence from the shop assistants themselves.

SUFFRAGE

Bill to remove the electoral disabilities of women, 1870, (31), iv, 799.
Bill for conferring the parliamentary franchise on duly qualified women, 1884–5, (39), iv, 363.
Bill to extend the parliamentary franchise to women occupiers, 1910, (180), iv, 325.
Bill to confer the parliamentary franchise on women, 1911, (6), v, 917; 1912–13, (3), iv, 201; 1913, (75), v, 613.
Prisoners' Temporary Discharge for Ill-health Act 1913, 3 & 4 Geo. 5, c. 4.

Representation of the People Act 1918, 8 & 9 Geo. 5, c. 64.
Representation of the People Act 1928, 18 & 19 Geo. 5, c. 12.
Lilian Lenton case: correspondence of the Home Office with the Royal College of Surgeons and Sir Victor Horsley with regard to the case of Lilian Lenton, 1913, (190), ii, 435.
Return showing the number of petitions to the House of Commons in favour of women's suffrage for each session from 1890 to 1906 inclusive; and the number of names attached to such petitions, 1906, (347), xcvi, 157.
Returns showing the number of women in England and Wales who are qualified to vote for county councils and for councillors in municipal boroughs etc, 1908, (364), xcii, 533.

The campaign for women's suffrage was single-minded in its aim to achieve the passing of a Bill in Parliament which would enable women to vote in general elections. The campaign was fought in various ways from the original Bill of 1870 presented by Jacob Bright to the successful Act of 1918 which enfranchised certain categories of women over the age of thirty. There were many suffrage Bills presented to Parliament between the years 1870 and 1928, several with a similar text. The original Jacob Bright Bill of 1870 sought to have 'the words which import the masculine gender, the same shall be held to include females for all purposes ...' and other Bills submitted during this decade used this or very similar wording. In 1884 William Woodall sponsored a Bill with the wording '... women shall have the same rights as men ...' and during the following years of the decade five similar bills were presented to Parliament. In the 1890s there were twenty-one Bills providing for women's suffrage, and although the wording varied the aim remained the same.

The turn of the century heralded a new aspect in the women's suffrage movement – the rise of the militants. However, despite a campaign of militancy, the imprisonment of many suffragettes and the introduction to Parliament of fourteen suffrage Bills, the right to vote had still not been gained. In 1910 the first 'Conciliation Bill' was introduced to Parliament by D. J. Shackleton. This Bill was sponsored by Members of Parliament of all parties, but it would only have given the vote to about a million women. It would have excluded the majority of married women, as the Bill was for the enfranchisement of women occupiers, and at that time husbands and wives could not qualify with respect to the same property. Following the failure of the Bill, a second 'Conciliation Bill' sponsored by Sir George Kemp was introduced in 1911. Between this Bill and the outbreak of war in 1914, four other suffrage Bills were introduced in Parliament. In addition to the Bills presented to the House of Commons, six Bills were introduced to the House of Lords between the years 1884–1914.

The First World War brought about great social changes; one result was the passing in February 1918 of the Representation of the People Act, which gave the vote to women over the age of thirty on equal terms with men. Full enfranchisement for women over the age of twenty-one came with the Act of 1928.

One other Act relevant to the suffrage movement was the Prisoners' Temporary Discharge for Ill-health Act of 1913, commonly known as the 'Cat and Mouse' Act. This allowed for prisoners whose health had been damaged by hunger striking to be released in order to recover, and then to be returned to prison; the period spent in prison only counting towards the fulfilment of the sentence.

A complete list of Bills and Acts presented to Parliament, together with their sponsors and relevant clauses, can be found in Constance Rover's *Women's suffrage and party politics.*

Other parliamentary papers relate to the case of Lilian Lenton who claimed that as a result of force feeding her health had been damaged; the papers give evidence for her case and resultant correspondence with the Home Office. The return relating to petitions presented to the House of Commons in favour of women's suffrage and the returns showing the number of women eligible to vote for county councils in England and Wales can also be found among official papers.

PERIODICALS

The periodicals included are those of women's organizations and societies, journals of the predominantly female professions of nursing and midwifery, trade union journals, and periodicals of a more general nature dealing with matters of importance to, and concerning, women. Locations have been kept to the minimum; as a general rule only the Fawcett Library and the Reference Division of the British Library are given. However, if a periodical is difficult to locate, other locations of important holdings are given. Dates are given only where a holding is incomplete. Each has been listed under its original title with any subsequent changes noted, in accordance with the policy adopted by the British Union Catalogue of Periodicals BUCOP.

GENERAL

(Those marked with an asterisk have occasional articles on women's interests).

Contemporary Review, from 1866. (British Library)
Edinburgh Review, Oct 1802–Oct 1929. (British Library)
The English woman, 1909–21 (vols 1–49). (British Library vols. 1–48; Fawcett Library)
Englishwoman's review of social and industrial questions, 1866–1910 (vols 1–41). (British Library; Fawcett Library, 1866–9, 1880; Girton College, 1870–1903)
The Eyeopener, superseded by *The Awakener*, superseded by *The Altruist*, organ of the Men's Society for Women's Rights, 1912–15. (Fawcett Library)
Fraser's magazine, Feb 1830–Oct 1882. (British Library)
The Freewoman, Nov 1911–Oct 1912, superseded by *The New Freewoman*, June–Dec 1912, superseded by *The Egoist*, Jan 1914–Dec 1919. (British Library; Fawcett Library, 1911–12)
Friendly Leaves, 1876–1917, superseded by *GFS Magazine*, 1917–51, superseded by *The Townsend*, from 1951. (all published by the Girls' Friendly Society for ordinary members). (British Library; Cambridge University Library)
Friendly work, 1883–94, superseded by *The Girls Quarterly: a paper for workers*, 1894–1901, superseded by *Friendly work for friendly workers*, 1902–17, then incorporated in *GFS Magazine* (all published by the Girls' Friendly Society for secondary members). (British Library)
GFS Advertiser, 1880–82, superseded by the *Girls' Friendly Society Associates' Journal (and advertiser)*, 1883–1919, superseded by *GFS Workers' Journal*,

1920–24, superseded by *The Workers' Journal*, 1925–34, superseded by *GFS Review*, from 1935. (British Library)

The Housewife: practical magazine concerning everything in and about the home, 1886–90. (British Library; Fawcett Library)

Iris: the organ of the Women's Progressive Society, 1892. (British Library)

Leisure Hour, 1852–1905. (British Library; Fawcett Library, 1852–61, 1864, 1867–81, 1895)

Quarterly Review, from 1806. (British Library)

Saturday Review of politics, literature, science and art, Nov 1885–July 1938. (British Library)

Shafts: a paper for women and the working classes, 1892–9. (British Library; Fawcett Library)

Victoria Magazine, 1863–80. (British Library)

Westminster Review, 1824–1914. (British Library)

Womanhood, 1892–1907. (Fawcett Library)

Woman workers, 1891–1924. Quarterly magazine of the Birmingham Ladies' Union of Workers amongst Women and Girls. (Birmingham Public Library)

Youngwomen, 1892–4. (British Library; Fawcett Library)

EDUCATION

The Governess (and Head Mistress), 1882–4. (British Library)

Journal of the Women's Education Union, 1873–82. (British Library; Girton College)

The School Mistress, 1881–1935, when it absorbed *Teachers' aid* which began publication in 1885; superseded by *Women teachers' world,* from 1935. (British Library)

EMIGRATION

Imperial Colonist, 1901–27; superseded by *Overseas settler,* 1927–30. (Fawcett Library)

Women's Gazette or News about work, 1875–9; superseded by *Work and leisure,* 1889–93. (British Library; Fawcett Library)

EMPLOYMENT

Association notes, 1906–20. Organ of the Association of Post Office Women Clerks. (Fawcett Library)

Opportunity, 1921–40. Organ of the Federation of Women Civil Servants. (British Library; Fawcett Library)

Woman and Work, 1874–6. (British Library)

Woman Clerk, 1925–31. Organ of the Association of Women Clerks and Secretaries. (British Library)

Woman Engineer, from 1919. Organ of the Women's Engineering Society. (British Library; Fawcett Library, 1919–25)

Woman health visitor, from 1926. Journal of the Women Sanitary Inspectors' and Health Visitors' Association and Women Public Health Officers' Association. (British Library)

Woman Teacher, 1919. Organ of the National Union of Women Teachers. (British Library)

Woman worker, 1907–10, 1916–21. Organ of the National Federation of Women Workers. (British Library; Fawcett Library, 1907–9)

Women's industrial news, 1895–1919. (British Library; Fawcett Library, 1903–19)

Women's Union Journal, 1876–90; superseded by *Quarterly report and review*, 1891; superseded by *Women's trade union review*, 1891–1919, the organ of the Women's Protective and Provident League. (British Library, few individual issues; Fawcett Library, 1876–80, 1891–1900, 1911–19; British Library of Political Science, 1910, 1917–19)

Armed services

The Link, from 1918. Monthly organ of the Queen Mary's Army Auxiliary Corps. (British Library)

Nursing

Nurses' Diary and Quarterly Review, 1896–7. (British Library)

Nurses Journal, 1891–1918. (British Library; Royal College of Nursing, 1891–1908)

Nurses Near and Far, from 1906. Organ of the Nurses' Missionary League. (British Library, No. 1 missing)

Nursing Mirror, from 1886. (British Library; Royal College of Nursing from 1907)

Nursing Notes, 1887–1945; superseded by *Midwives' Chronicle*, from 1945. (British Library; Royal College of Nursing from 1891)

Nursing Record, 1888–9; superseded by *International Nursing Record*, 1889–90; superseded by *Nursing Record and Hospital World*, 1890–1902; superseded by *British Journal of Nursing*, 1902–56. (British Library; Royal College of Nursing)

Nursing Times, from 1905. (Royal College of Nursing)

MORAL AND SOCIAL ISSUES

Birth control

Birth Control News, 1922–46. (British Library)

Contagious Diseases

The Dawn, 1882–96. (Fawcett Library)
Goodworks, 1875. A record of the proceedings of the Wesleyan and other societies
for the securing of the repeal of the Contagious Diseases Acts. (Fawcett Library)
The Sentinel, 1879–1900. (Fawcett Library)
The Shield, 1870–1916. (Fawcett Library) (Although this journal had the same
title throughout its existence it did in fact have several changes of sub-title, policy
and editors, it was the official journal of various anti-contagious diseases
organizations. The Fawcett Library has a complete list of all issues, their number
and date, and it is the major holder of the journal, all other holdings are
incomplete, probably as a result of irregular publication.)
The Storm-bell, 1898–1900. (Fawcett Library)

Missionaries

Baptist Zenana Magazine, 1904–11; incorporated in the *Herald: Journal of the
Baptist Missionary Society*. (Selly Oak Colleges, Birmingham 29)
*Female Missionary Intelligencer and Record of the Proceedings of the Society for
the Promotion of Female Education in China, Africa and the East*, 1858–99.
(British Library; University of Cambridge Library, some issues)
Nurses Near and Far, from 1906. Organ of the Nurses' Missionary League.
(British Library)
Our Indian Sisters, 1886–91. Quarterly magazine of the Ladies' Zenana
Missionary Society. (British Library, 1886–9, issues 3–14, 16)
Women's Work on the Missionary Field, 1904–32. Organ of the Women's
Auxiliary of the Wesleyan Methodist Society, superseded by *Woman's work*,
from 1933. (British Library from No. 22)

Politics

The Labour Woman, from 1913. Published by the Labour Party as a journal from
1913 but from 1911–13 published by the Women's Labour League as a leaflet.
(British Library from 1911, leaflet No. 1)
Women's Gazette and Weekly News, 1883–93. Organ of the Woman's Liberal
Federation. (Not located)
Women's Liberal Magazine, 1920; superseded by *Federation News*, 1921–4;
superseded by *Liberal Women's News*, from 1924. Organ of the Women's
Liberal Federation. (British Library from 1920; Fawcett Library, 1926–36)

Temperance

British Women's Temperance Journal, 1883–Sept 1892; superseded by *Wings: official journal of the Women's Total Abstinence Union*, Oct 1892–1925; superseded by *White Ribbon*, from 1926. (British Library, 1887–1925; National British Women's Total Abstinence Union, 1883–1902)

Woman's View, 1925–30. Organ of the Women's True Temperance Committee. (British Library)

Women's signal: Lady Somerset's New Paper, 1894–5. (National British Women's Total Abstinence Union; Fawcett Library)

Women's Penny Paper, 1888–93; superseded by *Women's Herald*, 1893–4; superseded by *The Journal*, 1894–9. (British Library; Fawcett Library)

SUFFRAGE

Anti-suffrage Review, 1908–18. (British Library, 1910–18; Fawcett Library, 1908–12 incomplete; Bodleian Library)

Church League for Women's Suffrage Monthly Paper, 1912–17; superseded by *Church militant*, 1918–28. (British Library; Fawcett Library, May–Nov 1912)

Common cause, 1909–13; superseded by *Women's suffrage: the common cause of humanity*, 1913–14; superseded by *Common Cause of Humanity*, 1914–20; superseded by *Woman's Leader and the Common Cause*, 1920–33. (British Library; Fawcett Library)

Conservative and Unionist Women's Franchise Review, 1910–15. (British Library)

Free Church Suffrage Times, 1913–15; superseded by *The Coming Day*, 1916–20. (British Library; Fawcett Library, June 1914, Feb 1915)

The Independent Suffragette, 1916–17. The organ of the Independent Women's Social and Political Union. (British Library, 1916 (Nos. 2 and 6 only); Fawcett Library, 1916–17 (Nos. 10, 22 and 23 only))

Jus suffragii, 1906–16. A monthly organ of the International Women's Suffrage Alliance; superseded by *International Women's Suffrage News*, 1923–30; superseded by *International Women's News*, from 1930. (British Library, 1912–; Fawcett Library, 1906–35)

Men's League for Women's Suffrage Monthly Paper, 1909–14. Organ of the Men's League for Women's Suffrage. (Fawcett Library)

The Suffragette, 1912–15. Organ of the Women's Social and Political Union, edited by Christabel Pankhurst; superseded by *Britannia*, 1915–18. (British Library; Fawcett Library, 1912–16)

The Vote, 1909–33. Organ of the Women's Freedom League. (British Library; Fawcett Library, 1909–31)

Votes for Women, 1907–18. (British Library; Fawcett Library, 1907–9)

Woman's Dreadnought, 1914–17; superseded by *Workers' Dreadnought*, 1917–24. (British Library)

Women's Franchise, 1907–11. (British Library; Fawcett Library, 1907–9)

Women's Suffrage, 1907 (5 issues). (British Library, issues 2–5)

Women's Suffrage Journal, 1870–90, edited by Lydia Becker. (British Library; Fawcett Library)

Women's Suffrage News, 1894 (6 issues); superseded by *Women's Suffrage Record*, 1903–6. (British Library, 1894, 1903–6; Fawcett Library, 1894, No. 2 only)

SUBJECT HISTORIES

Different aspects of women's history have been treated with varying degrees of thoroughness and authority over the years. The period 1908–13, for example, saw the publication of a large amount of material debating the pros and cons of women's suffrage; and following the limited enfranchisement of women in 1918 many volumes of reminiscences were published. These, however, tend merely to describe the formation and growth of the various suffrage organizations, rather than attempt to place the events within their social context. It is only in recent years that the various elements of the campaign for women's suffrage have been documented and analysed in such works as Antonia Raeburn's *The militant suffragettes* and Andrew Rosen's book on the Women's Social and Political Union, *Rise up women!* Other aspects of the history of women have recently become topics for academic discussion and an increasing number of books are being published. However, despite this interest McGregor's comment that no work on women's employment for the period after 1850 is comparable to Ivy Pinchbeck's *Woman workers and the Industrial Revolution 1750–1850* is still true (*British Journal of Sociology*, March 1955, p. 48), although current research is to some extent filling the gaps.

In all the sections and sub-sections contemporary accounts have been included as these are now in many cases treated as primary source material. This is particularly true of works on education and employment: books written in 1870 giving advice to women are very different from those published in 1928. The contrast between Josephine Butler's work *Woman's work and woman's culture*, 1869, and Sylvia Anthony's *Women's place in industry and home*, 1932, is particularly great as the former outlines the opportunities available to women in 1869 whereas the latter accepts that women are able to find employment in a wide range of trades and professions and is concerned with the problems of achieving equal pay and opportunities.

GENERAL

Anthony, Sylvia, *Woman's place in industry and home*, Routledge, 1932.
Banks, J. A. and O., 'Feminism and social change in a case study of a social movement' in G. K. Zollschan and W. Hirsch, eds, *Explorations in social change*, Routledge, 1964.
Blease, Walter Lyon, *The emancipation of English women*, Constable, 1910.

Branca, Patricia, *Silent sisterhood: Middle-class women in the Victorian home*, Croom Helm, 1975.

Branca, Patricia, *Women in Europe since 1750*, Croom Helm, 1978.

Brittain, Vera, *Lady into woman*, Andrew Dakers, 1953.

Butler, Josephine, *Woman's work and woman's culture: a series of essays*, Macmillan, 1869.

Caffrey, Kate, *The 1900s lady*, Gordon & Cremonesi, 1976.

Clephane, Irene, *Towards sex freedom*, John Lane, 1935.

Crepaz, Adele, *The emancipation of women and its probable consequences*, translated from the German by Ellis Wright, Sonnenschein, 1893.

Crow, D., *The Victorian woman*, Allen & Unwin, 1971.

Cunnington, C. W., *Women*, Burke, 1950.

Dahlström, E., ed, *The changing roles of men and women*, translated by G. and S. Anderman, Duckworth, 1967.

Delamont, Sara and Duffin, Lorna, eds, *The nineteenth-century woman: her cultural and physical world*, Croom Helm, 1978.

Evans, R. J., *The Feminists*, Croom Helm, 1977.

Higginson, T. W., *Common sense about women*, (1882), 4th edn, Sonnenschein, 1897.

Holtby, Winifred, *Women and a changing civilization*, John Lane, 1934.

Kamm, Josephine, *Rapiers and battleaxes: the women's movement and its aftermath*, Allen & Unwin, 1966.

Klein, Viola, *The feminine character: the history of an ideology*, 2nd edn, Routledge, 1971.

Lang, Elsie M., *British women in the twentieth century*, Werner Laurie, 1929.

Langdon-Davies, John, *A short history of women*, Cape, 1928.

Lennard, Vivian R., *Woman, her power, influence and mission: 21 sermons*, Skeffington, 1910.

Milburn, J. F., *Women as citizens: a comparative review*, Sage Publications, 1976.

Mitchell, Juliet and Oakley, Ann, *The rights and wrongs of women*, Penguin, 1976.

Ramelson, Marian, *The petticoat rebellion: a century of struggle for women's rights*, Lawrence & Wishart, 1977.

Rees, B., *The Victorian lady*, Gordon & Cremonesi, 1977.

Reeves, Magdalen Stuart (Mrs Pember), *Round about a pound a week*, Bell, 1913; new introduction by Sally Alexander, Virago, 1979.

Roe, J., 'Modernization and sexism: recent writings on Victorian women'. *Victorian Studies*, Winter 1977, 20, pp 179–92.

Stopes, Charlotte C., *British freewomen, their historical privilege*, (1894), 4th edn, Sonnenschein, 1909.

Strachey, Ray, *'The cause': a short history of the women's movement in Great Britain*, Bell, 1928; Virago, 1978.

Strachey, Ray, ed, *Our freedom and its results, by five women: Eleanor F.*

Rathbone, Erna Reiss, Ray Strachey, Alison Neilans, Mary Agnes Hamilton,
   L. and V. Woolf, 1936.
Swanwick, H. M., *The future of the woman's movement*, G. Bell, 1913.
Vicinus, Martha, ed, *Suffer and be still: women in the Victorian age*, Indiana
   University Press, 1972.
Vicinus, Martha, ed, *A widening sphere: changing roles of Victorian women*,
   Indiana University Press, 1977.

Following the great changes of the late nineteenth and early twentieth centuries with women gradually gaining access to education, the professions, the right to own property, employment opportunities and finally the vote, many books were published on either the history of these changes or on women's new role in society. These vary greatly and many contain only peripheral material. There has been no attempt here to cover all the works of a general nature relating to women but merely to record the more valuable, with some indication as to their scope, and to highlight the limitations of other publications. Published works on women cover a wide range of approaches, from Lennard's collection of sermons for women to Crepaz's anti-feminist work, translated from the German. Other works include those by Langdon-Davies, Lang and Cunnington but these, too, contain little of value. Many of the general works are written from a feminist point of view including those by Holtby and Brittain; earlier feminist works include Swanwick's and Blease's. Of the nineteenth-century works Higginson's *Common Sense about women* is a useful source. The more important works include Ray Strachey's *The cause*, recently reprinted, which is a retrospective review of the feminist movement up to 1928, as well as *Our freedom* which is a useful compilation of essays on changes in the role of women. Josephine Kamm's *Rapiers and battleaxes* provides a good popular background to women's history; and although Dahlström's book has an interesting title it is, in fact, translated from the Swedish and refers to experiences in Sweden. Klein's *The feminine character* is an analysis of theories relating to feminine psychology and includes a chapter on the role of women in the late nineteenth and early twentieth centuries which provides a useful concise review of the sociological history; it also has a useful bibliography. More valuable recent works include Vicinus's collections of essays on Victorian women and Crow's *The Victorian woman* which deals with various aspects of Victorian women. Vicinus collections of essays contrast greatly with such works as Rees' *The Victorian lady* and Caffrey's *The 1900s lady* which simply try to reinforce the stereotype images of women during this period. Branca's *The silent sisterhood* is an extremely useful book on the middle-class woman and covers all aspects of her way of life. It also shows the contrasts between the accepted image of the middle-class woman in Victorian England with what was probably the reality. *Clio's consciousness raised*, New York, Harper & Row, Torch Books, 1974 edited by Mary Hartman and Louisa Banner, contains several essays on Victorian England, including Patricia Branca's 'Image and reality: the myth of the idle Victorian woman', later expanded into *Silent Sisterhood*.

EDUCATION

In addition to general books, biographies of eminent women educationalists should be consulted for background information and these have been listed separately under Biographies, above.

Bremner, C. S., *Education of girls and women in Great Britain*, Swan Sonnenschein, 1897.

Burstall, Sara A., *Retrospect and Prospect: now and sixty years ago, a personal record*, Longmans, 1933.

Burstyn, J. N., 'Women's education in England during the nineteenth century: a review of literature', *History of Education*, 6, (1) February 1977, pp 11–19.

Kamm, Josephine, *Hope deferred: girls' education in English history*, Methuen, 1965.

Richardson, J., 'The great revolution: women's education in Victorian times', *History Today*, 24, 1974, pp 420–27.

Warwick, Countess of, ed, *Progress in women's education in the British Empire, being the report of the Education Section, Victorian Era Exhibition.* Longmans Green, 1898.

Zimmern, Alice, *The renaissance of girls' education in England: a record of fifty years' progress*, Innes, 1898.

Sara Burstall's *Retrospect and prospect*, whilst providing an interesting insight into one woman's career in education relies on personal reminiscences rather than on printed or archival sources. Of the older works, Alice Zimmern's work is particularly useful for the period up to 1898 as it relates the need for improved higher educational facilities to better employment opportunities; whilst Bremner's work is a general review of the education of girls and women, and outlines opportunities available; and the Countess of Warwick's book is a review of educational opportunities in the British Empire.

Primary and secondary

Burchell, D., *Miss Buss's second school*, Camden School for Girls, 1972.

Burstall, Sara A., *English High Schools for girls; their aims, organization and management 1871–1911.* Longmans, 1907.

Burstall, Sara A., *The story of the Manchester High School for Girls*, Manchester, Sherratt & Hughes, 1911.

Burstall, Sara A., and Douglas, M. A., *Public schools for girls; a series of papers on their history, aims and schemes of study*, Longmans, 1911.

Clarke, A. K., *A history of the Cheltenham Ladies' College 1853–1953*, Faber, 1953.

De Zouche, Dorothy E., *Roedean School 1885–1955*, private circulation, 1955.

Gurney, Mary, *Are we to have education for our middle-class girls?, or the history of Camden Collegiate Schools*, Women's Education Union, 1872.

Kamm, Josephine, *How different from us: a biography of Miss Buss and Miss Beale*, Bodley Head, 1958.

Kamm, Josephine, *Indicative past: A hundred years of the Girls' Public Day School Trust*, Allen & Unwin, 1972.

Magnus, L., *The Jubilee book of the Girls' Public Day School Trust, 1873–1923*, Cambridge University Press, 1923.

Milne, T. D., 'On the secondary education of girls', a paper read at the Social Science Congress, Aberdeen, 1877.

Scrimgeour, R. M., ed, *The North London Collegiate School 1850–1950: essays in honour of the centenary of the Frances Mary Buss Foundation*, Oxford University Press, 1950.

Early works on the secondary education of girls – such as Gurney's pamphlet and the paper read by T. D. Milne at the Social Science Congress – were mainly concerned with the provision of secondary schools for middle-class girls. The histories of the Girls' Public Day School Trust by Magnus, Kamm, and Burstall and Douglas, show how successful they were in achieving their ideals. Histories of individual schools, like those of the Cheltenham Ladies' College, of Manchester High School for Girls, and of Roedean School, provide good insights into the difficulties surrounding the establishment of these schools.

Further education

Bailey, E., *A short history of Lady Margaret Hall, 1879–1923*, printed by the Oxford University Press for private circulation, 1923.

Battiscombe, Georgina, *Reluctant pioneer: a life of Elizabeth Wordsworth*, Constable, 1978.

Bradbrook, M. C., *Barbara Bodichon, George Eliot and the limits of feminism*, Oxford, Somerville College, 1976.

Bradbrook, M. C., *That infidel place: a short history of Girton College, 1869–1969, with an essay on the collegiate university in the modern world*, Chatto & Windus, 1969.

Brittain, Vera, *The women at Oxford: a fragment of history*, Harrap, 1960.

Burstyn, Joan N., 'Education and sex: the medical case against higher education for women in England, 1870–1900'. *Proc. of American Philosophical Society*, 117, April 1974, pp 79–89.

Burstyn, Joan N., 'Religious arguments against the higher education for women in England 1840–1890', *Women's Studies*, 1 (1), 1972, pp 111–31.

Butler, R. F., *A history of St Anne's Society*, printed by the Oxford University Press, 1946, for private circulation.

Butler, R. F., and Pritchard, M. H., *The Society of Oxford Home Students: retrospects and recollection 1879–1921*, printed by the Oxford University Press, 1938, for private circulation.

Carus-Wilson, E., *Westfield College: University of London, 1882–1932*, private circulation, 1932.

Dyhouse, C., 'Social Darwinistic ideas and the development of women's education in England, 1880–1920', *History of Education*, 5 (1), 1976, pp 41–58.

Farnell, H., *A Somervillean looks back*, printed by the Oxford University Press, for private circulation, 1948.

Fawcett, M. G., 'The use of higher education to women', *Contemporary Review*, November, 1886, pp 719–28.

Gardner, Alice, *A short history of Newnham College, Cambridge*, Bowes & Bowes, 1921.

Grylls, R. G., *Queen's College 1848–1948*, Routledge, 1948.

Kaye, Elaine, *A history of Queen's College, London 1848–1972*, Chatto & Windus, 1972.

Lady Margaret Hall, A short history, edited by E. Bailey and issued on behalf of the Lady Margaret Hall Appeal Fund, Oxford University Press, 1923.

Major, K., 'St Hilda's College', *Amer. Oxonian*, 48, 1961, pp 57–60.

Ogilvie, Lady M. E., 'St Anne's College', *Amer. Oxonian*, 48, 1961, pp 118–122.

Peck, Lady Winifred, *A little learning, or, A Victorian childhood*, Faber, 1952.

Proctor, E. E. S., 'St Hugh's College', *Amer. Oxonian*, 48, 1961, pp 10–15.

Rogers, Annie M. A. H., *Degrees by degrees: the story of the admission of Oxford women students to membership of the University*, Oxford University Press, 1938.

St Clare Byrne, M., and Mansfield, C. H., *Somerville College, 1879–1921*, Oxford University Press, 1922.

Stephen, Barbara, *Emily Davies and Girton College*, Constable, 1927.

Thorne, Isabel, *Sketch of the foundation and development of the London School of Medicine for Women*, Women's Printing Society, 1916.

Tuke, M. J., *A history of Bedford College for Women, 1849–1937*, Oxford University Press, 1939.

Tylecote, Mabel, *The education of women at Manchester University 1883–1933*, Manchester University, 1941.

The first colleges for women were Queen's College and the Ladies' College, Bedford Square, now Bedford College. There is an excellent history of each, written by Grylls, Kaye and Tuke respectively, based on college records which record the modest beginnings. Of the histories of the colleges of Oxford and Cambridge, that of Girton College by Barbara Stephen is by far the most comprehensive, being based on archive material, and it includes a comprehensive bibliography. The histories of other Oxbridge colleges vary greatly, from Farnell's collection of reminiscences to short but adequate histories of colleges, like Gardner's history of Newnham College or Bailey's history of Lady Margaret Hall. Georgina Battiscombe's biography of Elizabeth Wordsworth also contains information relating to the early days of Lady Margaret Hall.

Teaching Associations

Glenday, N. and Price, M. *Reluctant revolutionaries: a century of head mistresses 1874–1974*, Pitman, 1974.

This provides a good history of the Head Mistresses' Association and was written for their centenary.

EMIGRATION

'Emigration', *Englishwoman's Journal*, 1874, pp 96–102.

Hammerton, A. James, *Emigrant gentlewomen: genteel poverty and female emigration 1830–1914*, Croom Helm, 1979.

Monk, Una, *New horizons: a hundred years of women's emigration*, HMSO, 1963.

Plant, G. F., *Overseas settlement: migration from the United Kingdom to the Dominions*, Oxford University Press, 1951.

Plant, G. F., *SOSBW: a survey of voluntary effort in women's empire emigration*, Society for the Oversea Settlement of British Women, 1950.

'Prospects of female emigrants to South Australia', *Englishwoman's Journal*, 1873, pp 271–2.

Ross, A., 'Emigration for women', *Macmillan's Magazine*, 45, 1882, pp 312–7.

Rye, Maria S., *Emigration of educated women ...: a paper read at the Social Science Congress in Dublin, 1861*, London, 1861.

Work and leisure, VIII, 8, 1882, pp 227–34.

The reprint of Maria Rye's paper on the need for qualified women to emigrate is listed because of its importance and the validity of its comments. The best general review of the emigration movement is Una Monk's *New Horizons* which gives a good concise history of the emigration of women from *c.* 1860–1960. A more detailed work is G. F. Plant's on the Society of Overseas Settlement for British Women while his *Overseas Settlement* deals with migration as a whole. In addition to published works, valuable primary source material can be found in contemporary periodical literature including articles in the *Englishwoman's Journal* in 1873 and 1874 and in *Macmillan's Magazine* and in the journal *Work and Leisure*.

EMPLOYMENT

In his bibliographical essay 'The social position of women in England, 1850–1914' (*British Journal of Sociology*, 1955, pp 48–60) Professor McGregor comments that 'the effects of early industrialism on women's employment have been investigated in great detail in Ivy Pinchbeck's pioneering study *Woman Workers and the Industrial Revolution*. There is no comparable book for the period after

1850.' His remarks are still true despite the newly aroused interest in women's studies. There have been many works published on women but there is still no overall study of women and employment, either studying the changing conditions of employment, the opening of employment opportunities to women or the sociological effects of these changes. Research is currently being undertaken into various aspects of women's employment and it is to be hoped that some of this will result in books of the calibre of Pinchbeck's excellent study of 1760–1850.

Although retrospective works covering the employment of women as a whole do not exist, there are many dealing with individual trades and professions. These vary greatly in their coverage, some are merely recollections and reminiscences of women active in a profession, whereas others, especially the pamphlets produced for the Women's Industrial Council, are extremely valuable sources giving details of rates of pay, hours of work, etc. In order to facilitate the use of this section, material has been further sub-divided into individual trades and professions. Several periodicals have been searched for useful articles, probably the most important being *Women's Industrial News* published by the Women's Industrial Council and *Work and Leisure* edited by Emily Faithfull.

General

Abbott, E., *Women in industry: a study in American history*, New York and London, Appleton, 1911.

Bird, M. Mostyn, *Woman at work: a study of the different ways of earning a living open to women*, Chapman & Hall, 1911.

Black, Clementina, *Married women's work: being the report of an enquiry undertaken by the Women's Industrial Council*, Bell, 1915.

Booth, C., *Life and labour of the people in London*, Macmillan, 1889–1903, 17 volumes.

Bulley, A. A. and Whitley, M., *Women's work*, Methuen, 1894.

Burnett, John, ed, *Useful toil: autobiographies of working people from the 1820s to the 1920s*, Allen Lane, 1974.

Butler, Josephine, *Woman's work and woman's culture: a series of essays*, Macmillan, 1869.

Cadbury, E. and others, *Women's work and wages: a phase of life in an industrial city*, Fisher Unwin, 1906.

Collet, Clara E., *Educated working women: essays on the economic position of women workers in the middle-classes*, P. S. King, 1902.

Collet, Clara E., *Women in industry*, Women's Printing Society, 1911.

Davies, Margaret L., ed, *Life as we have known it by Co-operative working women*, Introductory letter by Virginia Woolf, L. and V. Woolf, 1931; Virago, 1977.

Dawes, F., *A woman's place – women at work from 1830 to the present*, Wayland, 1976.

Faithfull, E., 'Women's work', a paper read at the Royal Society of Arts, 1871.

Hewitt, Margaret, *Wives and mothers in Victorian industry*, Rockcliff, 1958.

Holcombe, Lee, *Victorian ladies at work*, David & Charles, 1973.

Hollis, P., 'Working women'. *History*, 62 (October 1977), pp 439–45.

Hutchins, B. L., 'A note on the distribution of women in occupations'. *Journal of the Royal Statistical Society*, LXVII, 3, 1904, pp 479–90.

Hutchins, B. L., *Women's wages in England in the nineteenth century*, Women's Industrial Council, 1908.

Hutchins, B. L., *Women in modern industry*, Bell, 1915.

Martin, A., *The married working woman: a study*, National Union of Women's Suffrage Societies, 1911.

Morley, Edith J., *Working women in seven professions: a survey of their economic conditions and prospects*, Routledge, 1914.

Papworth, Lucy W. and Zimmern, Dorothy H., *The occupations of women*, Women's Industrial Council, 1914.

Pinchbeck, Ivy, *Woman workers and the Industrial Revolution 1750–1850*, Routledge, 1930.

Schreiner, Olive, *Woman and labour*, Fisher Unwin, 1911; Virago, 1978.

Wood, G. H., *The woman wage-earner*, Church League for Woman Suffrage, 1910.

Edinburgh Review 1802–1929.

Englishwoman's Review 1866–1910.

Fortnightly Review 1865–1954.

Westminster Review 1824–1914.

Women's Industrial News 1895–1919.

Work and Leisure 1880–93.

Of the general works, Pinchbeck's and Hewitt's are classics, but unfortunately both are of limited value for the period 1870–1928. However, for the study of middle-class women Lee Holcombe's work is a useful source including as it does parliamentary sources of information. Patricia Hollis's review article 'Working Women' is a useful guide to recent works on the subject, which is taken to be a broader heading than simply employment. Of the older material, Josephine Butler's work shows the attitudes and concern of the early feminists, and among the most useful is that by Clementina Black on married women's work, undertaken for the Women's Industrial Council, by Emily Faithfull on industrial employment, by B. L. Hutchins on women's wages, and on the newer opportunities created by the First World War, and by Papworth and Zimmern on the occupations of women which uses as its base statistics from the 1911 census. Two works by Clara Collet are also of value and Charles Booth's massive survey of labour in London is useful for conditions in the capital. Other interesting works are to be found among the pamphlet publications of women's organizations and societies; some are slender works which although providing only a brief outline of the subject give a particular opinion. Examples are Martin's review of working women published by the National Union of Women's Suffrage Societies, Wood's brief look at female wage-earners and Morley's coverage of seven professions for women. Other more general works such as those by Abbott, Bird, and Bulley and Whitley, are most superficial. Several periodicals contain useful contemporary information. The *Englishwoman's Review* has many articles on women's employment, both on conditions and opportunities. The review journals of the late nineteenth century contain material useful when observing reactions to the attempts by women's organizations to open up the professions for women. The *Edinburgh Review*, *Westminster Review* and *Fortnightly Review* are the most useful. The article by B. L. Hutchins in the *Journal of the Royal Statistical Society* deserves particular mention as it analyses the census figures of 1881–1901 for women's occupations.

PROFESSIONS AND TRADES

Almoners

Bell, E. M., *The story of hospital almoners: the birth of a profession*, Faber, 1961.

Armed services

Barton, Edith M., *Eve in khaki: the story of the women's army at home and abroad*, Part 1 In England; part 2 In France, by Marguerite Cody, Nelson, 1918.

Beauman, K. B., *Partners in blue: the story of women's service with the Royal Air Force*, Hutchinson, 1971.

Cowper, J. M., *A short history of the Queen Mary's Army Auxiliary Corps*, WRAC Association, 1966.

Douglas-Pennant, Violet, *Under the searchlight: a record of a great scandal*, Allen & Unwin, 1922.

Femina patriae defensor: woman in the service of her country, Interallied Veterans' Federation, 1934.

Gwynne-Vaughan, Helen, *Service with the army*, Hutchinson, 1942.

Hay, Ian, *One hundred years of army nursing*, Cassell, 1953.

Mason, Ursula S., *The Wrens 1917–1977*, Reading, Educational Explorers, 1977.

Mitchell, David, *Women on the warpath*, Cape, 1966.

Nursing in the army, Queen Alexandra's Imperial Military Nursing Service, Stationery Office, 1905.

Reminiscent sketches 1914–1919 by members of the QAIMNS, QAIMNS, 1922.

Women played a minor role in the armed services during the Boer War, when they were active mainly in nursing units attached to the army. But during the First World War owing to increasing shortages of men the decision was taken to employ women in the lines of communication in France. This led to the formation of the Women's Army Auxiliary Corps, later called Queen Mary's Army Auxiliary Corps

(QMAAC). Their story was written by the Chief Controller, Helen Gwynne-Vaughan. The official histories of the various women's units have been published, and although they contain detailed accounts of the early years they tend to be insular and to make little mention of outside events or changes in the services as a whole. The official history of the QAIMNS is in the form of reminiscences and includes an early recruiting leaflet.

Barmaids

Joint Committee on the Employment of Barmaids, *Women as barmaids*, King, 1906.

The conditions of women employed as barmaids in the late nineteenth and early twentieth centuries are well covered in this pamphlet.

Bookbinders

Guild of Women Bookbinders, *The bindery that Jill built*, Art Reproduction, 1901.
The bindings of tomorrow; a record of the work of the Guild of Women Binders and the Hampstead Bindery. Karslake, 1902.

Chainmakers

Cadbury E., and others, *Women's work and wages: a phase of life in an industrial city*, Fisher Unwin, 1906.
Sherard, R. *White slaves of England: true pictures of certain social conditions in 1897*, J. Bowden, 1897.

Civil Service

Blackburn, R., 'Women in the Civil Service'. *Englishwoman's Review*, 1875, pp 197–202.
Evans, Dorothy, *Women and the Civil Service*, Pitman, 1934.
Harkness, M. E., 'Women as Civil Servants', *Nineteenth Century*, 10, 1881, pp 369–81.
Manners, J., 'Employment of women in the public service', *Quarterly Review*, 151, 1881, pp 181–200.
Martindale, H., *Women servants of the state, 1871–1938: a history of women in the Civil Service*, Allen & Unwin, 1938.
Trollope, A., 'The young women at the telegraph office', *Good Words*, 18, 1877, pp 377–84.
Englishwoman's Review, VII, July 1871, p 221.

The first women telegraph workers employed by the Post Office when it was founded in 1870 were also the first women Civil Servants. Anthony Trollope's article is useful as it contains information on conditions of employment.

The story of the steady growth of the number of women employed up to the First World War and the effect both the war and its termination had on the numbers of women employed by the Civil Service has been covered in Dorothy Evans' book, while Hilda Martindale's, published some four years later, is a general survey of women's employment in the Civil Service for the years 1870–1938. A good general outline of the opening up of the Civil Service to women and of the improvements in conditions of service is to be found in the chapter on the Civil Service in Lee Holcombe's book (listed under General heading above) on the employment of middle-class women. In addition there are three notable periodical articles written in the late nineteenth century which outline the contemporary position.

Clerical work

Blackburn, H., 'Female clerks', *Englishwoman's Review*, 1878, pp 367–8.
'Ladies as clerks', *Fraser's Magazine*, NS 12, 1875, pp 335–40.
Mannin, Ethel, *Young in the twenties: a chapter of autobiography*, Hutchinson, 1971.
Silverstone, R., 'Office work for women: an historical review', *Business History*, 18, January 1976, pp 98–110.
'Telegraphists and clerks', *Bulletin of the Society for the Study of Labour History*, 26, Spring 1973, pp 7–9.

The census of 1871 showed that there were less than a thousand women clerks in the country, but by the 1911 census there were over 100,000. Lee Holcombe devotes a chapter to the subject in her work on middle-class women (listed under General heading above) and gives a brief account of the phenomenal use of women as clerks. The two contemporary articles outline the opportunities to women in the 1870s while the relationship between the founding of the Post Office and the rise in clerical opportunities during the same period is briefly covered in the article in the *Bulletin of the Society for the Study of Labour History*. Rosaline Silverstone's article uses census figures extensively, as does Lee Holcombe.

Cotton industry

Chapman, Sir Sydney J. *The Lancashire cotton industry: a study in economic development*, Manchester University, 1904.

This is an extremely useful work as it discusses the role of both men and women in the industry, using much valuable statistical data.

Domestic service

Adam, Ruth, *A woman's place, 1910–75*, Chatto & Windus, 1976.
Bateman, A. E., 'Discussion of A. L. Bowley's paper "Changes in average wages (Nominal and real) in the United Kingdom between 1860–1890." ' *Journal of the Royal Statistical Society*, LVIII, 1895, p 283.

Broadhurst, S. 'A plea for the domestic servant', *Macmillan's Magazine*, 80, 1899, pp 284–7.

Bunting, M. H. L., 'Mistress and maid', *Contemporary Review*, CVIII, 1910, pp 595–602.

Butler, C. V., *Domestic service: an inquiry by the Women's Industrial Council*, G. Bell, 1916.

Davidoff, L., and Hawthorn, R., *A day in the life of a Victorian domestic servant*, Allen & Unwin, 1976.

Dawes, Frank, *Not in front of the servants: domestic service in England, 1850–1939*, Wayland, 1973.

Ebery, Mark, *Domestic service in late Victorian and Edwardian England, 1871–1914*, University of Reading, 1977.

Franklin, J., 'Troops of servants', *Victorian Studies*, 19, 2, December 1975, pp 211–39.

Horn, Pamela, *The rise and fall of the Victorian servant*, Dublin, Gill & Macmillan, 1975.

Huggett, F. E., *Life below stairs: domestic servants in England from Victorian times*, John Murray, 1977.

Jermy, L., *Memories of a working woman*, Norwich, Goose, 1934.

Layard, G. S., 'Doom of the domestic cook', *Nineteenth Century*, 33, 1893, pp 309–19.

McBride, Theresa M., *The domestic revolution: the modernization of household service in England and France, 1820–1920*, Croom Helm, 1976.

Marshall, Dorothy, *The English domestic servant in history*, Historical Association, 1949.

'Solving the servant problem', *Women's Industrial News*, 1901, June, pp 236–9.

'Some difficulties of the domestic servant question', *Women's Industrial News*, 1900, March, pp 153–5.

Stephen, C. E., 'Mistresses and servants'. *Nineteenth Century*, 6, 1879, pp 1051–63.

Stuart, Dorothy M., *The English abigail*, Macmillan, 1946.

During the late nineteenth century approximately 40 per cent of all employed women were in domestic service. This situation was already changing before the First World War when women and girls were no longer prepared to do what they considered degrading work for low wages when they could find alternative employment, usually in factories. Articles on the resulting 'servant problem' are to be found in many contemporary journals, including the *Contemporary Review*, and the *Women's Industrial News*. The report of the Women's Industrial Council by C. V. Butler is an extremely valuable source of information, giving details of rates of pay and conditions of service for all types of domestic servants, as well as containing a bibliography. The *Journal of the Royal Statistical Society* article on rates of pay for domestic servants covering is excellent. Other works on domestic servants by Marshall and Stuart are of limited value in the present context as they are based on literary sources only, but recent works, although not specifically dealing with women, fill existing gaps in the coverage of the topic.

Engineering

Drake, Barbara, *Women in the engineering trades*, Labour Research Department, 1918.

This is the result of an enquiry by the Joint Committee of the Fabian Research Department and the Fabian Women's Group and is a most detailed account of women in the engineering industry during the First World War. It also considers the prospects for women at the end of the war.

Governesses and nannies

Gathorne-Hardy, J., *The rise and fall of the British nanny*, Hodder & Stoughton, 1972.
Howe, B., *A galaxy of governesses*, Derek Verschoyle, 1954.
Peterson, M. Jeanne, 'The Victorian governess: status and incongruence in family and society', in M. Vicinus, ed, *Suffer and be still*, Indiana University Press, 1972, pp 3–19.
West, Katharine, *Chapter of governesses: a study of the governess in English fiction 1800–1949*, Cohen & West, 1949.
Englishwoman's Review 1866–1910.

The story of the middle-class woman employed as a governess is a familiar one in English fiction and as a result two works, West's and Howe's, deal with this aspect. For more factual information the chapter by Peterson in *Suffer and be still* is useful and the *Englishwoman's Review* contains much contemporary material.

Health visiting

'Collectivism, regionalism and feminism: health visiting and British social policy 1850–1975', *Journal of Social Policy*, 6, 3, July 1977, pp 291–315.

Homework

Hutchins, B. L., *Homework and sweating: the causes and the remedies*, Fabian Tracts, 1918.
Knightley, Louisa M., 'Women as homeworkers', *Nineteenth Century*, 50, 1901, August, pp 287–92.

Lady Knightley's article on homework illustrates the middle-class, feminist point of view that any work, no matter how badly paid, was better than no work for working-class mothers.

Housework

Oakley, Ann, *The sociology of housework*, M. Robertson, 1974.
Oakley, Ann, *Housewife*, Allen Lane, 1974.

The inspectorate

Anderson, A., *Women in the factory: an administrative adventure*, Murray, 1922.
Boothroyd, H. E., *A history of the inspectorate*, Board of Education Inspectors, 1923.
Martindale, H., *From one generation to another*, Allen & Unwin, 1944.
Squire, Rose E., *Thirty years in the public service: an industrial retrospect*, Nisbet, 1927.

Adelaide Anderson's work covers the early days of the women inspectorate and gives a good account of conditions encountered in factories by the inspectorate; it also contains a list of dangerous and unhealthy trades. The works by Martindale and Squire are memoirs of early days in the inspectorate but do contain a view of women's work during the twenties and the thirties.

Journalism

Bennett, Arnold, *Journalism for women: a practical guide*, John Lane, 1898.
Drew, C., 'Women as journalists', *Englishwoman's Review*, October 1894, p 245.
'A Sphinx', *Journalism as a career for women*, Newnes, 1918.

The writing of articles for genteel magazines was a respectable occupation for middle-class Victorian women because of its connections with the field of literature. Arnold Bennett's work is intended as a practical guide for intending women journalists, but is concerned chiefly with literary matters. The position of women journalists in the 1890s is covered by the article in the *Englishwoman's Review* and in the 1920s by a book written under the pseudonym of 'A Sphinx'.

Laundry work

Laundry worker and legislation, Women's Industrial Council, 1908.
Life in the laundry, Fabian Society, 1902.
Macdonald, M. E., 'Report on enquiry into conditions of work in laundries'. *Women's Industrial News*, June 1907, pp 629–42.

The conditions of women employed in laundries were of concern to the Women's Industrial Council; this resulted in publication of the Report and articles in their journal, *Women's Industrial News*. The Fabian Society also issued a tract which is of value to anyone researching in this field.

Librarians

'Women in libraries', *Englishwoman's Review*, 1899, pp 240–4.

Medicine

Bell, E. C. H. Moberly, *Storming the citadel: the rise of the woman doctor*, Constable, 1953.

Blackwell, Elizabeth, *Pioneer work in opening the medical profession to women: autobiographical sketches*, Longmans, 1895.

Jex-Blake, S., *Medical women: a thesis and a history* (1872), 2nd edn, Edinburgh, Oliphant Anderson & Ferrier, 1886.

Lawrence, M., *Shadow of swords: a biography of Elsie Inglis*, Michael Joseph, 1971.

McLaren, Eva, *History of the Scottish Women's Hospitals*, Hodder & Stoughton, 1919.

Martindale, Louisa, *The woman doctor and her future*, Mills & Boon, 1922.

Murray, F., *Women as army surgeons*, Hodder & Stoughton, 1920.

British Medical Journal.

The Lancet.

Sophia Jex-Blake's and Elizabeth Blackwell's books tell of the early days of women's medicine, whilst Moberley Bell's is simply a chronological account of the fight for entry to the profession with the advantage of a short bibliography. Martindale's work is a useful contemporary account of women in the profession and includes statistical data. Flora Murray's work deals exclusively with the work done by the Endell Hospital and its sister hospital in Wimereux. In addition to Eva McLaren's work, information relating to the Scottish Women's Hospital can be found in Margot Lawrence's biography of Elsie Inglis.

The *British Medical Journal* and *The Lancet* contain articles relating to the admittance of women to the medical profession. *The Lancet* in particular has numerous letters to the editor on the subject, over a number of years and is the source for correspondence from the medical profession relating to women's place in medicine.

Midwifery

Aveline, J. H., *English midwives: their history and prospects*, Churchill, 1872.

Donnison, Jean, *Midwives and medical men: a history of inter-professional rivalries and women's rights*, Heinemann Educational, 1977.

Morland, Egbert. *Alice and the stork, or, the rise in the status of the midwife as exemplified in the life of Alice Gregory, 1867–1944*, Hodder & Stoughton, 1951.

Radcliffe, W., *Milestones in midwifery*, Bristol, Wright, 1967.

Jean Donnison's recent work fills a gap on this subject for although the period to

1872 was adequately covered by Aveline the only other book on the subject, Morland's *Alice and the Stork*, is an inadequate biography.

Nursing

Barton, Eleanor C., *The history and progress of Poor Law nursing*, Law & Local Government Publications, 192–.

Bendall, Eve and Raybould, Elizabeth, *A history of the General Nursing Council for England and Wales, 1919–1959*, H. K. Lewis, 1969.

Brainard, Annie M., *The evolution of public health nursing*, W. B. Saunders, 1922.

Charley, Irene H., *The birth of industrial nursing*. Baillière, Tindall & Cox, 1954.

Craven, D., *A guide to district nurses*, Macmillan, 1889.

Dock, Lavinia L., and Stewart, Isabel M., *A short history of nursing*, (1920) 4th edn., Putnam's, 1938.

Loane, M. E., *The next street but one*, Edward Arnold, 1907.

Nutting, Mary, and Dock, Lavinia L., *A history of nursing: the evolution of nursing systems from the earliest times to the foundation of the first English and American training schools for nurses*, 4 vols, Putnam's, 1907–12.

Pavey, A. E. *The story of the growth of nursing as an art, a vocation and a profession*, 4th edn, Faber, 1954.

De Pledge, J., 'The history and progress of nursing in Poor Law infirmaries', *Westminster Review*, CXLII, 1894, July–Dec, pp 173–82.

Rathbone, William, *Sketch of the history and progress of district nursing from 1859 to the present day*, Macmillan, 1890.

Seymour, L. R., *The general history of nursing*, 3rd edn, Faber, 1954.

Tooley, Sarah A., *History of nursing in the British Empire*, S. H. Bousfield, 1906.

Twining, L., 'Poor Law infirmaries and their needs', *National Review*, XIII, 1889, July, p 368.

Of all the histories of nursing the 'classics' are the works by Nutting and Dock, and Tooley, although they were published before state registration was achieved. Of the others, Seymour's is useful for its bibliography and Bendall and Raybould's is a more specific work on the General Nursing Council, published for its golden jubilee. There is no full history of district nursing, Craven's book is a guide for nurses as the title makes clear, Loane's is a book of reminiscences, and Rathbone's short history was published too early to be authoritative.

Policewomen

Allen, Commandant Mary S., *The pioneer policewomen*, edited and arranged by J. H. Heynemen, Chatto & Windus, 1925.

Carrier, J., 'The control of women by women: women police', *Bulletin of the Society for the Study of Labour History*, 26, Spring 1973, pp 16–19.

Tancred, Edith, *Women police, 1914–1950*. National Council of Women of Great
  Britain, 1951.
Women police. Women's Auxiliary Service, 1925.

The most general history of women police is that by Tancred although a brief
outline of the subject can be found in the *Society for the Study of Labour History's
Bulletin*. Mary Allen's work is basically the story of early difficulties.

Printing

Macdonald, J. R., ed, *Women in the printing trades: a sociological study*, P. S.
  King, 1904.

This was written as a result of a survey made by the Women's Industrial Council
and as with most of their publications gives good statistical data.

Retail trade

Adburgham, A., *Shops and shopping 1800–1914*, Allen & Unwin, 1964.
Benjamin, T. H., *London shops and shopping*, Herbert Joseph, 1934.
Black, Clementina, *Sweated industry and the minimum wage*, Duckworth, 1907.
Hallsworth, Sir Joseph, and Davies, R. J. *The working life of shop assistants: a
  study of conditions of labour in the distributive trades*, Manchester, National
  Labour Press, 1910.
Hoffman, P. C., *They also serve: the story of the shop worker*, Porcupine Press,
  1950.
Jefferys, J. B., *Retail trading in Britain, 1850–1950*, Cambridge University Press,
  1954.
Paine, W., *Shop slavery and emancipation: a revolutionary appeal to the educated
  young men of the middle class*, P. S. King, 1912.
Sutherst, T., *Death and disease behind the counter*, Kegan Paul, 1884.

The three major histories of the retail trade, by Adburgham, Benjamin and Jefferys,
all contain information relating to the conditions of employment for shop assistants
although each concentrates on a different aspect of the retail trade. Lee Holcombe
in a chapter in her book on the employment for middle-class women, (listed under
general heading above) gives the reasons for the predominance of female shop
assistants and also gives some indication of the poor conditions in which many of
these women worked, although this information can also be found in other works.
Sutherst's is one of the earliest works to specifically mention women.

Tailoring

Black, Clementina, 'London tailoresses', *Economic Journal*, 14, December 1904,
  pp 555–67.
Meyer, Mrs C., and Black, Clementina, *Makers of our clothes: a case for Trade
  Boards*, Duckworth, 1909.

Teaching

Fitch, M. G., 'The history of the training of teachers for secondary schools in England, 1836–1930', unpublished MA thesis, London, 1931.

Glenday, N., and Price, M., *Reluctant revolutionaries: a century of head mistresses 1874–1974.* Pitman, 1974.

Gosden, P. H. J. H., *The evolution of a profession: a study of the contribution of teachers' associations to the development of school-teaching as a professional occupation*, Oxford, Blackwell, 1972.

Milburn, J., 'The secondary schoolmistress: a study of her professional views 1895–1914', unpublished PhD thesis, London, 1969.

Pederson, J., 'School mistresses and headmistresses: elites and education in the nineteenth century', *Journal of British Studies*, 15, 1, November 1975, pp 135–62.

Tropp, A., *The school teachers: the growth of the teaching profession in England and Wales from 1800 to the present day*, Heinemann, 1957.

Williams, A. R., 'Teacher training: a Victorian ideal', *History of Education Society Bulletin*, 7, 1971, pp 19–23.

Although Tropp's work does not differentiate between men and women it is an excellent source of information because like the chapter in Lee Holcombe's book (listed under General heading above) it uses government sources extensively. Further information can be found in the general histories of women's education and particularly in Glenday and Price's work on the Head Mistresses' Association. Despite the word 'elite' in the title of Pederson's article, he does deal with the non-elite in his useful article. Gosden's work describes the struggle for equal pay and conditions while Williams describes the differences in teacher training for men and women. The two theses (by Fitch and Milburn) describe the training of secondary school teachers.

Trade Unions

Boone, Gladys, *The women's trade leagues in Great Britain and the United States of America*, New York, Columbia University Press, 1942.

Dilke, Lady Emilia F. S., *Trade unions for women*, Women's Trade Union League, 1893.

Drake, Barbara, *Women in trade unions*, Allen & Unwin, 1920.

Hamilton, Mary A., *Women at work*, Routledge, 1941.

Humphreys, Betty V., *Clerical unions in the Civil Service*, Oxford, Blackwell, 1958.

Jacoby, R., 'Feminism and class consciousness in the British and American women's trade union leagues, 1890–1925,' in B. A. Carroll, ed, *Liberating women's history: theoretical and critical essays.* University of Illinois Press, 1976, pp 137–60.

Lewenhak, Sheila, *Women and trade unions: an outline history of women in the British trade union movement*, Benn, 1977.

Olcott, T., 'Dead centre: the women's trade union movement in London', *London Journal*, 2, 1976, pp 30–50.

Soldon, Norbert C., *Women in British trade unions, 1874–1976*, Dublin, Gill & Macmillan, 1978.

Webb, B. and S., *The history of trade unionism*, Longmans Green, 1894.

Although the Webbs' book contains some background information relating to women in trade unions the best sources are Emilia Dilke's book, which gives the story of the early days of women's trade unions, and Barbara Drake's, which includes information relating to the First World War. Lewenhak's book gives an excellent review of the role of women in trade unions from the beginning and includes a useful bibliography. The other items contain a limited amount of information.

Waitresses

Drake, Barbara, *The tea-shop girl*, Women's Industrial Council, 1913.

Barbara Drake's pamphlet is the usual thoroughly researched document one associates with the Council and is the reprint of an article in *Women's Industrial News*.

FIRST WORLD WAR

This section indicates the type of available published material relating to women's role in the First World War. Unfortunately, however, much is in the form of contemporary accounts and personal reminiscences, and so is often superficial. Until Arthur Marwick's recent book, which is well-illustrated and covers all aspects of women's role in the First World War, the only retrospective account was by David Mitchell.

Bagnold, Enid A., *Diary without dates*, Heinemann, 1918; Virago, 1978.

Beauchamp, Pat W., *FANY goes to war*, Murray, 1919.

Bowser, Thekla, *The story of British VAD work in the Great War*, Melrose, 1917.

Dearmer, Jessie M., *Letters from a field hospital ... with a memoir of the author by Stephen Gwynn*, Macmillan, 1915.

Dent, Olive, *A VAD in France*, Grant Richards, 1917.

Fitzroy, Y., *With the Scottish nurses in Roumania*, Murray, 1918.

George, Gertrude A., *Eight months with the Women's Royal Air Force*, Heath Cranton, 1921.

Hamilton, Lady Peggy, *Three years of the duration: the memoirs of a munition worker, 1914–18*, Peter Owen, 1978.

Hutton, Lady Isabel, *Memories of a doctor in war and peace*, Heinemann, 1960.

Hutton, Lady Isabel, *With a women's unit in Serbia, Salonika and Sebastopol*, Williams & Norgate, 1928.
Lawrence, M., *Shadow of swords: a biography of Elsie Inglis*, Michael Joseph, 1971.
Luard, K. E., *Unknown warriors: extracts from the letters of K. E. L., nursing sister in France 1914–18*, Chatto & Windus, 1930.
MacLaren, Barbara, *Women of the war*, Hodder & Stoughton, 1917.
Martin-Nicholson, Sister, *My experiences on three fronts*, Allen & Unwin, 1916.
Marwick, Arthur, *Women at war, 1914–18*, Croom Helm for the Imperial War Museum, 1977.
Matthews, Caroline, *Experiences of a woman doctor in Serbia*, Mills & Boon, 1916.
Mitchell, David, *Women on the warpath*, Jonathan Cape, 1966.
Murray, Flora, *Women as army surgeons: the history of the Women's Hospital Corps in Paris, Wimereux and Endell Street, September 1914–October 1919*, Hodder & Stoughton, 1920.
Newberry, J. V., 'Anti-war suffragists', *History*, 62, October 1977, pp 411–25.
Onions, Maude, *A woman at war: being experiences of an Army signaller in France 1917–1919*, C. W. Daniel, 1929.
Stobart, Mrs St C., *The flaming sword in Serbia and elsewhere*, Hodder & Stoughton, 1916.
Stone, Gilbert, ed, *Women war workers: accounts contributed by representative workers*, Harrap, 1917.
Thurstan, Violetta, *The hounds of war unleashed*, St Ives, Cornwall, United Writers, 1978.
T'serclaes, Baroness de, and Chisholm, Mhairi, *The cellar-house of Pervyse*, A. & C. Black, 1916.
Usborne, H. M., *Women's work in war time: a handbook of employments*, Werner Laurie, 1918.
Ward, Irene, *FANY Invicta*, Hutchinson, 1955.
See also Diaries, First World War above.

THE LAW RELATING TO WOMEN

General

Bushe, S., *The legal position of women in England and Ireland*, Dublin, Chambers, 1878.
Chapman, A. B. W. and M. W., *The status of women under the English law*, Routledge, 1909.
Cleveland, A. R., *Women under English law: from the landing of the Saxons to the present time*, Hurst & Blackett, 1896.

Graveson, R. H., and Crane, F. R., *A century of family law, 1857–1957*. Sweet & Maxwell, 1957.

Ostrogorski, M., *Rights of women, a study in history and legislation*, Sonnenschein, 1893.

Reiss, Erna, *The rights and duties of Englishwomen: a study in law and public opinion*, Manchester, Sherratt & Hughes, 1934.

Stopes, C. C., *British freewomen, their historical privilege*, Sonnenschein, 1894.

Thicknesse, Ralph, *The rights and wrongs of women: a digest with practical illustrations and notes on the law in France*, Woman Citizen Publishing Society, 1909.

Changes in the law during the period 1870–1928 were many and varied. However, the major changes were in relation to marriage and divorce. Several of the general works devote large sections to these topics, Thicknesse's work, designed as a handbook for women and to illustrate the major differences in the law for men and women, is an example. The Chapmans' book is a general review of women's position in law from 1066 to 1909 but is particularly useful for a chronological table of the changes in law affecting women. Cleveland's book covers the position of women in English law from 'The landing of the Saxons', is more detailed than the Chapmans' book but holds the view that women cannot be fully equal with men under the law. Other general reviews are those by Bushe, which has a bias towards Irish law, the paper reprinted from the *Women's Herald* of 1892 is only a brief outline, and Stopes's *British freewomen* is chiefly an historical account. Ostrogorski's work on the rights of women has been translated from the French but is useful as a comparative study. The best book is *The rights and duties of Englishwomen* by Erna Reiss. This excellent work is an investigation into historical (from 1833) and current legislation affecting the rights and duties of women.

Criminal

Reiss, Erna, *The rights and duties of Englishwomen*, pp 162–86.

Wolstenholme-Elmy, G. C. *The criminal code in its relation to women*, Manchester, 1880.

Reiss gives an historical review of the position of women with regard to criminal law for the period 1833–1934 with frequent references to the relevant Acts.

Employment

Brownlow, Jane M. E., *Women and factory legislation*, Congleton, Women's Emancipation Union, 1896.

Harvey, E. C., *Labour laws for women and children in the United Kingdom*, Women's Industrial Council, 1909.

Labour laws for women, their reason and their result, Independent Labour Party, 1900.

Reiss, Erna, *The rights and duties of Englishwomen*, pp 162–86.

Report of the British Association for the Advancement of Science, 1901, John Murray, 1901, pp 399–402; 1902, John Murray, 1902, pp 286–313; 1903, John Murray, 1903, pp 315–64.

Swanwick, H. M., *Some points of English law affecting working women as wives and mothers*, Women's Co-operative Guild, 1914.

Tuckwell, Gertrude M., and Smith, Constance, *The worker's handbook*, Duckworth, 1908.

Vynne, Nora, and Blackburn, Helen, *Women under the Factory Act*, Williams Norgate, 1903.

Webb, Beatrice, *The case for the Factory Acts*, 2nd edn, Grant Richards, 1902.

Webb, Beatrice, *Women and the Factory Acts*, Fabian Society, 1896.

The best general review of the topic is again to be found in Reiss's work which covers all aspects of the law in relation to women's employment. For the period up to 1907 *The worker's handbook* includes the statutory regulations for individual trades. Of the others published in the 1900s, Beatrice Webb's are probably the most useful. The Reports of the committee appointed by the British Association are an extremely valuable source of information on the economic effect of legislation on women's employment. The 1901 Report of the committee outlines its scheme of investigation; the second, 1902, covers individual regions and their peculiar professions with detailed reports; and the final Report is an extremely valuable and authoritative source of information, particularly as it gives comparisons with foreign countries.

Family life

Hoggan, F. G., *The position of the mother in the family in its legal and scientific respects*, Manchester, A. Ireland, 1884.

Reiss, Erna, *The rights and duties of Englishwomen*, pp 93–123.

Marriage and divorce

Jenks, E., *Husband and wife in the law*, Dent, 1909.

Lush, Sir Charles M., *The law of husband and wife*, 3rd edn. by W. H. Griffith, Stevens, 1910.

McGregor, O. R., *Divorce in England: a centenary study*, Heinemann, 1957.

Matthews, Joseph A., *Manual of the law relating to married women*, Sweet & Maxwell, 1892.

Reiss, Erna, *The rights and duties of Englishwomen*, pp 45–92.

Reiss gives a short but thorough history of changes in the law relating to women and is the only book which spans the years 1870–1928. Matthews' *Manual of the law relating to married women* is a standard text and McGregor's work on divorce is most valuable and includes a study of the Victorian family.

Married women's property

Barrett-Lennard, T., *To married women and women about to be married.* Sampson, Low, Marston, 1882.

Graveson, R. A., and Crane, F. R., *A century of family law, 1857–1957*, Sweet & Maxwell, 1957.

Holcombe, L., 'Victorian wives and property, reform of the Married Women's Property law, 1875–1882', in Vicinus, M. ed, *A widening sphere*, Indiana University Press, 1977.

Redman, J. H., *A concise view of the law of husband and wife as modified by the Married Women's Property Acts*, Reeves & Turner, 1883.

Reiss, Erna, *The rights and duties of Englishwomen*, pp 124–46.

Reiss covers the subject well but there is as yet no major work on the effects of the Married Women's Property Acts as Barrett-Lennard's work is basically a guide for women on the workings of the 1882 Act.

MORAL AND SOCIAL ISSUES

Women were involved in many of the moral problems of the period and often played a major role in reform movements.

Rover, C., *Love, morals and the feminists*, Routledge, 1970.

Constance Rover's excellent work on the feminists gives a good general outline of the position of the feminist movement as a whole with regard to moral issues, and shows its viewpoint in the debate on birth control.

Abortion

Knight, Patricia, 'Women and abortion in Victorian and Edwardian England', *History Workshop*, 4, Autumn 1977, pp 57–68.

McLaren, Angus, 'Women's work and the regulation of family size: the question of abortion in nineteenth century England', *History Workshop*, 4, Autumn 1977, pp 70–8.

McLaren, Angus, 'Abortion in England 1900–1914', *Victorian Studies*, 20, 4, Summer 1977, pp 379–400.

Because abortion was illegal, it is a difficult subject. However Patricia Knight and Angus McLaren's articles in *History Workshop* show that women used abortion as a method of contraception. Knight's article draws mainly on the *British Medical Journal* during the 1890's and 1900's, whereas McLaren draws parallels between working women and family size, and the likelihood of working women using abortion as a method of birth control. McLaren's article in *Victorian Studies* reviews the drugs used and the ways in which women obtained illegal abortions.

Birth control

Arnstein, W. L., *The Bradlaugh case*, Oxford University Press, 1965.

Banks, Joseph A., *Prosperity and parenthood: a study of family planning among the Victorian middle classes*, Routledge, 1954.

Banks, J. A. and O., *Feminism and family planning in Victorian England*, Liverpool University Press, 1964.

Davies, Margaret Llewelyn, *Maternity letters from working women, collected by the Women's Co-operative Guild*, Bell, 1915; Virago, 1978.

Drysdale, Charles Vickery, *Freewomen and the birth rate*, Fifield, 1911.

Drysdale, Charles Vickery, *The small family system: is it injurious or immoral?* Fifield, 1913.

Fryer, P., *The birth controllers*, Secker & Warburg, 1965.

Glass, D. P., *Population: policies and movements in Europe*, Oxford, Clarendon Press, 1940.

How-Martyn, Edith, and Breed, Mary, *The Birth Control Movement in England*, John Bale, 1930.

Knowlton, Charles, *Fruits of Philosophy: an essay on the population question*, Freethought Publishing Co, 1877.

McLaren, Angus, *Birth control in nineteenth-century England*, Croom Helm, 1978.

Stocks, M., *Family limitation and women's organizations*, National Union of Societies for Equal Citizenship, 1925.

Stopes, M., *Early days of birth control*, Pitman, 1922.

Birth Control News, 1922–46.

The Bradlaugh case in 1877 over the publication of Knowlton's *Fruits of Philosophy* led to the formation of the Malthusian League. The story of the trial and the formation of the League are told in Fryers's *The birth controllers*; the significance of these events has been analysed in Banks' work *Prosperity and Parenthood* and in Glass's work on population movements in Europe. The story of the trial has also been dealt with in a separate work by Arnstein. The birth control movement was not a feminist movement and the links between the two were slight; Banks analyses the two movements, their developments and differences. Edith How-Martyn, one of the few suffrage campaigners interested in birth control, together with Miss Breed wrote a history of the movement. The published works taken as a whole cover the subject thoroughly.

Contagious Diseases

Butler, J. E., *Personal reminiscences of a great crusade*, Marshall, 1896.

Butler, J. E., *Simple words for simple folk, about the repeal of the Contagious Diseases Acts – Women*, Bristol, J. W. Arrowsmith, 1886.

Butler, J. E., *Some thoughts on the present aspect of the crusade against the state regulation of vice*, Liverpool, T. Brakell, 1874.

Hammond, J. L., and B., *James Stansfeld, a Victorian champion of sex equality*, Longmans, 1932.

Petrie, Glen, *A singular iniquity: the campaigns of Josephine Butler*, Macmillan, 1971.

Scott, B., *State iniquity: its rise, extension and overthrow*, Kegan Paul, 1890.

Walkowitz, J. R. and D. J., 'We are not beasts of the field: Prostitution and the poor in Plymouth and Southampton under the Contagious Diseases Acts.' in M. S. Hartman and L. Banner, eds, *Clio's consciousness raised: new perspectives on the history of women*, New York, Harper & Row, Torch Books, 1974.

Wilson, Henry J., *Copy of a rough record of events and incidents connected with the repeal of the Contagious Diseases Acts, 1864–6–9 in the United Kingdom, and of the movement against state regulation of vice in India and the Colonies 1858–1906*, private circulation, 1907.

Of the works published on the Repeal of the Contagious Diseases Acts the Hammonds' biography of James Stansfeld is the best record of the campaign, while those by Henry J. Wilson and Josephine Butler are personal accounts. Scott's work contains a useful bibliography of the literature of the movement, while the Walkowitz essay in Hartman and Banner's *Clio's consciousness raised* concentrates on the working of the Acts in two naval ports. Reference should also be made to the sections below on prostitution and sexuality as there is some overlap.

Prostitution

Acton, William, *Prostitution considered in its moral, social and sanitary aspects, in London and other large cities: with proposals for the mitigation and prevention of its attendant evils*, John Churchill, 1857.

Blackwell, Elizabeth, *Essays in medical sociology*, 2 vols, Bell, 1902.

Bristow, E. J., *Vice and vigilance: purity movements in Britain since 1700*, Dublin, Gill & Macmillan, 1977.

Chesney, Kellow, *The Victorian underworld*, Temple Smith, 1970; Penguin, 1972, pp 306–64.

Coote, William A., *A romance of philanthropy: being a record of some of the principal incidents connected with the exceptionally successful thirty years' work of the National Vigilance Association*, National Vigilance Association, 1916.

Creighton, Louise, *The social disease and how to fight it: a rejoinder*, Longmans, 1914.

Downward paths: an enquiry into the causes which contribute to the making of the prostitute, Bell, 1916.

Henriques, Fernando, *Prostitution and society*, vol 2, Europe and the New World, MacGibbon & Kee, 1963.

Logan, William, *The great social evil: its causes, extent, results and remedies*, Hodder & Stoughton, 1871.

Martindale, L., *Under the surface*, 6th edn, Southern Pub., 1920.

Mayhew, Henry (with John Binny and B. Hemyng), *London labour and the London poor*, London, 1862, vol IV.

Pankhurst, Christabel, *The great scourge and how to end it* [venereal disease], E. Pankhurst, 1913.

Pearsall, Ronald, *The worm in the bud: the world of Victorian sexuality*, Weidenfeld & Nicolson, 1969; Penguin, 1971, pp 245–313.

Scott, G. R., *A history of prostitution from antiquity to the present day*, Werner Laurie, 1936.

Sigsworth, G. M., and Wyke, T. J., 'A study of Victorian prostitution and venereal disease', in M. Vicinus, ed, *Suffer and be still*, Indiana University Press, 1972, pp 77–99.

Pall Mall Gazette, 6, 7, 8 and 10 July 1885.

Prostitution has been to a large extent neglected in studies of Victorian and Edwardian England and reliable contemporary accounts such as Acton's substantial work and Bracebridge Hemyng's chapter in Mayhew's *London labour and the London poor* relate to the pre-1870 period. These accounts do, however, provide the background to the Contagious Diseases Acts and early twentieth-century works such as those by Martindale, Royden and Creighton cannot compare. Of the secondary sources, Constance Rover deals briefly with the subject, as do Sigsworth and Wyke, while Henriques deals superficially with Victorian prostitution and the white slave trade. Chesney's work on the Victorian underworld has a chapter on prostitution and Pearsall's chapter on prostitution deals only with the famous 'personalities' involved in the profession.

Sexuality

Cominus, P. T., 'Late Victorian sexual respectability and the social system', *International Review of Social History*, VIII, 1963, pp 18–48, 216–250.

Ellis, Havelock, *Studies in the pyschology of sex*, University Press, 1897, 8 vols.

Hall, Ruth, *Dear Dr Stopes: sex in the 1920s*, Deutsch, 1978.

Harrison, Brian, 'Underneath the Victorians', *Victorian Studies*, X, 1967, March, pp 239–62.

Marcus, Steven, *The other Victorians*, Weidenfeld & Nicolson, 1967.

Pearsall, R., *Worm in the bud: the world of Victorian sexuality*, Weidenfeld & Nicolson, 1969; Penguin, 1971.

Stopes, Marie, *Birth control today: a practical handbook*, J. Bale, 1934.

Stopes, Marie, *Contraception (birth control): its theory, history and practice*, J. Bale, 1923.

Stopes, Marie, *Married love*, Fifield, 1918.

In common with prostitution this subject has been largely ignored by histories of the era and Brian Harrison in his excellent review essay on Marcus' work, *The other Victorians*, reviews the literature available, discusses the lack of research on Victorian sexuality and the possibilities for further research. Marcus' basically scholarly work on three nineteenth-century writers on sex, gives an insight into Victorian sexual attitudes from a new standpoint. Pearsall's book treats the subject somewhat sensationally, and the early twentieth-century works show a change from the Victorian attitude and lay the foundations for the more open approach in the post-First World War era.

Temperance

Burns, D., *Temperance history*, vol 2, 1862–90, National Temperance Publication Depot, 1891.

Burns, D., *Temperance in the Victorian Age: Sixty years of temperance, toil and triumph, from 1887 to the great Diamond Jubilee of Queen Victoria's reign*, Ideal Publishing Co, 1898.

Harrison, B., *Drink and the Victorians: the temperance question in England, 1815–1872*, Faber, 1971.

Hyslop, A., 'Temperance, Christianity and feminism', *Historical Studies*, 17, April 1976, pp 27–49.

Longmate, Norman, *The waterdrinkers: a history of temperance*, Hamish Hamilton, 1968.

The National British Women's Temperance Association, its origin and progress, Christie Malcolm, 1926.

Women's work in temperance, National Temperance League, 1868.

Hyslop's article is the only retrospective work dealing specifically with the temperance movement; of the more general works, Brian Harrison's deals with the 1815–72 period and Norman Longmate says little of the part played by women.

Vagrancy

Higgs, Mary, *Glimpses into the Abyss*, P. S. King, 1906.

Higgs, Mary, *Three nights in women's lodging houses*, Oldham, private circulation, 1905.

Mrs Higgs disguised herself in order to obtain first-hand information of women's lives as vagrants and of common lodging-houses.

ORGANIZATIONS

Bussey, Gertrude, and Tims, Margaret, *Women's International League for Peace and Freedom, 1915–1965: a record of fifty years' work*, Allen & Unwin, 1965.

Duguid, J., *The blue triangle*, [YWCA] Hodder & Stoughton, 1955.

L'Esperance, J., 'The work of the Ladies' National Association for the Repeal of the Contagious Diseases Acts', Society for the Study of Labour History, *Bulletin* 26, Spring 1973.

Gaffin, J., 'Evolution of the Women's Cooperative Guild' in Lucy Middleton, ed,

Women in the Labour movement: the British experience, Croom Helm, 1977.

Goodenough, Simon, *Jam and Jerusalem*, (Women's Institute) Collins, 1977.

Grant, I., *National Council of Women of Great Britain: the first sixty years, 1895–1955*, NCWGB, 1956.

Harrison, B., 'For church, Queen and family: the Girls' Friendly Society, 1874–1920', *Past and Present*, 16, November 1973, pp 107–38.

Hawksley, Cordelia J., *GFS, What does it mean?* Hatchards, 1882.

Heath-Stubbs, M., *Friendship's highway: being the history of the Girls' Friendly Society 1875–1925*, GFS, 1926.

A history of the British Federation of University Women, 1907–1957, BFUW, 1957.

Jenkins, Inez, *The history of the Women's Institute movement in England and Wales*, NFWI, 1953.

McLaren, E. S., *A history of the Scottish Women's Hospitals*, Hodder & Stoughton, 1919.

Money, Agnes L., ed, *History of the Girls' Friendly Society*, Gardner, 1897.

The National British Women's Temperance Association, its origin and progress, NBWTA, 1926.

Newsome, S., *The Women's Freedom League, 1907–1957*, WFL, 1960.

Over eighty years: historical sketches of the YWCA of Great Britain, YWCA, 1953.

Palmer, Mrs T. F., *Mothers' Union work: a vocation*, H. R. Allenson, 1910.

Parker, O., *For the family's sake: a history of the Mothers' Union, 1876–1976*, Folkstone, Bailey & Swinfen, 1976.

Rosen, Andrew, *Rise up women!* (Women's Social and Political Union), Routledge, 1974.

Scott, B., *The story of the Women's Institute movement in England and Wales*, Kingham, Village Press, 1925.

Stott, Mary, *Organization woman: the story of the National Union of Townswomen's Guilds*, Heinemann, 1978.

Strachey, R., *Women's suffrage and women's service* (London and National Suffrage Society), Fawcett Society, 1927.

Webb, Catherine, *The women with the basket: the history of the Women's Cooperative Guild, 1883–1927*, Manchester, Cooperative Wholesale Society, 1927.

'What has already been done?' *Women's Industrial News* (Women's Industrial Council), March 1904, pp 413–20.

The Women's Printing Society 1876–1913, WPS, 1913.

SUFFRACE

This section has been divided into three sub-sections, first, accounts of the campaign for women's suffrage published before 1918, secondly, histories of the campaign, and thirdly, anti-suffrage works. Biographies and reminiscences of the suffrage leaders which have been listed above in the biographical section are not repeated but works by some of the minor figures have been included where appropriate.

Contemporary accounts

Billington-Greig, Teresa, *The militant suffrage movement: emancipation in a hurry*, Palmer, 1911.

Blackburn, Helen, *Women's suffrage: a record of the women's suffrage movement in the British Isles with biographical sketches of Miss Becker*, Williams & Norgate, 1902.

Fawcett, M. G., *Women's suffrage: a short history of a great movement*, T. C. & E. C. Jack, 1911.

Lytton, Lady Constance, *Prisons and prisoners: some personal experiences*, Heinemann, 1914; Wakefield, EP Publishing, 1976.

Mason, Bertha, *The story of the women's suffrage movement*, Sherratt & Hughes, 1912.

Nevinson, Margaret W., *Five years' struggle for freedom: a history of the suffrage movement from 1908 to 1912*, Women's Freedom League, 1912.

Pankhurst, E. S., *The suffragette*, New York, Sturgis & Walton, 1911.

Pankhurst, E. S., *The suffragette movement*, Longmans, 1931; Virago, 1977.

Pethick-Lawrence, F. W., *Women's fight for the vote*, Women's Press, 1910.

Stanton, E. C. and others, eds, *History of woman suffrage*, New York, Fowler & Wells, 1881–1922, 6 vols.

Historical accounts

Fulford, Roger, *Votes for women: the story of a struggle*, Faber, 1957; White Lion, 1976.

Liddington, Jill, and Norris, Jill, *One hand tied behind us: the rise of the women's suffrage movement*, Virago, 1978.

Mackenzie, M. *Shoulder to shoulder: a documentary*, Penguin, 1975.

Morgan, David, *Suffragists and Liberals: the politics of woman suffrage in England*, Oxford, Blackwell, 1975.

Newsome, S., *The Women's Freedom League 1907–1957*, Women's Freedom League, 1960.

Pugh, M. D., 'Politics and the women's vote', *History*, 69, October 1974, pp 358–74.

Raeburn, Antonia, *The militant suffragettes*, Michael Joseph, 1973.

Raeburn, Antonia, *The suffragette view*, Newton Abbot, David & Charles, 1976.

Rosen, Andrew, *Rise up women!*, Routledge, 1975.

Rover, Constance, *Women's suffrage and party politics, 1866–1914*, Routledge, 1967.

Strachey, Ray, *'The cause': a short history of the woman's movement in Great Britain*, Bell, 1928; Virago, 1978.

Until recently histories of the suffrage movement concentrated on suffragettes rather than on the suffragist campaign, but Morgan's work has helped to redress the balance. Recent interest in the women's movement and in particular the suffrage movement has resulted in the publication of such works as Mackenzie's script of the television series of the same name and Raeburn's book of photographs which supplements her earlier book.

Anti-suffrage movement

Allen, J. M., *Women's suffrage, wrong in principle and practice*, Remington, 1891.
Dicey, A. V., *Letters to a friend on votes for women*, John Murray, 1909.
Harrison, Brian, *Separate spheres: the opposition to women's suffrage in Britain*, Croom Helm, 1978.
Hart, Heber, *Woman suffrage: a national danger*, P. S. King, 1912.
Lynn, Elizabeth Linton, *The girl of the period and other social essays*, Bentley, 1883.
Wright, Sir Almroth, *The unexpurgated case against woman suffrage*, Constable, 1913.
Saturday Review, 1855–1923.

Many other publications, particularly pamphlets, give the anti-suffrage view but the above are a representative selection. Until Brian Harrison's book was published, the anti-suffrage movement had been largely ignored.

PART 3

NON-BOOK MATERIAL

PART 3   CONTENTS

INTRODUCTION

The term non-book has been taken to cover newspaper cuttings and unpublished sources with the exception of archival manuscript material. Artefacts, such as banners and medals, films, oral history tapes and photographs are therefore included here. As with published sources the aim is to give an indication of the scope and type of material available and to indicate the main collections or sources.

The main difficulty in locating non-book material is the lack of bibliographical data. This was particularly true of film material which proved difficult to trace, and indeed little early film material has survived. Each type of material posed its particular problems. Although as many collections of archival and printed material were checked as possible, the locating of their non-book material is not straightforward. The newspaper-cuttings collections described were located in the main through personal visits to Collections. Oral history tapes are a valuable source and by far the best-documented of all non-book material. There is an annual review in the journal *Oral History*.

With regard to artefacts, no attempt has been made to provide more than a brief guide to the type and location of material available.

ARTEFACTS

During the course of the research for this project various collections of miscellanea have been discovered. The custodians of these materials were genuinely eager to display any items of relevance and all were keen for their existence to be more widely known and used. It is for this reason, as well as the fact that this material provides a useful visual record of events, particularly for schoolchildren who appreciate being able to view the toffee hammers actually used to smash windows by suffragettes, for instance, that this short section has been included.

As the material is so diverse no attempt has been made to classify artefacts. The holding libraries and institutions are listed alphabetically with a brief summary of the type of material held.

FAWCETT LIBRARY

The Fawcett Library has a substantial amount of miscellanea, including banners of the suffrage organizations, arm-bands worn by suffrage workers, portraits of leading members of various feminist movements, medals and other material. All were transferred with the archives and book collection to the City of London Polytechnic.

IMPERIAL WAR MUSEUM

The Imperial War Museum's Department of Exhibits and Firearms holds a comprehensive collection of uniforms worn by women in the services and voluntary organizations during the First World War.

LONDON MUSEUM

The London Museum has various articles connected with the militant movement, including such items as a prison knife, fork/spoon, cup and saucer, badges, medals awarded to suffragettes for imprisonment and hunger-striking, and chains used for tying themselves to railings. The library also has copies of some of the posters issued by the suffragettes in support of their campaign; banners about 8 ft × 7 ft embroidered in silks; sashes worn by the suffragettes; and samplers sewn by them in prison. There is also a 'Suffragette Roll of Honour' which lists the names of suffragettes who went to prison. It is inscribed, and bound in green leather.

MANCHESTER CENTRAL LIBRARY

When archive material relating to the societies like the Manchester Women's Suffrage Society was donated, the Library also received the banners used on marches and demonstrations by these organizations. These banners are embroidered in silks and are usually about 8–9 ft long, and are in remarkably good condition.

WOMEN'S ROYAL ARMY CORPS MUSEUM

The Museum at Guildford contains various items of interest relating to the early days of the women's armed services. These include examples of the uniforms worn by members of the Women's Army Auxiliary Corps and the changes in the uniforms made over the years. Medals awarded to members of the WAAC during the First World War are also on display. The Museum has a considerable amount of silver including various cups awarded for sports events that were organized within the WAAC during the First World War.

FILMS

Although news films were first made in the late nineteenth century much of this early material has perished because it was on nitrate film. Despite the establishment by the BBC in 1975 of an advisory committee on problem archive material under the chairmanship of Asa Briggs, there is still no British national system of classifying or preserving film archives. However, the National Film Archive has collected up some original films, including news-reels, in exchange for providing copies. Although the Archive does not permit the making of duplicates, it is a valuable source of early news-reel film if access to the collection can be gained. The EMI-Pathé Library does, however, allow public access to its collection of over fifteen million metres of 35mm and 16mm news-reels for the period 1896–1972. These include material relating to women. EMI-Pathé permit copies to be taken from negatives, although this can damage the original.

Other sources which allow public access are the Central Office of Information and the Imperial War Museum.

IMPERIAL WAR MUSEUM

The films listed below, with their reference numbers, contain material relating to women.

Domestic front

Factory and munition work

Nursing

Women's services

THE SOUTH ASIAN ARCHIVE

In addition to its archive material contains some film material showing the way of life in India, much of it relating to English women in India, in particular, films taken by Sir Eric Studd during the years 1917–19, which consist of forty-six reels, some of social events. The film of E. M. Hunter covers home and country life in India for the period 1928–32 and Mrs Montgomery's reels, made by her husband while Private Secretary to the Governor of Bihar and Orissa, include tiger shoots and Residency life. 'Films from the Raj' put together by the National Film Archive is a conglomerate film made from the collection. The originals are now held by the National Film Archive with copies in the South Asian Archive.

This material gives some indication of the type of information that must still be in private hands and would prove invaluable if only it could be located. A BBC television series in 1978 devoted to early home movies ('Caught in time', presented by James Cameron) contained valuable material lent by members of the public, much still in extremely good condition.

ILLUSTRATIONS

This material provides an insight, literally, into everyday activities, as well as portraying more important events. Illustrative material has in this context been taken to include photographs, portraits and other pictorial representations including cartoons of women and their role in society. Cartoons have been included for their sociological comment, this applies particularly to the *Punch* cartoons of the nineteenth century.

A useful guide to sources is Hilary Evans *The Picture researcher's handbook: an international guide to picture sources – and how to use them* (Newton Abbot, David & Charles, 1975). It is, however, biased towards commercial organizations and, where there is a commercial alternative, excludes museums and art galleries. The entries are arranged in broad subject groups with indexes for geographical names, subjects and a list of repositories. Each entry gives the name and address of the organization, scope and availability of the material, the procedure for obtaining prints, details of fees, etc. This is the best guide available, and is a useful check list for additional sources for specialized subjects.

FAWCETT LIBRARY

The Fawcett Library has a large amount of material, including portraits of the leaders of the feminist movements, a fine collection of photographs relating to various activities within the feminist movement but particularly relating to the suffrage campaign, also many cartoons.

IMPERIAL WAR MUSEUM

Excellent collection of photographs, known as the Women's Work Collection, showing women at work during the First World War. It is on the open shelves and can be consulted upon application to the Photographic Department.

The collection is contained in seven volumes:

Vol. 1: FANY; carpenters; drivers; forage; forestry. (This volume contains photographs of Baroness T'serclaes and Miss Mhairi Chisholm at Pervyse.) *See* Oral history, 1914–18 Archive, War front below.

Vol. 2: Girl Guides; Land Army; nurses.

Vol. 3: Nurses; WAAC; WRAF.

Vol. 4: Mostly WRNS; Industrial A–B Aircraft; bakery; blacksmithing; brewery.

Vol. 5: Industrial B–G Coke; cement; chemical work; glassworkers.
Vol. 6: Industrial G–M New Fuse Shop, Woolwich Arsenal.
Vol. 7: Industrial N–S Railways; shipbuilding.
Vol. 8: Industrial T–Z Vets.

London Museum

Houses the Suffragette Fellowship Collection, which has several hundred photographs covering all aspects of suffragette activities. The majority are of suffragettes and include many of the less known members of the movement as well as the more famous personalities. The Collection includes, too, photographs of processions and the resulting arrests, and of the funeral of Emily Wilding Davies, the suffragette who threw herself under the King's horse at the 1913 Derby. It has pictures of suffragette sympathizers, suffragettes in prison – including shots of Holloway prison of suffragettes exercising – and an unusual photograph showing Indian women marching in a suffragette procession.

In addition to the photographic collection the Museum has a fine collection of postcards relating to the suffragette movement.

OTHER SOURCES

The National Army Museum has over 100,000 photographs of the British army up to 1914, although very few are relevant to women.

Another source for women in the First World War is the 1914–18 Archive at Sunderland, organized by Peter Liddle. This includes copies of some Imperial War Museum photographs.

The Society of Friends library has a collection of over 100,000 illustrations some of which are valuable because they illustrate all aspects of Quaker life. The main collection is housed in 'Picture Boxes' with each individual box indexed. The boxes themselves are arranged in alphabetical order of subject content. Additional collections include the 'Picture Volumes' – three volumes indexed under personal name or place which include a great many portraits of men and women active in the Society. There are also photographs of the staff and students of schools belonging to the Society. The library also has a subject and name index to illustrations in *The Friend* 1895–1958, which gives a description of the photograph and is well cross-referenced. It would be useful for tracing illustrations of individual women. The library staff are extremely helpful.

The contemporary newspapers and magazines such as *Illustrated London News* also contain much valuable material, *Punch* magazine has long been famous for its radical comment during the nineteenth century, reflected not only in its articles but also in its political cartoons. Although not a supporter of 'women's rights' the journal often highlighted the inconsistencies in society's behaviour towards women. In *The Punch Book of Women's Rights* (Hutchinson, 1967) Constance Rover reviews *Punch's* attitude to the women's rights movement, including many of the *Punch* cartoons. Volumes 3 and 4 of Charles L. Graves's fuller work (*Mr Punch's history of modern England*, Cassell, 1921–2) on *Punch* as a source of English history are also useful.

PHOTOGRAPHIC AGENCIES

There are a number which have collections containing material relating to women. These agencies usually provide material on a loan or a copy basis; some allow individuals to search but the majority employ their own staff. The fees charged vary with the type of material, amount of staff research necessary, etc.

Probably the most famous agency is the Radio Times Hulton Picture Library, a collection of over six million items. These include photographs, prints, engravings, original paintings and drawings, covering all aspects of history, social life, events, places, technology, etc. It includes the Topical Press Library which is a photographic record of events, personalities and sport for the years 1903–36, and holds photographs of the suffrage activities up to the First World War.

The Mansell Collection is also a useful source with photographs, prints, and engravings covering matters of historical interest from pre-history to 1940.

Another well known commercial library, containing more than a million prints, is the Mary Evans Picture Library which deals predominantly with social conditions. The material is divided under broad subject headings and researchers are encouraged to consult the files personally. An article by Jill Turner in the *Library Association Record*, 78, 8 August 1976, pp 361–4, describes the collection and its background. It includes many valuable prints of women in the late nineteenth century. An illustrated history of prostitution is currently being prepared based on the collection's material, which will portray aspects of prostitutes' lives which are usually ignored, domestic scenes, for instance. Although a commercial concern, if costs are likely to be prohibitive the Picture Library does refer enquirers to public sources. With help and advice from Hilary Evans and his staff, this collection can be extremely valuable.

Other commercial sources are Barnaby's Picture Library which has a women's suffrage collection, and the Lords Gallery which among its collection of 2,000 posters includes many produced by the suffrage organizations from the 1890s onwards.

Addresses of the photographic agencies are given in Part 4.

NEWSPAPER-CUTTINGS

Several collections of newspaper-cuttings and items relating to specific aspects of women's role in society were compiled during the period 1870–1928 and have survived intact. The majority of these related to the campaign for women's suffrage and appear to have been compiled by women active within the movement. The Fawcett Library has a comprehensive collection and covers all aspects of women's way of life, including cuttings relating to individuals, of both sexes sympathetic to, and involved in, the various campaigns.

Many newspaper-cuttings collections, large and small, are to be found in archives and libraries throughout the country; they cover a variety of topics. The Labour Party archive contains a six-volume collection of press-cuttings relating to Ellen Wilkinson; the Blackburn Collection has cuttings relating to the Women's Suffrage Appeal of 1893. However, because of the number of small collections, especially those housed in local history sections of public libraries, many of them duplicated by the larger collections, only more comprehensive collections and those containing material of a more unusual nature have been described here in detail.

Some of the collections are predominantly newspaper-cuttings whilst others include a far wider range of material – letters, pamphlets, circulars, handbills and other ephemera. The newspapers and weeklies most commonly 'cut' were *The Times*, *Manchester Guardian*, *Sunday Times*, *New Statesman*, *Westminster Gazette* and *Pall Mall Gazette*. The suffrage collections – either suffragette or suffragist – contain a large percentage of material taken from the contemporary suffrage press. The Arncliffe-Sennett Collection in the British Library contains about one-third non-newspaper material – in the main letters and circulars relating to specific events reported in the press. These items are arranged in juxtaposition to the relevant cuttings and often give background information to the newspaper item. The more important collections are thus extremely valuable sources of contemporary material, particularly the suffrage collections, as they provide a day-to-day record of the campaign, which would otherwise prove difficult to obtain. As well as the material, so the emphasis of each collection varies, being generally compiled by an individual or for a particular purpose; the type and special emphasis in each collection are described below under the individual entries.

The value of the large collections lies in the wide range of material included and in the annotations frequently provided by the compiler. These notes can be of especial value in the case of photographs, as individuals are not always named. However, annotations should be treated with caution as the compilers were obviously subjective. Some collections which concentrate on an individual – like the Ellen Wilkinson material in the Labour Party Archive – provide useful potted biographies and an insight into an individual's interests and involvements. The material relating to Dame Millicent Garrett Fawcett (Fawcett Library) covers the period 1887–1929 and as it was collected by Dame Millicent herself reflects her particular concern with various aspects of the feminist movement.

The collections appear to have been under utilized, although the material in the John Rylands University Library, Manchester, was used extensively by Roger Fulford in *Votes for Women*, and that in the Arncliffe-Sennett Collection, by Andrew Rosen in *Rise up women!*

ARNCLIFFE-SENNETT COLLECTION

This is housed in the British Library (reference C121gP) and was collected by Maud Arncliffe-Sennett, the founder and president of the Northern Men's Federation for Women's Suffrage and also a member of the Women's Freedom League. The material reflects her interest in these organizations as well as her activities in the Artists' Franchise League, and in keeping up the campaign for women's suffrage during the war years. The Collection contains a wide variety of material including cartoons (often with Mrs Arncliffe-Sennett's comments), handbills, pamphlets, letters, complete issues of journals, receipts, rosettes, and newspaper-cuttings. A large amount of the material relates to the Men's League for Women's Suffrage and the Northern Men's Federation for Women's Suffrage; it also illustrates how the campaign for women's suffrage continued throughout the First World War.

The Collection consists of twenty-eight volumes plus two index volumes, for the years 1907–1918. The period covered by each volume varies: volume 26 covers Feb 1914–Dec 1915, volume 22 covers only May 1913. The index volumes are separate entities, with the exception of a complete list of portraits in volume 2, and so both should be consulted. The notes for guidance are as follows and give a further indication of the scope and range of material and also will enable researchers to familiarize themselves with the indexing methods used.

'(1) In looking up the name of any person look up also the heads (sic) meeting, letters to *The Times*. (2) For all Bills see Parliament; for Acts at work see the name of the Act, e.g. "Cat and Mouse" Act. (3) Articles are all under one head; author: paper: subject: volume: page. (4) Cartoons all under one head. (5) Letters to papers all under paper except Mrs Arncliffe-Sennett's which are under her name. (6) Meetings under the name of the society holding them, except a few which could not be so classified, which will be found under "meetings". (7) Roman figures refer to volume: arabics to pages: figures in brackets to page or extra inserts or loose paper.' Once these basic rules have been understood the index is relatively easy to use.

FAWCETT LIBRARY

The Library has by far the most comprehensive collection of newspaper-cuttings relating to women; its value lies in the breadth and depth of historical coverage and in the fact that it is an on-going collection, covering all aspects of women and their role in society, from the long-standing debate on women as clerics to the 'white slave trade'. The collection also has extensive material relating to women and literature, including items relating to biographies of women authors, book reviews, etc. A search through the collection soon reveals that it is a major source of contemporary comment and review. As well as material from the daily and weekly newspapers like the *Guardian*, *Observer*, *Times Educational* and *Literary Supplements*, which provides valuable contemporary record of the way the women's movement is reflected in the press, there are items from a wide range of women's publications and also ephemera – publicity handouts, minutes of meetings, memorial leaflets, etc. This policy has been followed for many years; in fact the same member of the library staff has collected cuttings and was herself active in the early days of the National Society for Women's Service, the forerunner of the Fawcett Society.

The collection is an extremely valuable source of biographical information for the less known members of women's organizations. The reason that the biographical section is so comprehensive is because the printed minutes of the various women's organizations have been searched and obituaries or memorials have been extracted and filed. These obituaries, etc, obviously vary greatly but on the whole they do give enough facts about an individual's interests and activities to indicate where further researches into society archives or documents should be made.

The arrangement of the collection is by UDC and the material itself is mounted on foolscap sheets and kept in envelopes. Any material unsuited for mounting, i.e., printed on both sides, is usually kept in suitably labelled envelopes. The collection as a whole is housed in deep drawers and can be consulted by readers in person.

In addition to its main collection the Fawcett Library has several useful smaller collections, including the scrap book of Mrs Millicent Garrett Fawcett which contains items of interest for the period 1875–1929. It is assumed that it was compiled by Mrs Fawcett herself. The library also has seventeen bound volumes and eight unbound volumes of newspaper-cuttings on suffrage arranged in chronological order. These have been taken from a variety of sources, including the daily press and the suffrage press.

The library also has a twenty-two volume collection on suffrage compiled by the St Joan's Political and Social Alliance covering the years 1911–52; this has items from a wide variety of newspapers including the Catholic press. Another bound volume presented by Helen Wilson, daughter of Henry J. Wilson, relates to suffrage activities around Sheffield from 1903. There are also one-volume collections relating to the 1897 Women's Suffrage Bill, compiled by the NUWSS for the period 1898–1907, including newspaper-cuttings and notices; another compiled by the LSWS and NUWSS jointly for the years 1907–9; and another compiled by the Women's Tax Resistance League for the years, 1910–12, which includes many cuttings on sales of possessions impounded for non-payment of taxes, as well as one on women members of the London School Boards, 1896–7, which contains cartoons, news items and photographs. There are two collections relating to the employment of women, three volumes relating to women's entry into the legal profession, covering the years 1912–20, 1912–29 and 1920. A bound volume of general cuttings for the period 1918–19 includes a wealth of material on various aspects of women's activities during the First World War including land work, nursing and the VAD. Another collection was made by the Birmingham Social Work Settlement, and relates to social work for the period 1908–18.

One final item worth mentioning is the three-volume collection of cuttings for the years 1910–20, 1914–16, and 1916–63, relating to women and the church.

JOHN RYLANDS UNIVERSITY LIBRARY OF MANCHESTER

The Women's Suffrage Collection, originally compiled by the National Union of Women's Suffrage Societies (later the National Union of Societies for Equal Citizenship) is now in the John Rylands Library (R56250 – library recall number) in thirty folio volumes and, although some of the bindings are a little the worse for wear, the contents are in very good condition. The press cuttings are arranged in chronological order from August 1910 and each has been carefully mounted and labelled with a note of the original source. The material includes printed articles, letters, records of meetings, etc, but unlike the Arncliffe-Sennett Collection does not contain leaflets or holographs. The earlier volumes cover all aspects of women's suffrage throughout the world but the majority of the volumes are concerned solely with the campaign for the vote for women in this country. The first volume contains cuttings relating to the Liberals' campaign for the General Election of 1910 as women's suffrage was included on their list of larger reforms to be debated by Parliament. The later volumes are a day-to-day account from the newspapers of the suffrage campaign. The daily newspapers searched include *The Times*, *Manchester Guardian*, *Daily Express*, *Daily Mail*, *Daily News*, *Morning Post*, *Daily Chronicle* and *Daily Herald*; the weeklies searched include The *Observer*, *Sunday Times*, The *People*, and *New Statesman*. Various local papers were cut, as were several of the review journals in addition to the suffragist journals. The collection provides a full record of the press coverage given to the suffrage campaign from 1910 to 1914.

LABOUR PARTY ARCHIVE

A collection of newspaper-cuttings relating to Ellen Wilkinson is housed in the Labour Party archive at Transport House. Although a relatively small collection – six volumes and two folders – it is valuable because her sister destroyed Ellen Wilkinson's own papers. The cuttings have been taken from numerous local and national newspapers, and are arranged in roughly chronological order. The two folders contain material relating to the Jarrow March in which Ellen Wilkinson took an active part.

The cuttings cover her political and public activities and the period when she was Labour Member of Parliament for Middlesbrough (East), 1924–1931, ending just after she was elected Member for Durham (Jarrow) in 1935. It is not know who made this collection.

MANCHESTER CENTRAL LIBRARY, ARCHIVES DEPARTMENT SUFFRAGE COLLECTION

Press-cuttings relating to Lydia Becker, founder of the Manchester Society for Women's Suffrage, for the years 1871–89, a small single-volume collection which includes reports of her speeches and lectures, her articles and letters to newspapers. These have been cut from a variety of sources but it is not known who compiled this collection.

Newspaper-cuttings on suffrage and other feminist topics. Miscellaneous volumes collected by various individuals and organizations.

Vols. 1–3 were probably collected by or on behalf of Lydia Becker for the Manchester National Society for Women's Suffrage. Some of the cuttings were made by an agency. The coverage varies in subject and the type of material included. The first volume covers the period 1867–8, and includes notices of the London National Society for Women's Suffrage and of affiliated suffrage societies. It also has cuttings on the claims of women to be put on electoral registers under the provisions of the Reform Act of 1867. The second volume covers the period 1869–70, and again relates mainly to suffrage issues, although it also contains items on the Married Women's Property Act, reviews of Josephine Butler's book, *Women's Work and Women's Culture*, and some *Punch* cartoons. The third volume covers the period 1870–71 and also contains predominantly suffrage material. It relates in the main to the Manchester National Society for Women's Suffrage but has additional material on women in the medical profession, including an article from *The Courant*, 19 January 1871 – 'The question of admitting female students to the wards'.

Vol. 4 covers the period 1876–8 and may also have been collected by Lydia Becker. It contains cuttings referring to suffrage societies, and also some items on cruelty to wives.

Vol. 5, now in poor condition, contains items relating to the 'Great Demonstration of Women' held in Bradford on 22 November 1881; they are chiefly from Bradford newspapers and refer to the demonstration itself and to meetings held in other West Yorkshire towns to promote the demonstration.

Vol. 6 contains material, mainly from local newspapers, relating to a second 'Great Demonstration' held in Sheffield in February 1882.

Vol. 7 covers 1884–5, with cuttings relating to Woodall's amendment to the
    Franchise Bill. Some material is undated and the volume itself is now in very
    poor condition.
Vol. 8 The Manchester National Society for Women's Suffrage compiled this
    volume, which includes material for the years 1894–7, the majority relating to
    the suffrage movement in the north-west.
Vol. 9 This was compiled by Rhoda and Agnes Garrett, but is only twenty-four
    pages of miscellaneous cuttings from a variety of sources.
Vol. 10 This and the first three volumes are the most valuable part of the collection.
    This volume contains Mrs. Fawcett's notes and newspaper cuttings for the
    period 1889–90, with a contents index in her own hand; and a large quantity of
    printed papers which also have underlinings and comments in Mrs Fawcett's
    handwriting. The cuttings cover a wide range of topics and reflect Mrs Fawcett's
    interest in such subjects as the Custody of Infants Bill as well as suffrage.
Vol. 11 is a miscellaneous collection on a wide range of topics, not all of which
    relate to women.

ORAL HISTORY

Oral history is comparatively new and many projects have recently been initiated in order to obtain first-hand evidence of ways of life. One major project was that of Dr and Mrs Thompson of the Department of Sociology, University of Essex, who up to 1975 collected over five hundred recorded interviews of persons born between 1870 and 1917. The project was set up to investigate the way of life in Britain and was supported by the Social Science Research Council for the interviewing stage. The classification and writing up are not yet complete and no specific date for completion or publication is available.

This project is of interest since half the interviewees were women and all the interviews contain a high proportion of material of relevance to women. The questions asked relate to family life, child-rearing, women's position in the home and women's activities outside the home both political and general. The majority of those interviewed were born between 1890 and 1903 and were chosen from urban, rural and city communities, and well distributed regionally according to the 1911 census. It was thus hoped to obtain as representative a sample as possible, although the age of those interviewed necessarily precluded a true random sample. When the results are available, this project will give an important insight into the Edwardian period and may noticeably change established views of the era, particularly with regard to the 'traditional roles' of men and women in the home.

Several other projects are underway, though few are of direct relevance to women, apart from another at Essex University on 'Employment and women in London in the twentieth century; industrial change and the sexual divisions of labour' which includes questions on the pre-1928 period. Research into the standard of living in Lancashire of working-class men and women between 1880 and 1930 was undertaken by Lancaster University; it included interviews with over ninety old people. Although widely publicized in the press the report is not easily obtainable.

In addition to specific research projects, two archives are currently collecting tape-recordings: the South Asian Archive in the Centre for South Asian Studies has interviewed women who were in India; and the 1914–18 Archive at Sunderland has interviewed many veterans of the First World War including a substantial number of women. Details appear at the end of this section.

Many local libraries and archives are showing an interest in this type of material (which is still not a fully accepted method of historical research due to the personal distortions which may appear) and are recording interviews with local people.

The main source of information about material available is the journal *Oral History* which includes an annual review, 'Current work in oral history', on research in progress as well as acquisitions. On the subject of women Joanna

Bornat's article 'Women's history and oral history: an outline bibliography', *Oral History*, 5, (2) pp 124–35 is useful. This essay includes references to early works which used interviewing techniques for social investigation, as well as listing the most important works of recent years, and concludes by describing work in progress.

Oral history interviews are being made use of by both radio and television, for example Charles Allen's *'Plain Tales from the Raj'*, which made extensive use of tape-recordings by British men and women formerly living and working in India. This was broadcast as a series of radio programmes in 1974 on BBC Radio 4 and has since been published in book form under the same title. A television series using extensive interviews was *'Yesterday's witness'*, produced by Stephen Peet. This included programmes on birth control in the twenties, British women medical volunteers with the Scottish Women's Hospital in Serbia during the First World War and 'Two Victorian girls', reminiscences of a novelist and a typist. *'Women at war'* was a series of six films produced by the BBC which showed the contribution made by women to the First World War effort and included interviews with women who worked on the land, in munitions works, as nurses, etc.

Listed below are the tape recordings by women held by the 1914–18 Archive at Sunderland and in the South Asian Archive. It should be borne in mind, however, that many local archives and record offices also contain material of this kind.

1914–18 ARCHIVE, SUNDERLAND

Like the Archive itself, the tape-recordings are divided into two distinct subdivisions: the war front and the domestic front. A brief note on the type of service discussed on the tapes has been included wherever possible.

Domestic front

Schoolgirls: K. Alexander*, in the Cotswolds 1914–18; Lady Ashton, East Anglia.
College Life: the Misses E. M. and M. L. Macleod; Miss Dorothy Straw, day student at Nottingham University College.
Domestic life: Mrs Davey*; Mrs Hammond, war widow; N. Liddle*; W. Liddle*, in Sunderland; Mrs Limon, in Hull, a war bride and a war widow; the Misses E. M. and M. L. Macleod; Mrs R. Morvelly, bombing and bereavement; Mrs U. K. Nimmo*, in a wealthy household; Miss Ridley, in Sunderland.
Billeting troops: Mrs Morgan Davies.
Intelligence work, naval and military: Lady Chamberlain*; Lady Champion*; Miss M. E. Jenkin; Mrs F. Munday.
Labour Party research: Dame Margaret Cole*.

*Tape-recordings made by Mr Peter Liddle.

Life in Germany: Mrs Lubinski, 1914–18.
Munition work: Mrs Ainsley*; Mrs Burnett, Gretna, 1916–17; Mrs Burton, Morecambe and Gretna, including the explosion at Gretna; Mrs Davis, Gretna; C. Dingle, making shells and nursing; M. Forster; Mrs Hubble, Gretna, including the accident and explosion; Mrs J. Robson*; Mrs E. M. Smith.
Nursing: Dowager Countess of Limerick*, VAD in the Home Counties; Miss M. Rankine, in Liverpool; Miss M. Thring, VAD in Ireland and France.
Teaching: Mrs Davey*, 1914–18; Miss S. Storr, 1914–18.
Recordings also by Mrs Brown and Mrs Douglas.

War front

FANY: Mrs Pat W. Beauchamp (author of *FANY goes to war*), 1914–17; Miss Toni Colston, 1909–16; Miss Hutchinson, 1914–18; Miss Puckle*; Miss Runciman, running a gas-mask factory in France, 1916–18.
Naval intelligence work: Miss M. Jenkin*, in UK and France; MI5 also, Mrs F. Munday.
Nursing: Mrs Baltrum, as Sister White she worked with Edith Cavell; Miss Mhairi Chisholm, with Baroness T'serclaes nursing in Belgium 1914–18; Mrs A. G. Elliott*, Australian nurse at Gallipoli; Miss Florence Farmborough (author of *Nurse at the Russian front*) on the Eastern front.
Scottish Women's Hospital: Mrs Stewart; Dr R. E. Verney.
VAD: Lady Mary Chance, in Salonika 1917–18; Lady Lenanton (*née* Carola Oman); Dowager Countess of Limerick, UK and France; Miss G. Milburn; Mrs Nimmo*, Western front; Miss Puckle*; Mrs Sarsfield Hall; Miss M. S. Thring*, in France; Mrs Wilsdon, UK and Egypt.
WAAC: Mrs Porter (also munition work); Miss Traynor.
WRNS: Lady Ashton*; Mrs A. J. Capel, 1918.

SOUTH ASIAN ARCHIVE

Memories of life in India

Mrs Kathleen B. Carter, Miss Winifred Kenny (both in the Rowding archives); Mrs C. Showers (1910)*; Mr and Mrs Tyler; Mrs Wells.
As an army officer's wife on the North West Frontier: Mrs Broad*.
As the wife of a member of the Indian Civil Service: Mrs Mullen*.
As Chief Inspector of Schools from 1908: Miss H. G. Stuart*.
As a Schools Inspector in 1922: Lady Stokes.
Experiences among the Untouchables: Miss Alice Stewart.
As a missionary and wife of a Public Works Department engineer, 1910–11: Mrs Summers.

*Tape-recordings made by Miss T. M. Thatcher.

PART 4

LIBRARIES AND RECORD OFFICES

Section 1   Major Collections
Section 2   List of Libraries and Record Offices

PART 4   CONTENTS

SECTION 1

FAWCETT LIBRARY

The Fawcett library was the library of Fawcett Society and its predecessors and as such has a unique collection of printed and manuscript material, including the papers of many of the leading figures in the women's movement. The library is open to members and operates a loan system. Further details regarding facilities can be found on page 200.

In March 1977 the Fawcett Library was transferred from its premises in Wilfred Street to the City of London Polytechnic. From that date the Polytechnic library has been responsible for the Fawcett Library. With funds provided by the government Job Creation Scheme the Polytechnic was able to appoint nine workers for a year. This enabled the stock to be sorted and rearranged. A stock check was also made and recently received unclassified books and pamphlets were catalogued. The check revealed that a large number of titles could not be traced; in some areas this accounted for as much as 25 per cent of the stock. Although all the books were classified and catalogued there still remain several thousand pamphlets and leaflets to be catalogued. Other work undertaken since the removal of the library to the City of London Polytechnic has included the sorting and indexing of the picture collection (the material has been indexed by individuals, events and subjects) and the compilation of a current index to periodicals. The newspaper-cuttings collection has been sorted and rehoused, and some attempt is being made to continue the collection although more selectively than hitherto.

Co-operation is developing between the library and the Equal Opportunities Commission, in particular the publication of *BiblioFem*. *BiblioFem* consists of the joint library catalogues of the Fawcett Library and the Equal Opportunities Commission together with a continuing bibliography of new books relating to women and equal opportunity published in the United Kingdom or catalogued by the Library of Congress. *BiblioFem* is a monthly cumulating microfilm publication and will eventually provide a complete list of the Fawcett Library's holdings readily available throughout the world.

The original Fawcett Library material is classified by the Universal Classification System (UDC) but material received since the collection was moved to the City of London Polytechnic is classified by the Dewey system. It is hoped that eventually all the original stock will be reclassified. At present the pamphlet collection and the newspaper-cutting collection are classified by UDC. The three special collections within the Fawcett Library – the Sadd Brown Collection, the Cavendish-Bentinck

Collection and the Josephine Butler Collection – are filed in separate sequences. The Library has both a name and subject catalogue, with archive material listed separately. The archive material is filed in boxes and kept in the material's original order, and it is available upon request. The material held by the Fawcett Library has been listed below under the subject headings used throughout this guide, with an additional section for papers of individuals. There are cross-references to the other Parts of the guide.

AUTOGRAPH LETTER COLLECTION

This Collection has been put together over a number of years and additions are still being made from material currently being donated to the Library. The material has been taken from a number of different sources including collections of papers relating to individuals. Whilst this makes the Collection valuable in its own right, the value of the original collection is diminished as in the majority of cases there is no indication that any material has been removed. It means that many of the letters can be quoted completely out of context.

The Autograph Letter Collection contains a large amount of material either written by, or relating to, both Mrs Josephine Butler and Mrs Fawcett taken from the archive material of their respective organizations and this should be borne in mind when consulting archives relating to their societies. The letters have been arranged in subject volumes, as listed below and each letter has a brief synopsis of its contents. Both author and addressee are indexed to give the volume and the letter number within the volume.

The arrangement of the volumes is arbitrary and the majority of the material would have been of more value in its original location, if only this were known, but in many cases the source has not been indicated.

1	Suffrage	14	Mrs Fawcett to Mrs Bidley
2	General women's movement	15	Women's Institutes
3	Emancipation of women	16	Hannah More
	(A) British Commonwealth	17	Women travellers
	(B) USA	18	Women in the arts
4	Education of women	19	Keir Hardie, the Webbs and
5	Women in medicine		Ramsay MacDonald
6	Women in the church	20	The militants
7	Literary ladies	21	Lady Constance Lytton
8	General and Personal	22	Scholars and learned ladies
9	Suffrage and women in industry	23	Alex V. Cotta's letters,
10	Dr Elizabeth Garrett Anderson		1870–1930
11	W. T. Stead's letters from prison	24	Letters from various Yorkshire
12	To Miss Louisa Hubbard		women concerned with
13	Mrs Harriet McIlquham		temperance, 1897–1921

25 Biographical notes made by Mrs
      Teresa Billington-Greig
      (arranged alphabetically)
26 Taylor Collection
27 Strachey letters

28 Becker Collection
29 Billingshurst letters
30 Tabor letters
31 Josephine Butler Collection

EDUCATION

Committee for Promoting the Higher Education of Women

Minutes 1869–71.
See also Autograph Letter Collection, above.

EMIGRATION

The library has a unique collection of emigration records, particularly relating to women. In addition to archive records of societies, the library has copies of the journals and many of the pamphlet publications of societies concerned with emigration.

British Women's Emigration Association *see* United Englishwomen's Emigration Register

Colonial Intelligence League 1910–19

Founded in 1910 under the leadership of the Hon Mrs Norman Grosvenor and Mrs John Buchan, who had worked for the South African Colonization Society who felt there was a need to help women with little capital wishing to establish small businesses in the Colonies. The aim of the League was to provide them with information. Started as the Committee of Colonial Intelligence for Educated Women, after negotiations with the Head Mistresses' Association, it was reorganized in 1911 as the Colonial Intelligence League. It soon became more than an information centre and began helping women to emigrate, chiefly to Canada. In 1919 it amalgamated with the British Women's Emigration Association and the South African Colonization Society to form the Society for the Overseas Settlement of British Women.

Annual Reports 1910–19.
Minutes: executive committee Feb 1910–June 1919; finance and settlement sub-committee Nov 1913–Dec 1919; county organization sub-committee March 1912–July 1914; literature sub-committee Nov 1913–July 1915.
Reference volume of extracts 1912–14, Canada.

Female Middle-class Emigration Society 1861–86

Founded by Miss Maria S. Rye and Miss Jane E. Lewin in 1861. In 1862 Miss Rye sailed to New Zealand with a party of emigrants sent by the Society. On her return she devoted much of her time to the emigration of children. Miss Lewin ran the Society until she retired in 1884. In that year the Colonial Emigration Society took over the affairs of the FMCES and in 1892 after no use had been made of the Society's funds since 1886 the United British Women's Emigration Association took over the remaining funds.

Annual reports 1862–85; letter books 1862–82.

Joint Council of Women's Emigration Societies 1917–19

The British Women's Emigration Association, the South African Colonization Society and the Colonial Intelligence League set up the Joint Council of Women's Emigration Societies in 1917, to coordinate their plans because the government was intending to encourage emigration, particularly of ex-servicemen and women, at the end of the First World War. This led to the formation in 1920 of the Society for the Overseas Settlement of British Women.

Minutes 1917–19.

Society for Overseas Settlement of British Women 1920–62

Founded in 1920 by an amalgamation of the British Women's Emigration Association, the South African Colonization Society and the Colonial Intelligence League. It became the Women's Department of the Oversea Settlement Committee of the former Colonial Office, now the Foreign and Commonwealth Office.

Annual Reports 1920–63
Minute Books: council 1919–37; executive committee 1920–67; finance committee 1919–64; sub-committees: 15 volumes mainly for the post-1928 period.
Documents of Title; finance files for hostels; correspondence files; legal files.

South African Colonization Society 1903–19.

When the Boer War ended in 1902 there was a rise in the number of emigrants to South Africa. In 1899 a council meeting of the United British Women's Emigration Association had recommended the establishment of a committee to deal with emigration to South Africa and in 1900 the South African Expansion Committee had been founded. In 1903 this became independent of its parent body, though they still worked in close co-operation. It amalgamated with the British

Women's Emigration Association and the Colonial Intelligence League in 1920 to form the Society for Overseas Settlement of British Women.

Annual Reports 1903–05, 1908–14.

Minutes: executive committee 1902–19; finance committee 1912–14; Rhodes Hostel committee 1908–11; shipping committee Dec 1912–Oct 1913; Cape Colony sub-committee 1901–15; Natal sub-committee 1901–7; Orange River sub-committee 1901–6; Rhodesia sub-committee 1901–8, 1912–23; Transvaal sub-committee 1901–9.

Correspondence 1902–4, 1907.

United British Women's Emigration Association

United Englishwomen's Emigration Register

There were frequent changes of name: United Englishwomen's Emigration Register 1884; United Englishwomen's Emigration Association 1885–6; United British Women's Emigration Association 1886–1901; British Women's Emigration Association 1901–19. There were disagreements within the Women's Emigration Society which caused its gradual dissolution. The dissolution of the Women's Emigration Society was, however, to result in the formation in 1884 of a register of independent emigrants. The early signatories on the Register met in 1884 and this lead to the establishment of the United English Women's Emigration Association, which was to become the strongest of such organizations. The Association, the South African Colonization Society and the Colonial Intelligence League merged in 1919 to become the Society for the Overseas Settlement of British Women.

Annual Reports 1888–1901, 1901–18.

Minutes: council 1896–1901, 1915–19; advisory committee 1914; factory scheme sub-committee 1903–4; finance committee 1885–6; hostel committee 1909–12; South African expansion committee 1901; sub-committee for diffusing information 1903–5.

Correspondence 1891, 1896, 1899–1900.

Lady Knox's Diary

Press-cuttings 1883–1915, 1887–96, 1894–1901. These volumes include some letters; the earliest appears to have been the personal scrapbook of Mrs A. Ross.

Women's Emigration Society 1880–90

When the Society was founded in 1880 it was a step of major importance as it brought together the major workers in the female emigration movement. Many branches were set up but unfortunately disagreement within the Society caused its decline. In 1884 its most active workers left to form the United English Women's Emigration Association. It is not known if any records have survived but the United

British Women's Emigration Association scrap book has copies of the documents listed below.

Preliminary paper setting out objects and rules; byelaws; printed address by Viscountess Strongford; letter from Thomas Tully, the Secretary.

EMPLOYMENT

Association of Post Office Clerks

Founded in 1901 as the Junior Women Clerks Association, it became affiliated to the Federation of Civil Service Women Clerks when that body was founded in 1913, and later merged into the National Association of Women Civil Servants.

Minutes: annual general meetings 1901–31; committee meetings 1901–31. Letters and papers 1908–24.
See also papers, Dorothea M. Barton below.

FIRST WORLD WAR

Scottish Women's Hospitals for Foreign Service, London Units

The Society sent doctors and nurses to its hospitals in France, Serbia and Russia. It also arranged fund-raising campaigns to finance this work; one of its methods was to encourage girls' schools and women's organizations to sponsor beds which were then named after the school or organization. The Society was affiliated to the National Union of Women's Suffrage Societies and the organizers of the SWHFS were all ex-suffrage workers, as were many of the nurses.

The material is at present housed in folders in six boxes and can be divided into the following divisions, although it is not arranged in this order.

1915: correspondence relating to the purchase of an ambulance and equipping it as an X-ray unit including a photograph of the ambulance; regarding accounts; relating to travelling arrangements, expenses, hotel arrangements, etc, for a party of doctors and nurses travelling to Salonika; with Serbian hospitals; with French hospitals.
Hospital lists, instruction sheets for nurses; application forms, agreement forms, lists of uniform requirements; passport application forms, some completed: circulars, press notices, etc; telegrams; accounts for 1915 arranged in monthly folders.
1916: requests for tickets, etc, for a meeting held at the Criterion Theatre on 4 April; letters requesting women to be stewards at this meeting; regarding financial matters, cheques and accounts; general correspondence.
1918: correspondence regarding the named beds subscribed to by various organizations. There are files for many of the individual beds.

Biographical notes of key personalities in the organization. Notes for speakers, including anecdotes to tell at meetings.

Typed copy of a lecture given by Miss Latham on her experience in Serbia during the great retreat.

Letters of Doctor Inglis, August 1916–17, including some addressed to Lady Ashmore, Miss Palliser and Miss Onslow. Reports I–XV (Sept 1916–Aug 1917) – the originals sent from field hospitals in Serbia; the early reports are in Dr Inglis's handwriting.

Copies of obituaries and letters of sympathy sent to the organization from various individuals and organizations.

Elsie Inglis Memorial Fund: correspondence: regarding subscriptions, and the inaugural meeting held in the Mansion House, July 1919; regarding stewards for this meeting; relating to donations and the membership of the General Committee including letters from Lord Balfour and Philippa Strachey.

Correspondence with branches in relation to meetings held in these areas in 1917 to publicize the work of the SWHFS: Brighton and Hove, Cowes, Eastbourne, Littlehampton, Portsmouth and Southsea, Ryde, Sandown and Shanklin, Southampton, Ventnor, Worthing and a file of general South Coast correspondence.

Other correspondence: Over one hundred letters from Miss Bury (secretary?) April–Sept 1915 regarding passports for nurses travelling to the various hospitals; relating to an article on the Scottish Women's Hospital written by Miss Burke for the journal *The Forum*; Croix Rouge correspondence with Miss Gosse regarding the supply of nurses, and accounts, April 1915; relating to meetings in 1916–17 held at various institutions such as schools and colleges, mainly for fund-raising; with schools regarding the naming of beds (this covers the war years and is kept in individual files for each school); with Miss Strachey, 1919; with Miss Compton regarding passports; regarding individual nurses and their suitability; regarding the naming of beds; miscellaneous, 1917.

Miscellaneous documents: bandaging instructions for nurses; list of decorations awarded to individuals and the recipient's name; organizing secretary's reports Oct 1916–Oct 1918 (incomplete); lists of the general committee, executive committee and the secretaries of London societies.

MORAL AND SOCIAL ISSUES

Association for Moral and Social Hygiene
1915–63

Formed by the amalgamation of the British Committee of the Continental and General Federation for the Abolition of State Regulation of Vice and the Ladies' National Association. In 1963 it became the Josephine Butler Society which is still in existence.

Minutes: executive committee 1915–48, (1915–18 are in the final volume of the minutes of the British committee); indexes to minutes 1897–1912, 1913–17, 1918, 1915–24, 1924.

Sub-committees: finance 1914–38; India and the East 1914–21; investigation and organization 1915–26; literature and Shield 1915–16; overseas 1921–6; Parliamentary 1915–17, includes a copy of the constitution following minutes regarding amalgamation; police court rota book 1917–19; 'Special effort' 1922–7.

Files: sexual morality inquiry 1920; manual of vigilance laws; Cape Hall Women's Colony 1920.

Finance: cash book 1913–18; income 1927–54; expenses 1918–42; Cheques drawn books 1919–30; petty cash summary analysis 1912–17, 1922–8; receipt books 1919–27; expenses committee of enquiry 1918–19; accounts: Queen's Hall protest meeting 1918; income expenditure in India 1929–31.

Josephine Butler Fellowship: appeal committee minutes 1928–9; committee minutes 1930–32; funds 1930–33.

British Committee for the Abolition of the State Regulation of Vice, in India and throughout the British Dominions, 1890–1915

With the success achieved in the repealing of the Contagious Diseases Acts in 1886, it was thought that the repeal would extend to the colonies, but this was not so. The British Committee was formed in order to campaign for the reform of the Acts for the State Regulation of Vice, particularly in India. This Committee and the Committee of the British branch of the British, Continental and General Federation for the Abolition of Governmental Regulation of Prostitution and the British, Continental and General Federation for the Abolition of Government Regulation of Prostitution were all run from the same office and by the same devoted 'repealers', and the histories of the societies are interwoven.

Minutes: British Committee 1890–1912; chairman's book and log-book 1897–1903.

Correspondence: letterbooks inwards 1890–5; outwards 1891–6; circulars 1909.

Report by Dr Kate Bushell and Mrs Andrew on their visit to India, 1892.

Indexes: to pamphlets 1874–1909; catalogue of regulation files; regulation files 1880s and 1890s; India file 1888, which deals with the Commission on the scandal of the cantonments in India.

British, Continental and General Federation for the Abolition of Governmental Regulation of Prostitution

Annual Reports 1875–80.
Minutes: executive committee 1887–8.

International Bureau for the Suppression of the Traffic in Persons

In 1899 the executive committee of the National Vigilance Association held an international conference. This conference passed a resolution for establishing a permanent international organization, which was founded the following year. There were close links between the British committee and the Bureau itself and as was the case with the National Vigilance Association, the same people were members of the various committees. This led to confusion and the British National Committee was formed. The work of the Bureau was suspended during the First World War but the National committees each carried on with their own work within their own countries. After the First World War the Bureau continued despite financial difficulties during the 1920s and 1930s.

Minutes 1899–1940.

Files: the Fawcett Library holds papers relating to international congresses 1926–65, as well as League of Nations files and documents. These mainly relate to the period after 1930, but there are individual files for the 1920s covering the traffic in women.

Ladies' National Association for the Abolition of the State Regulation of Vice and for Promotion of Social Purity 1870–1915

In its early days the Ladies' National Association was not a London-based organization. London branch members included Mrs Jacob Bright and Mrs Lucas. In 1881 the London branch became a distinct society with local committees.

Minutes: executive committee 1875–1915; special sub-committee minutes book 1912; special sub-committee to draft a memorial to the Royal Commission on Venereal Disease 1914; joint amalgamation sub-committee to consider the advisability of closer cooperation with the British Branch 1915; London branch LNA council 1883–95.

Ladies' National Association for the Repeal of the Contagious Diseases Acts 1870–1915

When in 1869 Mrs Josephine Butler was informed of the problem of the Contagious Diseases Acts by Miss E. C. Wolstenholme, who had been at the meeting of the British Association in Bristol, she helped in the establishment of the Ladies' National Association. The Association maintained close cooperation with the British Association, but justified its separate existence by proclaiming the need for a women's point of view. There were local correspondents and secretaries throughout the country and the meetings were held in various towns. After the repeal in 1886 of the Contagious Diseases Acts the LNA remained in existence to campaign against the continuance of regulation in the Empire, especially in India. It broadened its original title to include 'and for the promotion of social purity'. In 1915 the Association joined the British committee of the Continental and General Federation for the Abolition of Vice to form the Association for Moral and Social Hygiene.

Annual Reports 1871, 1888–98.
Journal: *Storm-bell*.

National Association for the Repeal of the Contagious Diseases Acts 1869–86

The campaign began in 1869 with the Social Science Congress of the British Association at Bristol and the passing of a resolution that the National Association for the Promotion of Social Science should protest against the Acts and take steps to resist their extension. The following day a meeting was held which resulted in the formation of the National Association for the Repeal of the Contagious Diseases Acts. Branches were set up throughout the country. The Association amalgamated with the Metropolitan Association in 1870. The Association continued in existence until the repeal of the Contagious Diseases Acts in 1886, when, its objects having been achieved, it disbanded itself, although it was not fully wound up until 1890.

Minutes of executive committee 1871–90.
Correspondence: letterbook 1883–6.
Journal, *The Shield*

National Vigilance Association 1885–1953

Following the publication of articles by W. T. Stead on the traffic in girls and young women in the *Pall Mall Gazette*, there was concern that there should be an organization that would ensure amendments in the criminal law. A meeting was held and a council was formed in August 1885. The Association took over the Minors' Protection Society and a few months later the Society for the Suppression of Vice. After lengthy discussions the Association merged with the Central Vigilance Society in 1891; its final merger was with the Travellers' Aid Society in 1939. Throughout this period while keeping its general aim, the constitution was amended several times. In 1953 the Association merged with the National Committee for the Suppression of Traffic in Persons to form the British Vigilance Association.

When this was wound up in 1971, a greater part of the records were transferred to the Fawcett Library. The Association gave some of its recent records to the Anti-Slavery Society. However it appears that some of the more important earlier records were sent in error to the Anti-Slavery Society which in 1973 deposited large quantities of material in the Fawcett Library including the Association's minute books.

Minutes of executive committee 1886–1928, 1928–56; finance committee 1885–8; general purpose sub-committee 1919–21.

The Library has a good deal of material relating to amalgamation with the British Vigilance Association, among the executive committee minutes.

Correspondence files: these are numerous and cover a range of subjects of interest to the Society over a considerable period of time. They also include individual case files.

Northern Electoral League for the Repeal of the Contagious Diseases Acts 1872–86 [?]

After the formation of the National Association, local associations were formed and included branches in the north, but it was felt that one association for the whole of the north would have a stronger influence. In 1872 the League was formed and quickly became a powerful force. Henry J. Wilson was the Honorary Secretary.

Annual reports 1873–83; correspondence.

Travellers' Aid Society 1885–1939

The inaugural meeting took place in October 1885 and in November the YWCA was asked to undertake the work of providing a 'scheme for aiding female passengers'. The Society worked in liaison with the Girls' Friendly Society, Metropolitan Association for Befriending Young Servants, National Vigilance Association and the Reformatory and Refuge Union. It eventually merged with the NVA in 1939 after a difficult period in the inter-war years when it had trouble raising finance, as the mainstays of the society died and were not replaced by younger members.

Minutes: general committee and sub-committee 1885–1939; executive committee 1886–1901; house and staff sub-committee 1896–1926.
Annual Reports 1886–1914.

PAPERS

Unfortunately it has not been possible to trace dates for some of the less known figures.

Barton, Dorothea M. *née* Zimmern

The material relates to the employment of women, with particular reference to wages and conditions of employment.

Notes on women's wages, for statistical papers 1914–19, including some correspondence; on the employment of women in higher posts in the Civil Service, and newspaper articles 1914–16.
Report of Inquiry into conditions of juvenile employment in the ready-made women's clothing trades in London, 1911, by Miss Collett, Senior Investigator

for women's industries. Report of sub-committee of Women's Industrial Council on Miss Jeannette Franklin's scheme for women's training.

Papers relating to women and their welfare 1912–17; on wages; on women in tailoring; on women's wages 1830–1914.

Comparison of wages 1886–1909.

Typescript of 'Changes in hours of labour for women and girls in the dressmaking industry in 1906 compared with 1863'.

Official notices for war service.

Newspaper-cuttings and printed material on hours of work, minimum wages and the value of the vote.

Becker, Lydia, 1829–1890

Diary for 1873, a day-to-day account.

Billingshurst, Mary

Letters, papers, newspapers and newspaper-cuttings 1890–1938, and diary.

Billington-Greig, Teresa 1877–1964

She joined the WSPU in 1903 and came to London with Annie Kenney. She left the Union after Mrs Pankhurst had taken control of the organization, and established the Women's Freedom League, but left it in 1911. She also formed the Manchester branch of the Equal Pay League. She spoke and wrote in favour of birth control and other topics of social and feminist interest. Her papers contain vast amounts of material including information collected for a biography of Mrs Charlotte Despard (see below).

Women's Freedom League: Notes on politics and the suffrage movement for the years 1903–12, and on the position of women 1900–14, quoting speeches and Royal Commissions.

Mrs Despard: autobiographical material – items relating to her early life, early memories, family background and traditions, and general, social and political setting, also a large number of quotations on a wide range of subjects, mainly from writers and politicians.

Notes on women pioneers from St Teresa to Mrs Pankhurst, including women prominent in the fields of education, political reform and human rights movement.

National Union of Societies for Equal Citizenship: correspondence with Dorothy Evans and the headquarters of all three major political parties (most are with the Liberal Party) to secure party support for an Equal Citizen (Blanket) Bill.

There is also a wide range of material relating to the organizations Teresa Billington-Greig belonged to after 1928. She was active in all aspects of women's emancipation and collected a vast amount of material.

Bowerman, Elsie

Letters 1910–20, personal, and relating to work with the Scottish Women's Hospital.

Burbury, Mrs Hawksley

She was a suffrage worker and subscribed to the Central Committee of the National Society for Women's Suffrage.

Eighteen letters c1872–c1893 including some from Miss Maria G. Grey and Miss Frances Buss; also letters from Mrs Fawcett.

Despard, Charlotte, 1844–1939

She was the 'elder statesman' of the suffrage movement and President of the Women's Freedom League. She had previously been a member of the WSPU but left when Mrs Pankhurst resumed complete control of that organization. She was imprisoned twice and was the author of various pamphlets and journal articles.

The following items are kept with Teresa Billington-Greig's papers who collected them for a biography of Mrs Despard that was never completed.

Mrs Despard's pamphlets, including typed copies; Teresa Billington-Greig's notes of interviews with Mrs Despard; first draft of the biography; correspondence with the Communist Party as to whether or not Mrs Despard had been a member; notes relating to the WSPU and WFL, and on Mrs Despard's character; photographs.

Duval, Elsie, 1892–1919

Her family were all involved in the suffrage movement and she was a member of the WSPU before 1907. She was arrested several times and force-fed, and never fully recovered from the experience. She escaped to the Continent while on release under the 'Cat and Mouse Act'. She married Hugh Arthur Franklin (see below) in 1915.

Correspondence, 1912, with Christabel Pankhurst, 1913–14, 1915–16, 1918; and relating to the WSPU; Circular letters, leaflets, etc, 1914–19 (useful for illuminating the development of WSPU policy during and immediately after the First World War); photograph album 1910–17; prison diaries 1911–12, 1913; Personal letters 1913, 1914 and 1918; List of mourners at her funeral; Pamphlets and miscellaneous items – menus, playing cards, 'Votes for Women', WSPU medals for prison and hunger strikes, banners, badges and colours.

Emmett, Lady Mary

Press-cuttings 1918–21; committee reports, 1918–21.

Evans, Dorothy M.

Drafts, typescripts and proofs of her book *Women and the Civil Service: a history of the development of the employment of women in The Civil Service and a guide to present day opportunities*, (Pitman, 1934).

Fawcett, Millicent Garrett, 1847–1929

Mrs Fawcett was interested in many aspects of women's role in society, but her major achievement and work was as a leader of the suffragist as distinct from the suffragette movement. Although she did not approve of the militancy movement, her letters show that at least in the beginning she was sympathetic to their aims. Her work in the suffrage movement lasted from its early days until her death. The Fawcett Library and Fawcett Society are named after her. As well as suffrage Mrs Fawcett was interested in many topics relating to women, for example in the Bryant & May match-girls' strike and in women's education.

1870–1922: Papers relating to a visit to South Africa during the Boer War to inspect concentration camps.

Part of the original manuscript (pp 68–80, pp 110–60) in Mrs Fawcett's handwriting of her book *What I Remember*.

Box of correspondence mainly with the National Union of Women's Suffrage Societies and members of the executive.

Material used by Ray Strachey in her book *Millicent Garrett Fawcett*. This includes letters from Women's Village Council Federation; letters on India 1915–18; letters from Vida Goldstein, Constance Lytton, the 'Armstrong' correspondence; personal letters, and letters received from various eminent suffrage workers. There are letters from the Revd Anna Shaw and Mrs Catt concerning Lady Cook; on the militancy shown by the Women's Suffrage and Political Union, including one to Lloyd George and the reply; a letter also on militancy from George Bernard Shaw.

Material relating to the International Women's Suffrage Alliance Conference in 1919; Mrs Fawcett's papers, and copies of letters from Margery Fry.

Items relating to the policy of the NUWSS in 1915; copy of an article by Mrs Fawcett on war work carried out by the NUWSS.

Material for the introduction to *Women's Year Book 1924*, including notes made by Mrs Fawcett for the introduction and quotations taken from various sources.

Notes for speeches.

Correspondence 1880–90 between Alfred Gilbert, sculptor of a memorial tablet to Mr Henry Fawcett, for Aldeburgh Church and Mr F. J. Dryhurst, private secretary to Mr Fawcett.

Typescript of interview of Mrs Fawcett and Miss Courtney with Ramsay MacDonald.

Copy of *Josephine Butler, an appreciation*.

Material relating to the Memorial Service for Mrs Fawcett held on 19 November

1929; order of service and list of representatives of organizations and individuals present.

Some undated material, probably pre-1900.

Correspondence regarding an article on her husband published by John Murray Ltd.

Note: All the above correspondence is listed chronologically with individual resumés of contents. There is also a vast amount of material housed in the Autograph Letter Collection, both written by her and to her, on a wide variety of topics.

See also Part 1, Archives, Suffrage, Papers.

Franklin, Hugh Arthur, 1889–1962

He became interested in the women's suffrage movement in 1909 after attending a meeting addressed by Mrs Pankhurst. The following year he joined the Men's Political Union for Women's Enfranchisement. He became very active in the WSPU and he it was who, incensed by Churchill's attitude to women's suffrage, attacked him with a dog whip. Franklin was imprisoned several times. In 1915 he married Elsie Duval (see above), a suffragette.

Notes of his speeches, and papers 1908–10; documents including a summons, press-cuttings, letters, etc, 1910–13, passports, visas and miscellaneous printed documents; correspondence 1910–14, mainly with suffragettes and other sympathisers, 1915–17, 1919, 1920s.

Holme, Vera

Correspondence; papers; paintings.

How-Martyn, Edith, 1875–1945

She was an active suffrage worker and was in the Women's Social and Political Union until the split which resulted in the formation of the Women's Freedom League. She became the Honorary Secretary of this for four years. She took part in many protests and demonstrations.

Twelve notebooks of news-cuttings, pictures, comments and miscellaneous papers.

Ramsay, Annie

Script of a talk on her part in the 1913 Suffrage March from Land's End to London entitled 'The women's pilgrimage'.

Royden, Agnes Maude, 1876–1956

Educated at the Cheltenham Ladies' College and Lady Margaret Hall, Oxford,

Agnes Maude Royden was a socialist and a suffrage worker. Her papers relate to religious matters in the 1920s and are at present unsorted.

Strachey, Jane Maria, 1840–1928

President of the Women's Local Government Society and on the Executive Committee of the NUWSS, Lady Strachey was also interested in the campaign for obtaining the state registration of Nurses.

Speeches on women's suffrage, women in local government and other subjects, 1903–14.
Correspondence: women's suffrage matters, chiefly copies of letters sent, 1907–17; NUWSS and other women's organizations, 1907–19; Women's Local Government Society, 1901–20; Lyceum Club, letters from and to Miss Smedly re Mrs Haselden, 1907.
Leaflets and notes, 1897–1907; annual reports, 1903–11; invitations to speak to suffrage societies, 1907–9; a few other miscellaneous papers and letters.
(There is also some material in the Autograph Letter Collection.)

Taylor, Mary Ellen

Mrs Taylor was a suffragette and was imprisoned in 1912 for her suffrage activities.

Letters from Mrs Taylor and to her from her daughter, Dr Dorothea Taylor, 1912 *see* Autograph Letter Collection 26 B.
Artefacts; Hand flag in suffragette colours; suffragette badge; water-colour.

Tuker, M. A. R.

Correspondence: literary and general, plus some newspaper-cuttings 1888–1912, 1913–39; On her book *Ecce Mater*, 1914–18; On her book about Cambridge, 1906–28; Articles.

Ward, Helen

A member of the Blanesburgh Committee on the parliamentary conditions of Crown servants, 1925.

Report of the Committee, minutes of evidence and miscellaneous papers, 1924–5.

SPECIAL COLLECTIONS

In addition to the archive material described in full below, and the general library stock, the Fawcett Library also contains a number of independent special collections, notably:

The Cavendish-Bentinck Collection

Was the personal collection of Ruth Cavendish-Bentinck, a prominent suffragist and active member of the Fawcett Library committee. It consists mainly of rare and antiquarian works relating to women. These are arranged in classified order.

The Josephine Butler Library

This was previously the library of the Association for Moral and Social Hygiene and contains material relating to the campaigns against state-regulated prostitution, particularly the Contagious Diseases Acts in this country and in India, and the white slave trade. The Library contains archives, books, periodicals and the journal, *The Shield*, which was the organ of the association. The collection is still being added to by the Josephine Butler Society and is amongst the material most frequently used in the Fawcett Library.

The Sadd Brown Collection

This is devoted to the role of women in the Commonwealth countries and was named after Mrs Myra Sadd Brown, a suffrage pioneer whose daughter, Mrs Myra Steadman, is now the Collection's chief sponsor.

SUFFRAGE

The most important of the Fawcett Library's holdings is the collection of archive material relating to the history of the Fawcett Society – a direct descendant of the London Society for Women's Suffrage, as the following diagram shows.

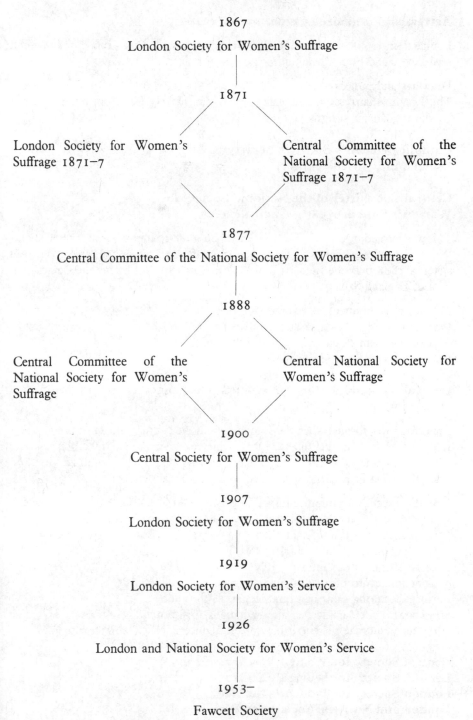

1867
London Society for Women's Suffrage

1871

London Society for Women's
Suffrage 1871–7

Central Committee of the
National Society for Women's
Suffrage 1871–7

1877
Central Committee of the National Society for Women's Suffrage

1888

Central Committee of the
National Society for Women's
Suffrage

Central National Society for
Women's Suffrage

1900
Central Society for Women's Suffrage

1907
London Society for Women's Suffrage

1919
London Society for Women's Service

1926
London and National Society for Women's Service

1953–
Fawcett Society

Actresses' Franchise League, 1908–c 1918

Founded in 1908 to attract and activate actresses. The League was neutral regarding tactics, but did not advocate strong militancy.

Drawings and posters
The League's correspondence with the London Society for Women's Suffrage is with the latter's records.

Catholic Women's Suffrage Society *see* **St Joan's Social and Political Alliance**

Central Committee of the National Society for Women's Suffrage, 1871–7 and 1877–97

This was formed by a breakaway movement after the split in the London Society for Women's Suffrage. In 1877 the two sides re-formed under this name, but split again in 1888 over the 'non-party line' issue; in 1897 it became the Central and East of England Society.

Minutes of committees: executive 1875–89; financial 1877–85.
Letters from Mrs M. G. Fawcett forwarding a loyal address to Queen Victoria; acknowledgement and reply June/July 1897.
Annual Reports 1871–8, 1883–8.

Central National Society for Women's Suffrage, 1888–1900

This group was formed when the second split in the suffrage movement took place. It placed its faith in the Liberal Party achieving women's suffrage. The Society changed its name to 'Central and Western Society for Women's Suffrage' in 1896 when the West of England was added to its sphere of activity.

Minutes: executive committee for 11 Dec 1888–March 1889. These are at the end of volume 3 of the Minutes of the Central Committee of the National Society as this was in use when the split on the 'non-party line' issue occurred. The volume was continued by the Central National Society.
Executive committee minutes July 1890–Jan 1892, June 1894–Dec 1895 (contains record of joint preliminary meeting, 10 June 1895).
Finance; lecturing campaign fund ledger 1896–1900.
Scrap books: circulars, leaflets and invitations, 1888–97. These books are from all the main suffrage societies, therefore it is uncertain who compiled them.

**Central Society for Women's Suffrage, 1900–7;
London Society for Women's Suffrage, 1907–19;
London Society for Women's Service, 1919–26;
London and National Society for Women's**

Service, 1926–53; Fawcett Society from 1953

In 1900 the two groups of the Central National Society reunited (see diagram above) to form the Central Society for Women's Suffrage. However the name changed frequently thereafter because various objectives were achieved and new causes were adopted.

Minutes of committees: executive 1903–17, 1927–41; finance 1918–20, 1930–6, Feb–July 1939; employment 1922–6, 1929–32; Bee Toymakers' (including rough financial statements) Oct 1914–April 1915; various committees and sub-committees 1912–18.

Correspondence: miscellaneous 1910–14; regarding attitude of LSWS to militancy; general files for the years 1906 and 1908–14; with branches 1908–14; with the Actresses' Franchise League; the Artists' Suffrage League; the International Women's Suffrage Alliance; the Men's League for Women's Suffrage; the Women's Tax Resistance League; the Women's Freedom League.

Correspondence between Maude Royden and Philippa Strachey and other LSWS officers. This has been taken from the files of general correspondence for the years 1911, 1912 and 1913.

Correspondence relating to by-elections and the pressures on MPs during World War I, 1913–17.

Status of Women: correspondence with MPs in connection with the British Nationality and Status of Aliens Amendment Bill. Letters from local political associations, mainly in London and surrounding districts, in reply to a circular regarding the representation of women in their organizations.

For some years the Society kept a complete series of the circular letters it issued. The signatures on the letters that were signed are noted at the end of each entry. 1906–07, 1909–12 (these cover a wide range of subjects including financial matters, notices of conferences, etc); (mainly agendas) concerning executive committee, 1911–12; press secretary's circulars 1912 – letters requesting help and assistance; Election policy/activities general correspondence, 1908–10; draft circulars and printed material, various dates.

Classified correspondence and papers: Executive Committee 1906–12.

Common Cause 1909–11, 1914.

Anti-suffrage opinion and activities 1907–14.

Suffrage plays 1909–13.

Conciliation Bills 1910–12.

Constituency books: The London Society stepped up its intervention in parliamentary elections 1908–9 and to make this more effective, workers in constituencies were asked to complete a profile of information for their constituency to be used during election campaigns. Thirty-four books of various dates for London Constituencies.

Whitechapel and St George-in-the-East branch of the London Society for Women's Suffrage: minutes Jan 1913-July 1914.

Hitchin, Stevenage and District Women's Suffrage Society (previously North Hertfordshire WSS) 1909–18

Minutes: March 1909–May 1909 (rough), Feb 1909–March 1913, March 1913–Aug 1915, Sept 1915–Sept 1918, Oct 1918–April 1919; Stevenage committee, Dec 1913–Oct 1916.
Attendance Book April 1911–April 1919.

London Society for Women's Suffrage, 1867–77

When John Stuart Mill was elected to Parliament in 1865, he promised to present a petition to Parliament on behalf of women's suffrage, provided that it had a reasonable number of signatures. The Women's Suffrage Provisional Committee was formed in 1865 to collect these signatures. This committee was dissolved in 1867 and re-formed as the London Society for Women's Suffrage. The Society established women's suffrage committees throughout the United Kingdom, but a split occurred because some of the members were active in the Contagious Diseases campaign. Apart from printed annual reports for the years 1871–3 and 1883–8, no active records for this Society have been traced.

National Union of Societies for Equal Citizenship, from 1918

Minutes: executive committee 1920–8; status of wives and mothers sub-committee 1921–4; committee on employment of married women 1921–3; Married women's drafting committee 1924–6; married women (Parliamentary Bills) committee July 1925–July 1926; general purposes, organization and finance committee, minutes for meeting 10 Dec 1924; Sub-committee on Equal Franchise March–June 1926; widows' pensions special committee 11 July 1919–Dec 1919; equal guardianship special committee 9 Sept 1919; widows' pensions and equal guardianship special committee (one later sub-committee) 1919–21; equal moral standard sub-committee 1920–21; publicity and education committee March–June 1920; economic independence of women sub-committee May 1920–Jan 1921; programme and coordination committee April–Nov 1920; literature and education sub-committee 27 Oct 1920; parliamentary sub-committee/later committee 1928–31.
Correspondence: summer school, St Hilda's College, Oxford, regarding press coverage, August 1922; letters sent to various organizations 31 Dec 1926–22 Feb 1927 regarding mass meeting on Equal Franchise, Central Hall, London, 3 March 1927; circular letter from the Young Suffragists regarding mass meeting at House of Commons, 28 Feb 1927; demonstration on Equal Franchise at Queen's Hall, London; duplicated letters sent to various organizations 28 July–9 Dec 1927 regarding their representative appointed to serve on the advisory council set up by the NUSEC; correspondence with individuals Nov 1927–May 1928 invited to serve on the advisory council.

National Union of Women's Suffrage Societies, 1896–1918

By 1896 there were a number of suffrage societies representing the major areas of the British Isles and it was felt that a coordinating body was needed. The National Union was founded and had a general council upon which all affiliated societies were represented according to their membership strength. In the first years sixteen societies were affiliated to the NUWSS; this number grew steadily and by 1909 there were seventy in the United Kingdom.

The Union revised its constitution to make cooperation between the societies more effective. This resulted in an organization with a regional basis rather than one centred in London because the constitution allowed federations of affiliated societies. Each federation committee included at least one representative from each of the affiliated societies in the area and at least one member of the executive committee of the National Union. The functions of the federations were the promotion of new local societies and the handling of election work in the constituencies within their areas. By 1910 there were fifteen federations.

In 1909 *Common Cause*, the official journal of the society containing items of policy, began publication. On the outbreak of war in 1914 the NUWSS and its affiliated members suspended political activities but remained in existence to organize women in the war effort and to be ready to resume activities when the war was over. When limited franchise was granted in 1918, like other suffrage societies, the NUWSS widened its aims and changed its constitution, and its name to the National Union of Societies for Equal Citizenship. Its object was now 'to obtain all such reforms as were necessary to secure real equality of liberties, status and opportunities between men and women'. Its organization, however, remained the same.

Minutes: executive committee 1899–1918; sub-committees: 10 volumes 22 Jan 1896–2 Dec 1897 (these are for meetings which lead to the formation of the NUWSS); various sub-committees 1896–1901, 1903–6 including the minutes of meetings to draft the new constitution in 1906; 1907–9 (this volume includes the international executive planning committee for an international women's congress held in London).

Various subcommittees 1913–15 (for 1915 only, women's interest committee with some correspondence); Professional Women's Patriotic Fund committee Jan–Nov 1915; women's employment committee 1917–18; election fighting fund committee Jan–Dec 1912 (this volume is indexed).

Annual council meetings: preliminary agenda, 21–3 Feb 1917; report of the committee appointed to consider the reform of the constitution and procedure of council, Jan 1917; redraft of the rules of the NUWSS, Feb 1917; final agenda for meeting and proceedings of the annual council, 21–3 Feb 1917; preliminary agenda for meeting, 12–15 March 1918; and for special and half-yearly meeting, 27–9 Nov 1918.

Circular letters from head office to societies and federations on reorganization and

parliamentary matters, also the London Society of Women's Suffrage replies to
these letters.

Council reports, quarterly and yearly.

Scrap-book of notices of meetings, leaflets, etc, 1909–13; copies of official reports,
pamphlets and information sheets, 1913–17.

National Women's Citizens' Association, 1918–73

Now incorporated in the National Council for Equal Citizenship and Women for
Westminster.

Records were deposited by Mrs Nina Copps, former General Secretary, on behalf
of her Association, 11 June 1974. Most of the material refers to post 1928, but
there are many branch files which contain information for the early years of their
existence.

North Hertfordshire Women's Suffrage Society
see **Hitchin, Stevenage and District Women's Suffrage Society**

Oldham Women's Suffrage Society, 1910–18

Records 1910–18. Account in diary form kept by Mary Lees, of the activities of
the society; at the back are notes of speeches.

St Joan's Social and Political Alliance, 1911–52

This was named the Catholic Women's Suffrage Society from 1911–23. It was
originally founded by Mrs Gabrielle Jeffrey and Miss Mary Kendall to answer
attacks on women's suffrage from a Catholic viewpoint. It had several branches;
Liverpool, Brighton, Hastings and East Sussex, Bristol, and Edinburgh.

Minutes of the committee 1911–44, 7 volumes; records 1911–44; diary 1914–28
of activities and callers at the office, etc; news-cutting book (23 volumes), mainly
yearly compilations, 1911–52.

Women's Freedom League, 1907–57

This was formed after Mrs Pankhurst announced that the WSPU annual conference
for 1907 would not take place and that she was taking control. Led by Mrs
Despard, a group of prominent members – like Mrs How-Martyn and the Pethick-
Lawrences – continued with the October conference and formed the Women's
Freedom League. The policy of the WFL was militancy confined to attacking the
government. The League published its own journal, *The Vote*, from 1909.

Minutes: National Executive Committee Nov 1908–July 1941, Jan 1947–61;

political and militant department, 1910–20 including correspondence and news releases, 1910; finance sub-committee 1907–9; press committee 1908–10; social committee 1908–9; parliamentary committee 1908–9; organizing committee 1908–9; Green, White and Gold Fair committee; vote brigade 1913–14.

Annual conference reports: verbatim minutes (1st, 2nd, 14th, 27th, 29th and 32nd excepted). Programmes: Anglo-Belgian meeting, 18 June 1915; of entertainment, 8 June 1916; Green, White and Gold Fair, 24–5 Nov 1916.

See also Papers, Teresa Billington-Greig, above.

Women's Tax Resistance League, 1909–18

Formed with the object of forming 'a society for organized resistance to taxation by the earnest women interested in the suffrage movement ...' (from the 1909–13 minute book). They promoted their cause by meetings, distributing pamphlets and non-payment of taxes. On the outbreak of war they suspended activities and eventually folded up.

Minutes of committee meetings 1909–18; annual reports 1912.

Women's Local Government Society for the United Kingdom, 1888–1925

The Society was established in 1888 after the passing of the County Council Act to promote the eligibility of women to elect to, and serve on all local governing bodies.

See also Papers, Lady Strachey, above.

BLACKBURN COLLECTION

This is housed in the Library of Girton College, Cambridge, and is basically the material collected by Helen Blackburn during her activities in the women's movement and used in her writings. There may have been later additions, but the Collection remains much as it was when donated to the College. It consists of books and other printed material on various topics relating to women and includes a good deal of material that is difficult to locate outside the Fawcett Library. It contains works in French and German in addition to English publications, on such topics as suffrage, employment, education and temperance. Apart from the books, the main items of interest are as follows:

Pamphlets: bound volumes on medical education of women, women in India, women's suffrage and social and domestic topics.

Parliamentary papers relating to women, including copies of suffrage Bills 1889–98; records of voting on suffrage Bills; electoral statistics 1871–1901; and reports on parliamentary papers in foreign countries including Australia and New Zealand.

Periodicals relating to, or published by women, in English, French, German and Swedish, including *Englishwoman's Review, Journal of Women's Education Union, The Shield, Work and Leisure* and *The Suffragette*.

Reports: annual conference of women workers, 1893–1900; National Society for Women's Suffrage central committee 1891–1900; Society for Promoting the Employment of Women as Poor Law Guardians, 1882–1902.

Scrapbook entitled 'Circulars and memoranda of the Women's Suffrage Societies in the first ten years of the movement', and including copies of petitions, posters, prospectuses for societies, papers and circulars, chiefly of the Manchester Society.

Women's Suffrage Appeal, 1893: Newspaper-cuttings, books for collection of signatories and notices.

Women's suffrage book of autographs: arranged in subject order of individual's interests, contains cuttings of signatures with no indication of source. The majority appear to have been taken from a list appended to a petition, possibly the Women's Suffrage Appeal of 1893.

SECTION 2

LIBRARIES AND RECORD OFFICES

This section gives the addresses and facilities of extant libraries, record offices and other repositories which have material relating to women. Facilities vary widely because private institutions are frequently unable to commit themselves to definite hours of opening, etc. Although hours of opening are given in some instances, many libraries request that individuals check before visiting as staff shortages sometimes make changes necessary. Where prior permission is necessary, it should be requested in writing giving as much notice as possible and stating the kind of documents which will be required. The majority of librarians, archivists and secretaries of societies are happy to make their holdings available, but it should be remembered that much of the material is irreplaceable and must be treated with care.

Association of Assistant Mistresses

29 Gordon Square, London WC1H 0PU   (01-387 5674)

Access may occasionally be granted to researchers provided they make written application to the secretary at the above address.

Association of Head Mistresses

29 Gordon Square, London WC1H 0PU   (01-387 1361)

All applications should be addressed to the Secretary who deals with each on its merit.

Baptist Missionary Association

93–97 Gloucester Place, London W1H 4AA   (01-935 1482)

Prior notice must be given for a visit to consult archive material.

Barnaby's Picture Library

19 Rathbone Street, London W1P 1AF   (01-636 6128)

Written authorization required to consult the collection which is open Monday to Friday 9.00–18.00.

Bedfordshire Record Office

County Hall, Cauldwell Street, Bedford MK42 9AP   (06683 63222)

Open normal office hours for reference use only.

Berkshire Record Office

Shire Hall, The Forbury, Reading RG1 3EX   (0734 55981)

Open normal office hours for reference only, if possible application giving area of interest should be given.

Birmingham Central Library

Paradise, Birmingham B3 3HQ   (021-235 4511)

Open to the general public Monday to Friday 9.00–21.00, Saturday 9.00–17.00. Photocopying facilities available.

Birmingham University Library

P.O. Box 363, Edgbaston, Birmingham B15 2TT   (021-472 1301)

Prior application should be made to the librarian. The Library's opening hours are 9.00–21.00 during term and 9.00–17.00 during the vacations.

Blackburn Collection *See Section 1 above*

Bodleian Library

Oxford OX1 3BG   (0865 44675)

The Library is open to genuine research workers who should apply for a reader's ticket; this is essential for admission.

British Red Cross Society

9 Grosvenor Crescent, London SW1X 7ET   (01-235 5454)

Requests to consult the material should be made to the Hon. Secretary in advance.

British Library: Reference Division

Department of Printed Books and Department of Manuscripts, Great Russell Street, London WC1B 3DG   (01-636 1544)

British Library: Newspaper Library

Colindale Avenue, London NW9   (01-200 5515)

Open Monday, Friday and Saturday 9.30–17.00; Tuesday, Wednesday and Thursday 9.30–21.00; closed Good Friday, Christmas Eve, Christmas Day, Boxing Day and New Year's Day, and the week beginning the last Monday in October. Admission is by reader's ticket only. Photocopying facilities are available. Fuller details can be obtained from the British Library which produces a series of leaflets describing its facilities.

British Library of Political and Economic Science

London School of Economics, Houghton Street, London WC2A 2AC (01-405 7686)

Because of lack of space the Library has to restrict the number of external readers so prior permission to use the Library must always be sought.

Cambridge University Library

West Road, Cambridge CB3 9DR   (0223 61441)

Open to researchers for reference only upon prior application, opening hours during term time Monday to Friday 9.00–19.00, Saturday 9.00–13.00.

Camden School for Girls (Frances Mary Buss Foundation)

Sandall Road, London NW5 2BD   (01-485 3414)

As this is a school, it is not open to members of the public, so permission to see the archive must be sought from the head mistress.

Churchill College Archives Centre and Library

Storey's Way, Cambridge CB3 0DS   (0223 61200, Ext 338)

Unfortunately this Library is not open to public but in special cases permission to consult specific records may be granted. The library is open 9.00–13.00, 14.15–17.00 term time only.

Church Missionary Society

157 Waterloo Road, London SE1 8UU   (01-928 8681)

Application to consult these archives must be made to the Librarian, Miss Rosemary Keen. Records are only made available to the public after a lapse of fifty years.

Congregational Council for World Mission

Housed in the School of Oriental and African Studies Library, Malet Street, London WC1E 7HP   (01-637 2388)

All enquiries should be addressed to the Librarian at the above address.

Cooperative Women's Guild

342 Hoe Street, Walthamstow, London E17 9PX   (01-520 4902)

Its records are housed in the British Library of Political and Economic Science and Hull University Library.

Devon Record Office

14 Tavistock Place, Plymouth PL4 8AN   (0752 28293)

Open Monday to Friday 9.00–17.00 for reference use only.

Dorset County Record Office

County Hall, Dorchester DT1 1XJ   (0305 3131)

Open Monday to Friday 9.00–17.00 for reference use only.

Edward Hall Collection

Wigan Record Office, Wigan Central Library, Rodney Street, Wigan WN1 1DQ (0942 36141)

As this Collection is housed in a public library it is open to the public for consultation. As some of the less-used material is housed separately, it is advisable to contact the archivist in advance so that the required material can be made available. The Collection, given to the Library in 1947, is still being added to by Edward Hall, an antiquarian bookseller who donates to Wigan Record Office any diaries he discovers in the course of his business.

Family Planning Association

27–35 Mortimer Street, London W1N 8BQ   (01-636 7866)

Applications to use the material, which is at present being arranged, should be made to the above address.

Fawcett Library

City of London Polytechnic, Old Castle Street, London E1 7NT (01-283 1030, Ext 570)

Open to members Wednesdays and Thursdays 10.00–17.00, at other times by prior arrangement with the Librarian. Annual subscription payable. The Library allows up to six books to be borrowed at any one time, provided they have been published since 1920, are in good physical condition, and are not especially rare or valuable. Pamphlets, periodicals and archives are not normally available for loan. The loan period is three weeks and books not required by other readers may be renewed by visit, post or telephone.

Girls' Friendly Society

126 Queens Gate, South Kensington, London SW7 5LQ   (01-589 9628)

Enquiries should be directed to the National Register of Archives (see below) where the material is at present being arranged and listed.

Girton College Library

Girton College, Cambridge CB3 0JG   (0223 76219)

Application to consult the Emily Davies papers and Blackburn Collection should be made to the Librarian who will assist in any way she can.

Gloucestershire County Record Office

Worcester Street, Kingsholm, Gloucester GL1 3DW   (0452 21444)

Open for reference only 9.00–17.00 Monday to Friday.

Greater London Council Record Office

County Hall, London SE1 7PB   (01-633 5000)

Open Monday–Friday 9.00–17.00. The Record Office is open to the public for reference and the use of its documents and has a large, well-trained staff to assist readers with its complicated and often out-of-date indexing system.

Health Visitors' Association

36 Eccleston Square, London SW1Y 1PF   (01-834 9523)

Anyone wishing to consult their records should contact the General Secretary at the above address for an appointment.

House of Lords Library

Clerk of the Records, Record Office, House of Lords, London SW1A 0AA (01-219 3074)

Papers in the House of Lords Library are open to researchers after a lapse of thirty years but permission to use the facilities must first be obtained from the Clerk of the Records. Permission is also required to quote from any of the papers.

Huddersfield Public Library

Central Library, Huddersfield HD1 2SU   (0484 21356)

Hours of opening on application to the Librarian.

Hull University Library

The Brynmor Jones Library, The University, Cottingham Road, Hull HU6 7RY
(0482 46311)

Prior application must be made to the Librarian, who will also advise on opening
times.

Imperial War Museum

Lambeth Road, London SE1 6HZ		(01-735 3922)

The Museum's collections are open to the public although prior arrangements to
use the collections must be made. The departments are open weekdays only,
10.00–17.00. Photocopying facilities are available.

India Office Library and Records

Orbit House, Blackfriars Road, London SE1 8NG		(01-928 9531)

The Record Office should be contacted in advance. It is open Monday to Friday,
9.30–18.00, and Saturday 9.30–13.00, throughout the year except for public
holidays and two weeks in early October. Archives are open, subject to the thirty-
year rule. The Library has photocopying facilities.

Internationaal Instituut voor Sociale Geschiedenis

Herengracht 262–266, Amsterdam C, The Netherlands

Material can be consulted upon prior application to the England North American
Department.

John Rylands University Library of Manchester

Oxford Road, Manchester M13 9PP		(061-273 3333)

Kent County Record Office

County Hall, Maidstone ME14 1XQ		(0622 671411)

Labour Party Library

Transport House, Smith Square, London SW1P 3JA		(01-834 9434)

Open to genuine researchers upon application, but this must be made well in
advance as space is limited. A small monthly fee is charged per individual for
consulting archive material.

Lady Margaret Hall

Oxford OX2 6QA   (0865 54353)

The Library is basically a general academic library run by a qualified librarian catering for the needs of the students resident in the College. The College archives are not yet organized and permission to consult these will only be granted for genuine research if the material cannot be obtained elsewhere. Permission to consult archive material must be obtained from the Principal and Governing Body of the College.

Lambeth Palace Library

Lambeth Palace Road, London SE1 7JU   (01-928 6222)

Open Monday–Friday 10.00–17.00. The Library is open to *bona-fide* students, although special permission is needed for access to some categories of manuscripts. New readers need to provide a letter of introduction from a person or institution of recognized standing. Although the Library has no photographic staff the Librarian will endeavour to obtain photographs on condition that the negative or microfilm becomes the property of the Library. The Librarian will not accept responsibility for charges or payment for photographs. Requests to reproduce photographs should be addressed to the Librarian. Where extensive use of material has been made in a publication, readers are invited to present a copy of their work to the Library.

Leeds Central Library

Municipal Buildings, Leeds LS1 3AB   (0532 462062)

This is a public library and its records are open to the public, although enquiries regarding archive material should be addressed to the Librarian before consultation.

Liverpool University Library

Harold Cohen Library, Ashton Street, PO Box 123, Liverpool L69 3DA (051-709 6022)

Open in the term Monday–Saturday 9.00–21.30; vacation Monday–Friday 9.30–18.00. The Library is open for consultation by postgraduates and research workers upon letters of application.

London Museum *See* Museum of London

Lords Gallery

26 Wellington Road, London NW8 9SP   (01-722 4444)

Requests accepted by letter, telephone or visit. Written authorization required for visit, and appointments necessary. Open Monday–Friday 10.00–18.00.

Manchester Central Library

St Peter's Square, Manchester M2 5PD   (061-236 9422)

Open Monday–Friday 9.00–21.00, Saturday 9.00–17.00. The archive department, open Monday–Friday 9.00–12.00, 13.00–17.00, is open to the general public, but the material is obviously only available for reference. Photocopying facilities are available at current rates.

Mansell Collection

42 Linden Gardens, London W2 4ER   (01-229 5475)

Open for commercial and professional use only. Requests should be made in writing and visits can only be made by appointment, usual wait 1–2 weeks, open Monday–Friday 9.00–18.00.

Mary Evans Picture Library

Samuel Smiles House, 11 Granville Park, London SE13 7DY   (01-852 5040)

Requests by letter, telephone or visits, appointments must be made. Open Monday–Friday 9.00–18.00.

Methodist Missionary Society

25 Marylebone Road, London NW1 5JR   (01-935 2541)

All enquiries to consult the archive material should be made to the Archivist, the Revd John C. Bowmer.

Mill Memorial Library

McMaster University, Hamilton 16, Ontario, L88 4L8 Canada

A description of the contents of the Bertrand Russell collection in this Library is given in B. Feinberg's *The archives of Bertrand Russell* (Continuum Ltd, 1967).

Minet Library

Knatchbull Road, London SE5 9QR   (01-733 3279, Archivist)

A branch of Lambeth Public Library and therefore open to the public. Opening hours upon application to the Librarian.

Museum of London

150 London Wall, London EC2Y 5HN   (01-600 3699)

The material held here is available to researchers; application should first be made to the Director.

National Army Museum

Royal Hospital Road, London SW3 4HT   (01-730 0717/9)

Prior application must be made for use of the Reading Room. Open Monday–Saturday 10.00–17.30

National British Women's Total Abstinence Union

Rosalind Carlisle House, 23 Dawson Place, London W2 4T8   (01-229 0804)

Genuine researchers are allowed to use the archives; but permission must first be sought from the General Secretary (Mrs Sharp) as the Union is a busy place and can only accommodate a few researchers in the office.

National Council of Women of Great Britain

36 Lower Sloane Street, London SW1W 8BP   (01-730 0619)

The material is available for reference on application to the General Secretary.

National Federation of Women's Institutes

39 Eccleston Street, London SW1W 9NT   (01-730 7212)

All applications to consult material must be made to the Press and Public Relations Officer.

National Register of Archives

Quality House, Quality Court, Chancery Lane, London WC2A 1HP   (01-242 1198)

The Register contains lists of archive holdings in libraries and record offices, indexed under subjects and personal names. These indices are constantly updated. The Register is open Monday–Friday 10.00–16.30. It can be consulted by letter or telephone, as well as by personal visit.

1914–18 Archive

Sunderland Polytechnic, Chester Road, Sunderland, Tyne and Wear SR1 3SD (0783 76191)

The 1914–18 Archive is virtually a private archive collected by Mr Peter Liddle. Applications should be made to him before visiting the Archive and if possible some indication of the type and amount of material required should be given.

The Archive consists of diaries, papers and recollections relating to the First World War, together with books and a collection of newspapers published during the war, although financial considerations have limited the number. The personal recollections, by far the most useful part, take two forms: first, letters written to Mr

Liddle by individuals recounting their experiences and the way the war brought them into contact with situations and circumstances they had never before encountered (notably in the field hospitals of France and Serbia but also in munition factories and the armed services); and secondly, tape-recorded recollections. As a source of information this material is incomparable.

North London Collegiate School for Girls

Canons Park, Edgware, Middlesex HA8 7RJ   (01-952 0912)

The collection is organized and administered by two archivists. They welcome genuine researchers and are extremely knowledgeable about the material housed at the School. Prior permission must be sought; photocopies can be supplied.

Northamptonshire Record Office

Delapre Abbey, Northampton NN4 9AW   (0604 34833)

Nuffield College Library

Oxford OX1 1NF   (0865 48014)

Only suitably accredited researchers may use the Library so prior application should be made to the Librarian. Open Monday–Friday 9.00–13.00, 14.00–18.00.

Public Record Office

Chancery Lane, London WC2A 1LR   (01-405 0741)
Ruskin Avenue, Kew, Richmond   (01-876 3444)

Open to readers Monday–Friday 9.00–17.00, and Saturday 9.30–13.00. Documents required for use on Saturday must be ordered on Friday. In order to use the facilities one must be a 'reader'; an application form must be countersigned by a person in a responsible position.

Radio Times Hulton Picture Library

35 Marylebone High Street, London W1M 4AA   (01-580 5577)

Available for commercial and professional use only. Requests for information can be made in writing, by telephone or in person. Written authorization must be obtained for visit to the collection. All requests must be specific and detailed. Normal opening hours Monday–Friday 9.30–17.30.

Religious Society of Friends

Friends House, Euston Road, London NW1 2BJ   (01-387 3601)

Open to researchers upon production of identification or introduction but preferably prior application should be made stating requirements. Open Monday–Friday 10.00–17.00.

Rhodes House Library

South Parks Road, Oxford OX1 3RG   (0865 55762)

Admission by recommendation only.

Royal College of Midwives

15 Mansfield Street, London W1M 0BE   (01-580 6523)

The Library is open to genuine research workers upon written application to the Librarian.

Royal College of Nursing

1 Henrietta Place, London W1M 9AF   (01-580 2646)

Open to researchers upon letter of application.

William Salt Library

Eastgate Street, Stafford ST16 2LZ   (0785 52276)

Open to the public Tuesday–Saturday 10.00–12.45, 13.45–17.00 throughout the year.

School of Oriental and African Studies Library

Malet Street, London WC1 7HP   (01-637 2388)

Open to researchers upon written application to the Librarian.

Selly Oak Colleges

Birmingham B79 6LE   (021-472 4231)

Prior application must be made to consult archival material. The Library is open Monday–Friday 9.00–13.00, 14.00–17.00.

Sheffield Central Library

Department of Local History and Archives, Sheffield City Library, Surrey Street, Sheffield S1 1YZ   (0742 73411)

Open Monday–Friday 9.00–17.30, Saturday 9.00–17.00. As this is a public Library the material is freely available to members of the public, and the Department has facilities for photocopying.

Sheffield University Library

University of Sheffield, Sheffield S10 2TN　　(0742 78555)

Open Monday–Friday term 9.00–21.30, vacation 9.00–17.00. Prior permission to consult any of the University's archive material must be sought from the Librarian. A letter of introduction is also required. A coin-operated photocopying machine is available.

Somerville College

Oxford OX2 6HD　　(0865 57595)

The Library is in the main for the undergraduates of the College. It does, however, own the John Stuart Mill Collection, which contains copies of all his published works on women. The Library has no manuscripts and his printed copies contain no manuscript marginal notes. The College is conservative in allowing individuals to consult its archives, but usually allows serious researchers access to some material. The library can provide information on individual past members of the College compiled from its own sources. Application should first be made to the Librarian.

South Asian Archive

Centre of South Asian Studies, University of Cambridge, Laundress Lane, Cambridge CB2 1SD　　(0223 65621)

The Archive and Library are open Monday–Friday 9.30–13.00, 14.00–17.30. Prior permission to study there should be sought. Photocopies can be obtained. Neither the archive material nor books can be borrowed.

Suffragette Fellowship Collection *See* London
Museum

Thomas Cook Ltd

45 Berkeley Street, London W1A 1EB　　(01-499 4000)

Material not normally available but application can be made to the above address.

Trades Union Congress

Congress House, Great Russell Street, London WC1B 3LS　　(01-636 4030)

Records can be consulted after application to the Librarian; owing to shortage of space this should be made as early as possible.

United Reformed Church

86 Tavistock Place, London WC1H 9RT　　(01-837 7661)

An appointment must first be made to study the records.

United Society for the Propagation of the Gospel

15 Tufton Street, London SW1 3QQ   (01-222 4222)

Application to see the records, available after forty years, must be made in writing.

University College

Gower Street, London WC1E 6BT   (01-387 7050)

Library open to the public upon written application at the Librarian's discretion. Open Monday–Friday 9.30–21.00 term time, 9.30–19.00 Christmas and Easter vacations and 9.30–17.00 during the long vacation. Open Saturday 9.30–12.30 except during the long vacation.

University of St Andrews

College Gate, St Andrews, Fife, Scotland KY16 9AJ   (033-481 4411)

Permission to use the Library must first be sought from the Librarian.

Warwickshire Record Office

Priory Park, Cape Road, Warwick CV34 4JS   (0926 43431)

Open to the public during normal office hours for reference only. If possible, prior application should be made to the County Archivist.

Westfield College

Kidderpore Avenue, Hampstead, London NW3 7ST   (01-435 7141)

The material held by the College is not freely available for use, but any genuine research enquiries should be directed to the Principal who will deal with each on its merit.

West Sussex County Record Office

West Street, Chichester, West Sussex PO19 1RN   (0243 85100)

West Yorkshire County Record Office

County Hall, Bond Street, Wakefield WF2 2QN   (0924 67111)

Women's Co-operative Guild *See* Co-operative Women's Guild

Women's Research and Resources Centre

190 Upper Street, London N1 1RQ   (01-359 5773)

The Centre is run collectively by women; its facilities and meetings are open to men. It maintains a register of research projects relating to women's studies in progress, holds research seminars, and has a library of books, periodicals, pamphlets and leaflets. It produces a monthly news-letter. The Centre is open to members on a subscription basis and members are able to borrow books. The Centre is normally open Wednesday–Saturday 10.30–17.30, but intending visitors should first telephone as the Centre is run mainly by volunteers.

Women's Royal Army Corps Museum

WRAC Centre, Queen Elizabeth Park, Guildford, Surrey GU2 6QH   (0483 71201)

Application to visit the Museum must be made in advance to the Curator.

AUTHOR AND SELECTED TITLE INDEX

SUBJECT INDEX